Study Guide

MICROECONOMICS

Study Guide

MICROECONOMICS:
Principles and Tools
Fourth Edition

Arthur O'Sullivan
Steven M. Sheffrin

Janice Boucher Breuer
University of South Carolina

Upper Saddle River, New Jersey 07458

VP/Editorial Director: David Alexander
Acquisitions Editor: Jon Axelrod
Project Manager: Marie McHale
Manager, Print Production: Christy Mahon
Production Editor & Buyer: Wanda Rockwell
Printer/Binder: Courier, Bookmart Press

10   9   8   7   6   5   4   3   2   1
ISBN 0-13-153607-9

Contents

PART 5: THE LABOR MARKET AND INCOME DISTRIBUTION

PART 6: THE INTERNATIONAL ECONOMY

PREFACE

About the Study Guide

This study guide has been designed especially for you as a student of economics. This is a place where you can practice the material that you have learned. The study guide is designed to promote your comprehension of economic principles and your ability to apply them to different problems since these are skills you will be required to use when you take economics exams and other economics courses.

The study guide is different from any other economics principles study guide for a few reasons. First, it contains a section on performance enhancing tips (PETS). The PETS are tips that may help you through some of the rougher material in each chapter as well as with some basic principles that are used over and over again throughout the course. Second, the study guide is different from other study guides because it contains an answer key to the practice exam multiple choice questions and to the essay questions. For the multiple choice questions, the correct answer is explained in detail and explanations are given for why the other options are not correct. In this way, you learn a lot more because you learn not only why an answer is right but why other answers are wrong. This should help you out when it comes time to take an exam. The study guide also provides detailed answers to the essay questions. Finally, since your professor may use terms different than those used in text, equivalent terms that your professor may use have been put in parentheses. For example, some professors use the term "resources" to mean "land, labor, and capital" whereas other professors use the term "factors of production."

The study guide is not a tool to help you memorize economic principles, nor should it be used as a tool for memorization. It has been my experience as an instructor that students who understand basic economic principles perform much better than students who attempt to learn by memorizing material.

Some words of wisdom...

When I was a sophomore at the University of Delaware, I took my first principles of economics course in the Spring of 1980. I had heard from my roommates and other classmates that economics was a very difficult course, made only more difficult because the professor who was to be teaching the course, Professor Harry Hutchinson, was supposedly very hard on the students. Naturally, I was scared since it seemed like there was a real possibility that this might be one course that I (and a lot of other students) might fail. Much to my surprise, I actually liked economics and thought Professor Hutchinson was a great teacher. In fact, I ended up majoring in economics and going onto graduate school to earn a Ph.D. in it! The words of wisdom I'd like to impart to you I owe a great deal to Professor Hutchinson. These are words of wisdom I share every semester with the students whom I teach at the University of South Carolina.

#1   Attend class.

Don't think to yourself "I don't have to attend class to learn; I can learn this material by reading the textbook." First, professors cover material in class that they will put on the exam. This means two things: (1) professors may include material in their lectures that is not in the textbook and test you on it; and (2) material not covered in class will probably not show up on the exam. By attending class, you will have a better idea about what to spend time studying and what not to and your study time will be more focused and thus more productive.

#2 Take notes in class and recopy them within three days after each class.

For me, recopying my notes was the most useful practice for learning that I engaged in during my college and graduate school career. Recopying notes forces you to review the material and confront any points on which you are not clear. You learn by recopying your notes. Also, by recopying your notes, you will have a well-organized, clear set of notes from which to study. And, that makes studying much easier.

When you re-copy your notes, elaborate on major points from the lecture and supplement them with relevant material from the text. Write down questions about the material directly in your notes so that you can ask the professor later on. Use colored pens, stars, stickers, or whatever else you want to make your notes unique.

#3 Read, or at least, skim the assigned chapter(s) to be covered in each class before the class meets. Within three days after class, re-read the chapter(s).

#4 Jump the gun with studying.

Begin studying for the exam four to five days prior to the exam date. You'd be surprised how much easier it is to learn when you don't feel pressured for time. Plus, the extra time to study gives you an opportunity to review the material more than once or twice and to work through the study guide. You'll also have time to meet with your professor and ask questions about material which gives you trouble.

#5 Do things in reverse.

When your professor works through an example in class for which an "increase" is considered, work through the reverse case of a "decrease." When you are working through the practice exam multiple choice questions and essay questions in the study guide, it may also be useful for you to consider the reverse of each question. For example, if the multiple choice question asks you to consider an "increase," instead consider a "decrease" and then figure out whether there is any correct answer or how an answer would have to be modified to be correct. You should do likewise for questions where you are asked to consider a "rightward" shift in a curve, or a "negative" relationship, or which statement is "true."

#6 Meet with your professor to discuss material that you have trouble with.

All of these words of wisdom may be summed up as:

Expect to work hard if you want to do well. Hard work, in this course, or any course, usually has its rewards.

In my experience as a student and then later as a professor who has interacted with students, I have observed firsthand, how hard work has transformed a D student into a C or B student, and a C student into a B or A student.

ACKNOWLEDGEMENTS

There are a number of people whom I would like to acknowledge for their participation in the fourth edition of the study guide. I would like to thank Laney Grubbs for preparing the graphs and formatting the text for me, and Marie McHale for helping keep me on top of things. I would like to thank my students over the past fifteen years for exposing me to their questions, travails, and triumphs in learning economics. I would also like to thank the many economics professors that I had as an undergraduate student at the University of Delaware and as a graduate student at the University of North Carolina-Chapel Hill. I would especially like to name Professor Harry Hutchinson, Professor Stanley Black, Professor Randy Nelson, Professor Knox Lovell, and Professor Dennis Appleyard.

Dedicated to my son, J. Martin, and my daughter, Lena.

PART 1: INTRODUCTION AND KEY PRINCIPLES

CHAPTER 1
INTRODUCTION: WHAT IS ECONOMICS?

I. OVERVIEW

In this chapter, you will be introduced to economics. You will learn about the basic economic problem of scarcity and how it relates to what products a country produces, how it produces them, and who consumes them. You will be introduced to questions that economists answer and how economic analysis can be used. You will also learn about some of the terms and techniques economists use for thinking about problems that an individual, a firm, or a government faces.

II. CHECK LIST

By the end of this chapter, you should be able to:

✓ Explain the concept of scarcity and provide examples of it.

✓ Describe the difference between positive and normative economics.

✓ List the three basic economic questions that individuals, firms, and the government must answer.

✓ Describe the usefulness of making assumptions.

✓ Explain what is meant by "*ceteris paribus*."

✓ Explain what a "marginal change" is.

✓ Explain the concept of rationality used by economists.

✓ Describe ways in which economic thinking can be used.

✓ Distinguish between microeconomic and macroeconomic issues.

III. KEY TERMS

ceteris paribus: the Latin expression meaning other variables being held fixed.

economics: the study of choice when there is scarcity, that is, a situation in which resources are limited and can be used in different ways.

marginal change: a small, one-unit change in value.

macroeconomics: the study of the nation's economy as a whole.

microeconomics: the study of the choices made by households, firms, and government and of how these choices affect the markets for goods and services.

normative economics: Analysis that answers the question, "What ought to be?"

positive economics: Analysis that answering the questions, "What is or what will be?"

scarcity: a situation in which resources are limited in quantity and can be used in different ways.

variable: a measure of something that can take on different values.

IV. PERFORMANCE ENHANCING TIPS (PETS)

PET #1

The term 'ceteris paribus' means 'holding other factors constant', i.e. keeping other factors at the same level before and after a change in a relationship between two other variables.

For example, you may read an article in the newspaper that says "student test scores rise by 10 points from reading 3 more hours a week." The relationship between tests scores and reading assumes some other factors are held constant. For example, the relationship between reading and test scores may be based on students getting eight hours of sleep a night before and after the additional reading time is logged. Let's put some numbers to the example to illustrate the point. Suppose that on a standardized verbal test, students score 78% based on reading five hours a week. Further suppose that when students increase their reading to eight hours a week (three more hours), standardized verbal test scores rise to 84. The relationship assumes that nothing else relevant to the relationship has changed. For example, it assumes that students get the same hours of sleep per night in the case where they were reading five hours a week and in the case where they were reading eight hours a week. If this was not assumed, then the article would have to indicate that student test scores rise when students read three more hours a week and, say, get more than eight hours of sleep a night.

For another example, you may hear an ad on the radio that says that "walking 3 miles a day four days a week will, over the course of a year, lead to weight loss of 10 pounds." The relationship between walking and weight loss assumes some 'other factors held constant.' Those 'other factors held constant' might be that eating habits remain unchanged over the year and/or that no diet supplements are taken.

V. PRACTICE EXAM: MULTIPLE CHOICE

1. Economics is:

a) the study of money.
b) the study of financial decisions.
c) the science of choice in the face of limits.
d) the study of production.
e) the science of efficiency.

2. Limits or constraints on the resources we have:

a) is defined as 'scarcity.'
b) forces individuals and society to make tradeoffs.
c) prevent an economy from growing.
d)   create inefficiencies in production.
e) (a) and (b).

3. Which one of the following does NOT represent the concept of "scarcity"?

a) a decision by your parents to put more of their savings to fund college expenses and less to life insurance.
b) public policy in the state of Washington to reduce timber production so that more wildlife species will be preserved.
c) a decision by a company to increase advertising expense for a new board game by decreasing its budget for telephone expense.
d) a decision to commit more time to perfecting your volleyball serve and more time to perfecting your tennis serve.
e) a decision by a student to spend more time studying and less time partying.

4. Which one(s) of the following questions is an example of normative economics?

a) by how much will spending on housing decline when interest rates rise?
b) if an electronics store lowers the price of DVD players, how many more will be sold?
c) should lottery money be used to fund scholarships to attend college?
d) should I start saving now for my retirement?
e) (c) and (d).

5.   Which one(s) of the following questions is an example of positive economics?

a)   health care costs will rise by 7% if universal health insurance is adopted.

b)   countries that adopt free-market policies should grow faster than those that do not.

c)   the government should increase the minimum wage to reduce poverty.

d)   the central bank should lower interest rates to get the economy out of recession.

e)   banks should be permitted to sell mutual funds.

6.   All of the following are elements of the economic way of thinking EXCEPT:

a)   simplifying assumptions.

b)   individuals acting in their self-interest.

c)   thinking at the margin.

d)   the need for government intervention.

e)   all of the above.

7.   Which of the following statements illustrates the use of the *ceteris paribus* assumption?

a)   "If I increase the amount of time spent reading my economics textbook and working through the study guide, my course grade in economics should improve."

b)   "If the U.S. budget deficit was reduced, then interest rates would be lower."

c)   "If the tax on cigarettes was increased, fewer packages of cigarettes would be sold."

d)   "If my company lowers the price of its product, it should sell more, assuming that our competitors don't do likewise."

e)   "Lower interest rates will lead to consumers taking out more car loans."

8.   Economists:

a)   often disagree over conclusions from positive economic analysis.

b)   debate policy.

c)   help inform individuals, businesses, and the government about tradeoffs in the choices they face.

d)   attempt to quantify observations about economic relationships.

e)   all of the above.

9. Suppose we were interested in studying the relationship between grade point average and hours studied. Which of the following would be important to hold constant in order to clearly understand the relationship?

a) number of classes attended.

b) grade point average.

c) hours studied.

d) phases of the moon.

e) all of the above are held constant.

10. Suppose you volunteer at a local food bank and find that for every additional 100 brochures you send out seeking financial donations, the food bank sees an increase in the donations received of $1,500. If you convince the executive director of the food bank to send out 200 more brochures this year than last year, what would you predict is the change in donations?

a) $3,000.

b) $750.

c) $30.

d) $135.

e) cannot be determined from information given.

VI. PRACTICE EXAM: ESSAY QUESTIONS

1. Consider a society that is producing two types of goods: birdhouses and pianos. Explain what happens in a society if a decision is made to produce more birdhouses.

2. Suppose you hear a commentator on the radio cite a study that says that when Vitamin A is taken daily, people are less likely to get stomach cancer. List some factors that need to be held constant in order to be able to clearly establish the relationship.

VII. ANSWER KEY: MULTIPLE CHOICE

1. Correct answer: c.

Discussion: Economics is the science of choice. More specifically, economics is about how choices are made in the face of limited or scarce resources. Economics studies not only how a country will choose to use its resources to produce goods and services from, e.g. wheat, to clothing, to toys, to computers, but how an individual will choose to use their income to the consumption of goods and services. While statements (a), (b), (d) and (e) are topics that come up in economics, the main point is that economics is a field of study that investigates choice.

2.   Correct answer: e.

Discussion: Scarcity is defined as limits or constraints on the resources we have available to produce or consume goods and services. Because of scarcity, individuals, businesses, and the government confront tradeoffs in making choices. Scarcity makes it difficult to satisfy all wants and needs. Consequently, individuals and society are faced with choices. In making choices, tradeoffs must be made. For example, a choice by a student athlete to attend college may mean that playing a professional sport is given up. Thus, statements (a) and (b) are correct.

Statements (c) and (d) are not necessarily true. Limits on resources don't necessarily prevent an economy from growing but choices about how they are used might. Also, limits on resources don't necessarily lead to inefficiencies in production. But again, choices about how they are used might.

3.   Correct answer: d.

Discussion: This statement does not represent the concept of scarcity because it does not reflect any sacrifice or trade-off. That is, you have decided to commit more of your limited amount of time to both activities. Thus, you are not giving up anything. Of course, you will obviously have to cut back time on other activities, (perhaps to sleeping, studying, shopping, or whatever) but such trade-offs are not expressed in the answer.

Statements a, b, and c all represent the concept of scarcity. Statement a represents the concept of scarcity because it reflects a sacrifice or tradeoff made by your parents. Their decision to put more of their savings toward college expenses means that they will have less savings to devote to life insurance. That is, while your parents have to give up some funding of life insurance, in return, they are able to increase funding for college expenses. Statement b represents the concept of scarcity because it reflects a sacrifice or tradeoff made by legislators representing the state's interests. The sacrifice is that some timber companies will be put out of business. In return, more wildlife species will be preserved. Statement c represents the concept of scarcity because it reflects a sacrifice or tradeoff made by a business. The sacrifice is that its telephone budget will be reduced. In return, the company will be able to beef up its advertising expenses for the new board game.

Note: while there is a sacrifice, there is also something earned in return. Perhaps, another way to think of sacrifice is "trade-off" whereby something must be given up in order to obtain more of something else.

4.   Correct answer: e.

Discussion: Normative economics questions deal with what 'should' or 'ought' to be. They typically deal with policy issues, be it for an individual, firm, or government. Statement c deals with whether a government should fund college scholarships with lottery money. Statement d deals with whether an individual should start saving for retirement. In contrast, positive economic questions deal with what is or will be. Statements a and b are questions about what will be.

5. Correct answer: a.

Discussion: Statement a is an example of a positive economics statement because it describes and quantifies an economic relationship between health care costs and the adoption of universal health insurance. Statements b, c, d, and e are all examples of normative economics statements since they are statements of judgment about what should be done. Normative economic statements have the ring of opinion.

6. Correct answer: d.

Discussion: The elements of the economic way of thinking are not based on the need for government intervention. In fact, in many cases, the economic way of thinking proceeds under the assumption that government intervention is unnecessary.

Statements a, b, and c are all used in the economic way of thinking.

7. Correct answer: d.

Discussion: Statement d is the most accurate because it is the only statement that qualifies the relationship between the two variables, price and amount sold. For example, without the qualifier, a company may lower its price but find that its sales do not increase. This situation may arise because the company's competitors may also lower their price making it harder for the company to sell more even though it has lowered its price. The qualifier, in effect, holds fixed other variables that may be relevant to the relationship between price and amount sold. The qualifier thus makes clearer what the expected relationship is between the two variables.

Statements a, b, and c are not as accurate as statement d because none of these answers adheres to the "ceteris paribus" condition of holding other variables fixed that might also be important to a relationship between two variables. Statement a would be more accurate if it was qualified with a clause like "assuming that I continue to attend class regularly and take and recopy my notes." That is, even if you spend more time reading the textbook and using the study guide, if you decide at the same time, to skip class and stop taking notes, you may not see any improvement in your grade at all. Statement b would be more accurate if it was qualified with a clause like "assuming that the central bank decides not to raise interest rates." That is, a lower budget deficit may not necessarily lead to lower interest rates if something else happens in the economy to change them. Statement c would be more accurate if it was qualified with a clause like "assuming tobacco companies do not increase their advertising and/or do not lower the price they charge for a pack of cigarettes." That is, an increased tax on cigarettes may not have the desired effect of reducing the packages of cigarettes sold if tobacco producers respond by, say, lowering the price they charge for a pack of cigarettes.

8. Correct answer: e.

Discussion: Economists often disagree over conclusions from positive economic analysis. Their disagreement over conclusions from positive economic analysis often leads to difference of opinion regarding policy. Consequently, economists debate policy. Economists also help provide information to individuals, businesses, and the government about tradeoffs in the choices they face. They help to inform them by quantifying observations about economic relationships. Thus, statements a - d are all correct.

9.   Correct answer: a.

Discussion: Number of classes attended is the only variable being held constant in this example. If it were not held constant, it would be difficult to know what the contribution of increased study time was to the grade point average. For example, if at the same time, a student increased study time and increased their class attendance, the grade point average may increase because both of these factors changed. To know the effect of increased study time on grade point average, therefore, class attendance must be held constant. Statements b and c are not correct because they are the variables in the relationship being described. Statement d is not correct because the phases of the moon are not relevant to the relationship between the two variables and so it doesn't matter whether it is assumed to be held constant or not. Statement e is not correct by virtue of the fact that number of classes attended is held constant, as stated in a.

10. Correct answer: a.

Discussion: The answer relies on using marginal analysis. The information in the question reveals that the change in donations received is $1,500 for every 100 additional brochures mailed out. That is, every 1 additional brochure sent out returns $15 in donations. ($1,500 donations/100 brochures = $15 donations/1 brochure). The marginal change in donations per 1 brochure is $15. So, if the food bank mails out 200 more brochures, it can expect to raise $15 per brochure X 200 brochures = $3,000.

Statements b, c, and d are not correct based on the explanation above. Statement e is not correct because there is enough information to figure out the answer.

VIII. ANSWER KEY: ESSAY QUESTIONS

1.   If the society decides it wants to produce more birdhouses, then it must give up (sacrifice) the production of some pianos. Since the resources that a society has available to help produce output are scarce (limited, fixed amount) at a point in time, the only way the society can produce more birdhouses would be to cut back piano production. By cutting back piano production, the society frees up resources from producing pianos and can then allocate those resources into birdhouse production. However, if the amount of resources available to the society were to increase, then these new resources could be devoted to producing more birdhouses without having to cut back on piano production.

2.   The commentator is pointing out that a study finds a relationship between two variables – a daily dose of Vitamin A and the likelihood of getting stomach cancer. Though not stated in the relationship, there may be underlying assumptions about what other factors relevant to the relationship are assumed to be held constant. For example, the relationship may assume that individuals taking a daily dose of Vitamin A are not taking any medications. The study may assume

that individuals exercise three times a week. These other factors, were they to change, could affect the reported relationship between Vitamin A and stomach cancer.

We invite you to visit the book's Companion Website at:
http://www.prenhall.com/osullivan/
for further exercises and practice quizzes.

CHAPTER 2
THE KEY PRINCIPLES OF ECONOMICS

I. OVERVIEW

In this chapter, you will learn fundamental economic principles that will be used throughout this course. You will learn that decisions made by a household, business, or government generally involve an opportunity cost; choosing one option means that other options must be given up or sacrificed or foregone. You will learn about the marginal principle. The marginal principle can be used to guide decisions. It requires that the marginal benefit be compared to the marginal cost of undertaking an activity. You will learn about the principle of voluntary exchange. The principle of voluntary exchange says that when two or more people engage in voluntary exchange with each other, they are all necessarily better off. You will learn about the principle of diminishing returns. The principle of diminishing returns means that more and more effort devoted to an activity leads to smaller and smaller increases (or improvements) in the activity. Diminishing returns arise when more and more effort is exerted but there is no change in other factors which affect the activity. Lastly, you will learn about the real-nominal principle. The real-nominal principle requires that you think in "inflation-adjusted" terms. That is, you must always consider the effects of rising prices (inflation) on your income, pay raises, and interest and dividend earnings from financial investments, as well as on your debt. A true picture of the national economy also requires that you think of its performance in inflation-adjusted terms.

II. CHECK LIST

By the end of this chapter, you should be able to do the following:

✓ Evaluate the opportunity cost that is encountered when choosing an activity (e.g. attending a party on Saturday night, furthering your education, opening up a new factory, building more schools, cutting tax rates).

✓ Use the production possibilities curve to compute the opportunity cost of producing one good or bundles of goods instead of another.

✓ Explain why opportunity costs increase in moving either up or down the production possibilities curve.

✓ Use marginal analysis to decide the level at which an activity should be undertaken.

✓ Explain why picking an activity level where "marginal benefit" = "marginal cost" is the best choice.

✓ Explain why fixed costs are not relevant for marginal analysis, i.e. why it is that fixed costs do not matter in selecting an activity level.

✓ Explain why voluntary exchanges (or trades) between people necessarily make them better off.

✓ Explain the circumstances under which diminishing returns occur and under what circumstances it does not occur.

✓ Use the real-nominal principle to assess how well off you are based on the income you earn, any pay raises you might get, or any interest earnings you might receive from financial investments.

✓ Use the real-nominal principle to get a true picture of the state of the economy.

✓ Explain the difference between nominal and real variables.

III. KEY TERMS

long run: A period of time long enough that a firm can change all the factors of production, meaning that a firm can modify its existing production facility or build a new one.

marginal benefit: The extra benefit resulting from a small increase in some activity.

marginal cost: The additional cost resulting from a small increase in some activity.

marginal product of labor: The change in output from one additional worker.

nominal value: The face value of an amount of money.

opportunity cost: What you sacrifice to get something.

real value: The value of an amount of money in terms of what it can buy.

short run: A period of time over which one or more factors of production is fixed; in most cases, a period of time over which a firm cannot modify an existing facility or build a new one.

external cost: A cost borne by someone other than the people directly involved in the transaction.

external benefit: A benefit experienced by someone other than the people directly involved in the transaction.

externality: The effect of a transaction on a third party.

IV. PERFORMANCE ENHANCING TIPS (PETS)

PET #1

Throughout this course, it is wise to always consider the best foregone alternative (option that is given up) when a household, firm, or government makes a decision. An understanding of what is being given up in order to have something else may alter your opinion about the proper course of action.

For example, suppose that a political candidate is proposing that household income tax rates be cut. What opportunity costs might arise if the proposal is adopted? On the surface, you might think that a tax cut is great because your take-home pay will be higher and allow you to buy more goods and services (assuming prices don't rise, remember the real-nominal principle). However, as with most decisions, there is a cost -- something that is given up. In this case, a tax cut means that the government has less money to spend. So, the government may have to cut funding for space programs, or education, or highway repair, or police protection or whatever. These are opportunity costs of the tax cut. Which one of these government programs is the "best" foregone alternative depends on your viewpoint. If you value good schools, then the cut in education would be considered the opportunity cost associated with the tax cut. As you can see, debate over the opportunity costs of the proposal to cut taxes can lead to quite a lively discussion and may mean that not everybody agrees that a tax cut is such a good thing.

PET #2

*When you see the term "marginal," you should always think of computing the **change** in a variable. Computing the change requires that you have some numeric value before the change and some numeric value after the change. The difference between the two is the change in the variable.*

For example, suppose the revenue your company earns from selling 5,000 jewelry boxes is $100,000. Furthermore, you have forecasted that if the company sells 6,000 jewelry boxes the revenue will be $108,000. What is the addition to revenue (marginal) revenue? It is $8,000 (for 1,000 more boxes). Suppose that the cost of producing 5,000 jewelry boxes is $90,000 and you forecast that the cost of producing 6,000 boxes will be $95,000. What is the addition to cost (marginal cost) associated with producing 1,000 more jewelry boxes? It is $5,000.

Now, use the marginal principle to answer whether your company would be better off by increasing production by 1,000 boxes. Since the marginal revenue (benefit to the company) is $8,000 and the marginal cost (cost to the company) is $5,000, the marginal principle dictates that production be increased since the marginal benefit exceeds the marginal cost. That is, the company will add more to its revenue than it will incur in costs by raising production. This means that the company's profits will increase.

PET #3

*The marginal cost or marginal benefit associated with **fixed** costs or fixed benefits is zero. When costs and/or benefits are fixed, the change in the costs or benefits must, by definition, be zero. This is why fixed costs and benefits are not considered when using the marginal principle to decide the best activity level.*

For example, suppose that the fixed costs of operating a factory are the rent and interest on loans (debt) that it must pay every month. Suppose these fixed costs total $3,400 per month. Consider the other monthly costs of operating a factory, including paying employees and paying for raw materials. Suppose these costs are $6,600. If the factory decides to increase production, it must hire more employees and purchase more raw materials. Suppose these costs rise to $8,900. What about rent and interest? Do they change when the company decided to produce more? No, they are fixed costs. So, what is the *marginal* cost associated with increasing production? All you have to do is compute the change in costs -- the cost of rent and interest on loans went from $3,400 to $3,400, which is a change of zero. There is no addition to fixed costs and thus no marginal cost associated with them. The costs of employees and raw materials have increased from $6,600 to $8,900 which is an increase of $2,300. The change in costs or marginal cost associated with increasing production is $0 + $2,300 = $2,300.

PET #4

*Diminishing marginal returns means that as an activity level (such as production) is **increased**, it increases but at a **decreasing** rate. Just because the term "diminishing" is used does NOT mean that an activity level (such as production) decreases or diminishes.*

For example, which table below illustrates the principle of diminishing returns?

Table A		Table B	
# of workers	Output	# of workers	Output
1	100	1	100
2	98	2	110
3	95	3	117
4	91	4	122

The correct answer is Table B. In Table B, output is increasing as more workers are hired. However, the rate at which output is increasing is decreasing. Output increases by 10 units (110-100) from hiring one additional worker, then by 7 units (117-110), and then by 5 (122-117). In Table A, output is decreasing as more workers are hired. This is not the definition of diminishing marginal returns.

PET #5

*Compare the inflation rate to the rate of change in any nominal variable to determine whether it has increased, decreased, or remained unchanged in **real** terms.*

For example, suppose your boss gives you a raise of 15% for the coming year. You may be quite happy about this until one of your economist friends points out that inflation is expected to be 18% this year. In this case, while your nominal income will grow by 15%, your real income (inflation-adjusted) will be expected to decrease by 3% (15%-18%). Maybe you should go back to your boss and ask for a bigger raise!

For another example, suppose that you invested $1,000 in the stock market at the beginning of this year. At the end of the year, your investment is now worth $1,200. What is the percent return on your investment? In nominal terms, it is 20% = [(1,200 - 1,000)/1,000] X 100. What is the percent increase in real terms? First, you'll need the inflation rate for that year. Suppose inflation was 4%. Then, in real terms, your investment has increased in value by 16% (20% - 4%).

V. PRACTICE EXAM: MULTIPLE CHOICE QUESTIONS

1.   The "bowed out" shape of the production possibilities curve (PPC) arises because:

a)   as we move farther inside the PPC, an economy loses increasing amounts of both goods.

b)   the opportunity cost associated with a move from a point on the PPC to a point outside the PPC increases in terms of what must be given up to get there.

c)   to continue to get the same increment in the production of a particular good requires that more and more of the other good be given up.

d)   since resources are scarce, producing more of one good means we must produce less of another.

e)   none of the above.

2.   Based on the diagram below, which statement is correct?

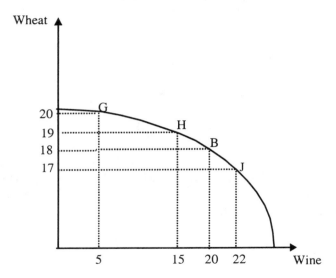

a)   moving from G to H incurs an opportunity cost of 1 bushel of wheat.

b)   as the economy moves along the PPC, more wheat can be obtained along with more wine.

c)   the opportunity cost of moving from G to H to B increases while the opportunity cost of moving from B to H to G decreases.

d)   moving from H to B incurs an opportunity cost of 5 barrels of wine.

e)   moving from G to J entails no opportunity cost.

3. Which one of the statements is true of the graph below?

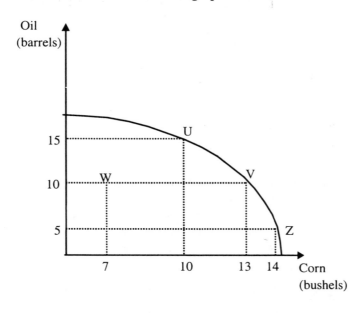

a) the opportunity cost of moving from U to V is 3 bushels of corn.
b) the opportunity cost of moving from Z to V is 5 barrels of oil.
c) the opportunity cost of moving from W to U is zero.
d) resources are not being efficiently used at point V.
e) all of the above are true.

4. You are deciding whether to stay at home and study from 3:00 p.m. - 8:00 p.m. or go to a park with friends. The park charges no admission fee. If you go to the park, which one of the following is not likely to be an opportunity cost associated with your decision?

a) your time away from studying. ✓
b) the $1 you spent on a soda shortly after you arrived. ✓
c) time spent eating dinner at the park.
d) cost of the gasoline used by your automobile to get to the park. ✓
e) all of the above.

5. Which one of the following is an example of a fixed cost?

a) electricity.
b) raw materials.
c) telephone.
d) supplies.
e) rent.

6. Which one of the following would NOT be considered a factor of production (or resource) for an economy?

a) a conveyor belt.

b) a financial analyst with a B.A. degree.

c) tin.

d) a new house.

e) A computer.

7. Suppose Fred computes the marginal benefit of working one more hour as a salesclerk in an electronics store to be $7.75. However, by working one more hour, he must give up the opportunity to attend a free, one-hour workshop on how to start your own business. However, Fred believes he will learn a lot by attending the workshop. Based on this information, which one of the following statements is correct?

a) Fred should work one more hour in the electronics shop since the workshop is free.

b) Fred should not work that one more hour in the electronics shop if the implicit value of what he will learn by attending the workshop is $25.00.

c) Fred should not work that one more hour in the electronics shop if the implicit value of what he will learn by attending the workshop is $5.00.

d) Fred should work one more hour in the electronics shop if the implicit value of what he will earn by attending the workshop is $5.00.

e) (b) and (d) are correct statements.

8. Use the table below to answer the following question.

# of workers	Output
1	5
2	15
3	30
4	37
5	40
6	38

Diminishing returns occurs:

a) between the first and second worker.

b) between the second and third worker.

c) between the third and fourth worker.

d) between the fourth and fifth worker.

e) between the fifth and sixth worker.

9. Which one of the following statements is true?

a) diminishing returns occur when a firm can change the amount of all of the factors of production it uses. ✗

b) if Helena finds that the marginal benefit of eating an ice cream cone is equal to the marginal cost of eating an ice cream cone, then Helena would be better off to eat one more ice cream cone.

c) if Jay works at a job he dislikes and is paid for his work, both he and the employer are better off.

d) the production possibilities curve is positively sloped. ✗

e) none of the above statements are true.

10. Suppose that your boss just informed you that you will be receiving a raise of 8% for this coming year. Suppose further that you have heard economic forecasts that the inflation rate for this coming year will be 9%. Based on this information, you might think to yourself:

a) "Wow, they must really like me - I'm effectively getting a 17% pay raise! I need to call home and tell mom!"

b) "Gee, thanks for the raise but the raise isn't actually a raise at all since my real income will decline by 1%."

c) "This isn't much of a raise but at least my real income will increase by 1%."

d) "Well, this isn't really a raise - my real income is going to decline by 0.72%."

e) "This isn't really a raise - my real income is going to decline by 7.2%."

11. If your salary increases from $28,000 per year to $29,400, then the percentage increase in your salary is ____%. If inflation is 6% a year, then your "real" or "purchasing power" income has changed by ____%.

a) 5%; 11%.

b) 14%; 8%.

c) 5%; -1%.

d) 50%; 45%.

e) 5%; 1%.

12. Suppose an old high school friend calls you up and desperately pleads to borrow $1,000 from you. You've been out working for a few years and have a little bundle in savings and decide that this is a good friend who really needs your help. So, you lend them $1,000 with the promise that they pay you the $1,000 back, without interest, at the end of the year. In one year after you are paid back:

a) In real terms, the money you will be paid back will be worth less than $1,000 if inflation was greater than 0%.

b) In real terms, the money you will be paid back will be worth more than $1,000 if inflation was greater than 0%.

c) In real and nominal terms, you will be paid back $1,000.

d) In nominal terms, the money you will be paid back will be worth less than $1,000 if inflation was greater than 0%.

e) In nominal terms, the money you will be paid back will be worth more than $1,000 if inflation was greater than 0%.

VI. PRACTICE EXAM: ESSAY QUESTIONS

1. Explain what happens when a country decides to move from one point on its production possibilities curve to another. Be sure to discuss opportunity cost and the allocation of scarce resources.

2. What advice would you give to a friend who has received two job offers both of which offer the same starting salary of $30,000 and the same benefits package? The jobs are basically the same. However, one job is located in Boston and the other job in Columbia, S.C.

VII. ANSWER KEY: MULTIPLE CHOICE QUESTIONS

1. Correct Answer: c.

Discussion: The bowed out shape of the PPC reflects increasing opportunity costs (which arise because resources are not equally-well adapted to producing one good as another). Statement c is the only one that expresses that opportunity costs are increasing, i.e. that more and more of one good must be given up in order to get back the same increment (say 1 unit) of the other good. For example, to produce 1 more motorboat may require that an economy give up producing 100 rolls of carpet; if the economy wants to produce another 1 more boat, the economy now has to give up producing 125 rolls of carpet; and if the economy wants to produce yet 1 more motorboat, the economy now has to give up producing 175 rolls of carpet.

The question asks about the bowed out shape of the PPC and so requires an answer that addresses a movement along the PPC, not to or from it. Statements a and b are incorrect because they address movements from a point not on the PPC to a point on it (or vice-versa), neither of which deals with a movement along the PPC. Statement d is incorrect because it only explains why the PPC has a negative slope, not why it has a bowed out shape. Statement e is incorrect because answer c is correct.

2.   Correct answer: a.

Discussion: Opportunity cost is measured by how much is given up or sacrificed. In this case, the graph shows that in moving from G to H, the economy foregoes producing (reduces production by) 1 bushel of wheat. In return, however, the economy is able to produce 10 more barrels of wine.

Statement b is incorrect because it is not true that as the economy moves along the PPC more wheat can be obtained along with more wine. The concept of opportunity cost means that the economy can only have more wheat if it produces less wine (and vice-versa). Statement c is incorrect because increasing opportunity costs are encountered moving in both directions along the PPC. To see this, note that as the economy moves from G to H, it must give up producing 1 bushel of wheat but gets back 10 barrels of wine. As the economy moves from H to B, it must give up 1 bushel of wheat, but this time only gets back 5 barrels of wine. That is, it is more costly to produce wine because less is gotten back in return for the same 1 bushel of wheat. Thus, opportunity costs of producing more wine are increasing as the economy moves from G to H to B. If the economy moves from B to H to G, opportunity costs will also be increasing. To see this, note that as the economy moves from B to H, it must give up producing 5 barrels of wine, while it gets back 1 bushel of wheat. In moving from H to G, the economy must now give up 10 barrels of wine while still only getting back 1 bushel of wheat. This just means that producing wheat has become more costly (i.e. the opportunity cost has increased). Statement d is not correct. Opportunity cost is measured by how much is given up; in moving from H to B, the economy has gotten back (not given up) 5 barrels of wine. Statement e is not correct because there is an opportunity cost; the opportunity cost is 3 bushels of wheat.

3.   Correct answer: c.

Discussion: Statement c is correct because at a point inside the production possibilities curve, resources are unemployed and/or not being efficiently used. This means that there are resources available to produce more of both corn and oil. That is, production in one commodity does not require sacrificing or giving up production of another commodity. Since there is no sacrifice in moving from W to U, there is no opportunity cost associated with the movement.

Statements a and b are not correct because opportunity cost is based on what is given up, not what is gained. Statement a is not correct because in moving from U to V, three bushels of corn are gained. In moving from U to V, the opportunity cost is the reduction in oil production, which in this case is five barrels of oil. Statement b is not correct because in moving from Z to V, five barrels of oil are gained. In moving from Z to V, the opportunity cost is the reduction in corn production, which in this case is one bushel of corn. Statement d is not correct because at a point on the production possibilities curve all resources are fully-employed and efficiently used. Statement e is not correct because statements a, b, and d are not true.

4.   Correct answer: c.

Discussion: Statement c is correct because regardless of whether you stayed at home and studied from 3:00 p.m. - 8:00 p.m. or stayed at the park, you would have had to take time to eat dinner.

Statement a is not correct because time spent away from studying is an opportunity cost. By being at the park with friends, you give up that time for studying. Statement b is not correct because that $1 spent could have been spent on something else. Statement d is not correct because the cost of the gasoline could have been saved had you stayed home and that used money on something else. Statement e is not correct because statement c is not an example of an opportunity cost.

5. Correct answer: e.

Discussion: Rent is the only example of a cost that will not change with a firm's production level. That is, whether a firm produces 0, 1, or 1,000,000 e.g. skateboards will not change the cost of the rent the firm pays for the production facility.

Electricity, raw materials, telephone, and supplies are all examples of costs that will change with a firm's production level. The more a firm produces, the more electricity it will need to operate the factory, the more raw materials it will need to produce the product, the more telephone calls it will have to make to coordinate distribution and sales, and the more supplies (packaging, etc.) it will need in production.

6. Correct answer: d.

Discussion: A resource or factor of production is any good, service, or talent that enables a society to produce output -- other goods and services. A new house does not enable society to increase production of other goods and services.

Statements a, b, c, and e are all examples of factors of production. A conveyor belt is physical capital. It may be used by a factory in its production process. A financial analyst is both labor and human capital. The financial analyst provides physical and mental effort on the job and also brings with him or her skills acquired through formal education. Tin is a natural resource. It may be used in many different production processes -- bottling, sheeting, etc. A computer may be used in the production process of a service like banking or in manufacturing.

7. Correct answer: e.

Discussion: Statement e is correct because statements b and d are both correct. Statement b is correct because the marginal cost of not working one more hour (or of attending the workshop) is $7.75, i.e. Fred will give up $7.75 by attending the workshop. However, Fred will benefit. The marginal benefit of using that one hour to attend the workshop has a value of $25.00. In this case, the marginal benefit of attending the workshop exceeds the marginal cost of attending the workshop so Fred would be better off by attending the workshop. Statement d is also correct but for the reverse reasons. In this case, if Fred assesses the marginal benefit of the one hour of attending the workshop at $5.00, the marginal benefit exceeds the marginal cost of attending the workshop ($7.75 loss in wages from not working that one hour). Here, Fred would be better off working and not attending the workshop.

Statement a is not correct. Even though the workshop is free, it does not mean that there is no benefit to attending it. Thus, it is not correct to compare the marginal cost of attending the workshop of $7.75 to a zero benefit. Statement c is not correct. If the marginal benefit of attending the one-hour workshop is $5.00 and the marginal cost of attending it is $7.75 (loss in wages from not working that one hour), then Fred would be better off working that one hour. Here, the marginal benefit of attending the workshop is less than the marginal cost of attending the workshop. So, the workshop should not be attended.

Statements b and d are both correct; however, option e allows you to pick both statements so that it is the correct answer.

8. Correct answer: c.

Discussion: Diminishing returns occurs when the addition of one more input (a worker in this example) adds less to output than the previous worker. Between the third and fourth worker, output increases by 7 units but had previously increased by 15 units (from 15 to 30). Thus, diminishing returns has set in.

Statement a is incorrect. Output has increased by 10 units from hiring one more worker but diminishing returns cannot yet be inferred until you are able to make one more comparison. Statement b is incorrect because, in this case, output has increased by 15 units from hiring one more worker (2 to 3 workers) and had previously increased by 10 units. This is an example of output increasing at an increasing rate, not a decreasing rate as is true of diminishing returns. (See PET #4). Statement d is not correct because the point at which diminishing returns has set in is where the rate of increase in output slows down; this happens between the third and fourth worker, not the fourth and fifth worker. While statement d does show that the addition to output is decreasing (it had been 7 units from the previous worker and is now 3), it is not the point at which diminishing returns has set in. Statement e is not correct because output actually *decreases* by hiring one more worker. That is, output goes from 40 units to 38 units (-2) by hiring one more worker. This is not an example of diminishing returns (see PET #4).

9. Correct answer: c.

Discussion: Statements a, b, d, and e are not true.

Statement c is correct even though Jay dislikes the job he has. The example illustrates the principle of voluntary exchange. Jay voluntarily works at a job he dislikes, and the employer pays Jay for the work he performs for the company. Both Jay and the employer must be better off since both are engaged in trading with each other. Jay trades his time to the employer for pay (money) and the employer in turn trades money for Jay's time.

Statement a is incorrect because diminishing returns occurs because a firm CANNOT change the amount of all of the factors of production it uses. Statement b is incorrect because if Helena found the marginal benefit to eating an ice cream cone just equal to the marginal cost, then she is as well-off (or happy) as she can be. She should neither eat one more ice cream cone nor one fewer. She is eating just the right amount. Statement d is incorrect because the production possibilities curve is negatively sloped. Statement e cannot be true since statement c is true.

10. Correct answer: b.

Discussion: Since your nominal income is going to grow by 8% but prices are expected to go up by 9%, then in real terms, your income will decline by 1% (8% - 9%). (See PET #5).

Statement a is not correct. This statement assumes that you have added the two numbers. It is not correct to add the growth rate of your nominal income and the inflation rate to determine the effect on your real income. Statement c is not correct. This statement assumes that you should take the inflation rate and subtract the growth rate of the nominal variable. This is not correct; it is the other way around.

Statements d and e are not correct. These statements assume that you have multiplied the numbers which is not the correct method for computing the real value of a variable.

11. Correct answer: d.

Discussion: You can calculate the percentage change in your nominal income by using the formula to calculate percentage change found in the Appendix to Chapter 1. The percentage change in your salary is calculated as [($29,400 - $28,000)/$28,000] X 100 = +5%. However, since inflation has increased by 6%, then the real or purchasing power value of your salary increase is 5% - 6% = -1%. Since the inflation rate has outpaced your salary increase, your real income has actually declined by 1%. Based on these calculations, none of the other options are correct. Do remember, however, that you must subtract the inflation rate from the increase in the nominal value to obtain the percentage change in the real value.

12. Correct answer: a.

Discussion: If you have agreed to be paid back $1,000 without interest and inflation is greater than 0%, then in real terms, your $1,000 will be worth less than $1,000. In other words, your $1,000 will not be able to buy as much as it had the year before if inflation was greater than 0%. You should note that in nominal terms, you are still getting back $1,000 but in real terms, you are getting back less than $1,000.

Statement b is incorrect. If inflation is greater than 0%, then the $1,000 you are paid back will not be able to buy as much as the year before. Thus, in real terms, the money you will be paid back is less than $1,000. Statement c is not correct. In nominal terms, you will be receiving $1,000. However, in real terms, you may be getting back more or less than $1,000 depending on whether prices have fallen (deflation) or risen (inflation). Statement d is not correct because in nominal terms, you will be getting back $1,000. Statement e is not correct because again, you will be getting back $1,000 in nominal terms. Inflation affects how much you earn in real terms, not nominal terms.

VIII. ANSWER KEY: ESSAY QUESTIONS

1. When a country moves from one point on its production possibilities curve to another, it has made a decision to produce fewer units of one good (e.g. apparel) and more of another (e.g. electronics). The country faces an opportunity cost -- the opportunity cost is that the country must cut back on production of apparel goods if it wants to produce more electronics. This is because resources are scarce. In order to produce more electronics, more resources -- land, labor, capital -- will have to be devoted to the electronics industry which means that there will be fewer resources available to produce apparel goods. That is, there will be a re-allocation of resources from the apparel industry to the electronics industry. With fewer resources available to the apparel industry, apparel production will contract; the opposite will happen in the electronics industry. While the movement along the production possibilities curve assumes that resources remain fully-employed (and efficiently used), there may be an adjustment phase (setting up new factory floors, training apparel workers to work in the electronics industry) during which some resources may become idle.

2. The advice I would give to my friend would be to consider the cost of living in Boston compared to that in Columbia, S.C. That is, I would have them consider the price of food, rent, clothing, etc. in the one city compared to the other in determining which job offer provides the higher "real" salary.

Since Boston is known to be a very expensive city and Columbia is in the Southeast, where the cost of living is typically lower than in the Northeast, I would suggest to my friend that in real terms, the salary offer from the company in Columbia is better than the other offer. I would suggest to my friend that if they really want her to live in Boston, she tell the company that they will have to offer a higher nominal salary to entice her to work for them.

We invite you to visit the book's Companion Website at:
http://www.prenhall.com/osullivan/
for further exercises and practice quizzes.

CHAPTER 3
EXCHANGE AND MARKETS

I. OVERVIEW

In this chapter, you will learn what markets are. You will learn that markets exist because people find it easier and mutually beneficial to specialize in producing certain types of goods, and to exchange what they have produced with what others have produced, than to produce for all of their own needs. You will learn that specialization and exchange arise because of differences in the productivity. You will learn that specialization and exchange can increase the set and amount of goods and services that each participating party may ultimately acquire. You will learn about comparative advantage which is an application of the principle of opportunity cost. You will learn that comparative advantage can be used to determine which goods should be produced by whom and which should be exchanged. You will learn that international trade may also be based on comparative advantage and that it too, can be mutually beneficial. You will also learn about the differences between a market-based economy and a centrally-planned economy and about the role of the government in a market economy. Along the way, you will learn about the virtues and shortcomings of markets.

II. CHECK LIST

By the end of this chapter, you should be able to do the following:

✓ Explain why specialization and exchange can benefit all participating parties.
✓ Determine comparative advantage by comparing opportunity costs of production.
✓ Discuss the principle of voluntary exchange and what it means.
✓ Draw consumption and production possibilities curves and illustrate the gains from exchange.
✓ Explain why specialization increases the productivity of workers.
✓ Explain how comparative advantage can be used to understand international trade.
✓ Explain why governments might intervene in international trade.
✓ Describe some features of a market economy that makes them function better.
✓ Compare and contrast a centrally-planned economy to a market economy.
✓ Describe the virtues and shortcomings of a market economy.
✓ Explain the role of prices in a market economy.
✓ Explain the role of entrepreneurs in a market economy.
✓ Discuss the role of government in a market economy.
✓ Explain how a government may reduce uncertainty in a market economy.

III. KEY TERMS

Comparative advantage: The ability of one person or nation to produce a good at a lower opportunity cost than another person or nation.

Absolute advantage: The ability of one person or nation to produce a good at a lower absolute cost than another person or nation.

Centrally planned economy: An economy in which a government bureaucracy decides how much of each good to produce, how to produce the goods, and who gets them.

IV. PERFORMANCE ENHANCING TIPS (PETS)

PET #1

Opportunity cost calculations used to determine comparative advantage should be based on a per unit comparison.

Suppose you are given the following information:

	Country A	Country B
Wood Products	10/hour $\frac{3}{2}$ high tech	8/hour $\frac{1}{2}$ h-t
High-tech products	15/hour $\frac{2}{3}$ woods	4/hour 2 woods

The information in the table tells you that Country A can produce 10 units of wood products in one hour (with its resources) and 15 units of high-tech products in one hour. Country B can produce 8 units of wood products in one hour (with its resources) and 4 units of high-tech products in one hour. How can this information be used to determine which country has a comparative advantage in wood production and which country has a comparative advantage in high-tech production?

As a side point, you may wish to note that Country A has an absolute advantage in the production of both wood and high-tech products since it can produce more per hour of either good than can Country B. But, absolute advantage does NOT determine the basis for trade.

The easiest way to compute comparative advantage is to determine what the opportunity cost of production is for each good for each country, on a per unit basis. To do this, you must first answer how much Country A must give up if it were to specialize in the production of wood. For every additional hour of effort devoted to producing wood products, Country A would give up the production of 15 units of high-tech products. (Of course, it is then able to produce 10 more units of wood products). On a per unit basis, Country A must give up 1.5 units of high-tech products for each 1 unit of wood products = (15 high-tech products/hour)/ (10 wood products/hour) = 1.5 high tech products/1 wood product. You would read this as "for Country A, the opportunity cost of 1 wood product is 1.5 high-tech products." For

Country B, for every additional hour of effort devoted to producing wood products, it must give up 4 units of high tech products. (Of course, it is then able to produce 8 more units of wood products). On a per unit basis, Country B must give up 0.5 units of high-tech products for each 1 unit of wood products = (4 high-tech products/hour)/ (8 wood products/hour). You would read this as "for Country B, the opportunity cost of 1 wood product is 0.5 high-tech products." Thus, Country B has the lower opportunity cost of producing wood products since it has to give up fewer high-tech products.

Since Country B has the lower opportunity cost of wood production, it should specialize in wood production. (Wood production is "less costly" in Country B than in Country A). If this is true, then it must also be true that Country A has the lower opportunity cost of high-tech production and thus should specialize in producing high-tech goods.

Let's see if this is true using the numbers from the table above. For Country A, the opportunity cost of producing more high-tech products is that for every additional hour of producing high-tech products, it must give up producing 10 units of wood products. (Of course, it is then able to produce 15 more units of high-tech products). On a per unit basis, Country A must give up 0.67 wood products for every 1 high-tech product = (10 wood products/hour)/ (15 high-tech products per hour). You would read this as "for Country A, the opportunity cost of 1 high-tech product is 0.67 wood products." For Country B, the opportunity cost of producing more high-tech products is that for every additional hour of producing high-tech products, it must give up producing 8 units of wood products. (Of course, it is then able to produce 4 more units of high-tech products). On a per unit basis, Country B must give up 2 wood products for every one unit of high-tech products = (8 wood products/hour)/ (4 high-tech products/hour). Thus, Country A has the lower opportunity cost of producing high-tech products since it has to give up fewer wood products. (High-tech production is "less costly" in Country A than in Country B).

PET #2

The endpoints of a production possibilities curve illustrate how much of one good could be produced if all time (and resources) were devoted to the production of that good, and none to the other good. The line connecting the points illustrates the possible combinations that could be produced if some time (and resources) were devoted to the production of one good and some to the other. The slope illustrates the trade-off in production between the two goods.

Suppose over the course of one week, Jan can bake 50 loaves of bread or she can make 200 cups of coffee. That is, if Jan devotes all of her time to bread production, she can bake 50 loaves of bread and zero cups of coffee. If, instead, she devotes all her time to coffee production, she can make 200 cups of coffee and zero loaves of bread.

A (linear or straight-line) graph illustrating Jan's production possibilities would therefore look like:

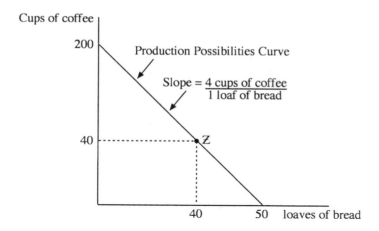

The slope of the line shows how many more cups of coffee Jan could produce if she cut back production of bread by one loaf. In this case, the slope is 4 cups of coffee/1 loaf of bread (200/50) which shows that for every four more cups of coffee Jan wants to produce, she must give up producing one loaf of bread. Alternatively, we could say that Jan will be able to produce one more loaf of bread for every four cups of coffee she is willing to cut back the production of.

All points between the endpoints illustrate combinations of the two goods that Jan could produce in a given day. For example, suppose Jan cuts back bread production by 10 loaves, from fifty to forty, she would now have the time to produce 40 cups of coffee (based on the trade-off) instead of zero. Thus, one combination of goods Jan could produce is 40 loaves of bread and 40 cups of coffee. This is illustrated as point Z on the production possibilities curve.

PET #3

The consumption possibilities curve will have an endpoint based on the good the individual is more capable of producing (more productive at) and will be above the production possibilities curve. The slope of the consumption possibilities curve will depend on the rate of exchange in goods between one individual and another.

Let's continue with the example from PET #2. Suppose another individual, Alex, can produce 25 loaves of bread in one day and 500 cups of coffee in one day. A calculation of comparative advantage shows that Jan is more productive in baking bread (since the opportunity cost to her is four cups of coffee per loaf of bread) and that Alex is more productive in making cups of coffee (since the opportunity cost to him of making one *loaf of bread* is twenty cups of coffee). Based on comparative advantage, Jan will specialize in making bread (and thus no coffee) and Alex will specialize in making coffee (and thus no bread). So, Jan will produce 50 loaves of bread per day and Alex will produce 500 cups of coffee per day. Let's say Jan is willing to trade 10 loaves of bread with Alex. This time, instead of getting back 40 cups of coffee (as in PET #2 where Jan does not exchange), Alex may be willing to give Jan, e.g. 100 cups of coffee. Thus, another point on Jan's consumption possibilities curve is point G which is a combination of goods better than had she not exchanged with Alex. So, Jan's consumption possibilities curve is above her production possibilities curve (except at the end point).

The graph below illustrates the consumption possibilities curve for Jan based on Alex' willingness to trade 100 cups of coffee for 1 loaf of bread.

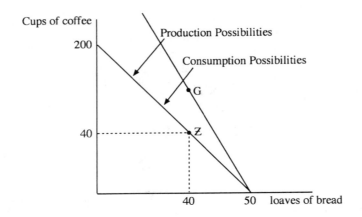

V. PRACTICE EXAM: MULTIPLE CHOICE QUESTIONS

1.   Use the information below to determine which answer is correct.

	Lena	J. Martin
Brownies produced per week	4 ½ painting	5 2 paintings
Pictures painted per week	2 2 brown	10 ½ brownies

a)   the opportunity cost of one picture for Lena is 1/2 brownies. ×
b)   the opportunity cost of one picture for J. Martin is 2 brownies. ×
c)   Lena has a comparative advantage in brownies production.
d)   Lena's opportunity cost of brownies is greater than J. Martin's.
e)   (c) and (d).

2.   Using the information from question (1), which one of the following statements is correct?

a)   Lena will specialize in brownies.
b)   J. Martin will specialize in brownies.
c)   Lena will specialize in painting pictures.
d)   J. Martin will specialize in painting pictures.
e)   (a) and (d).

3. Use the table below to answer the following question.

	Country A	Country B
A Toys	50 per day $\frac{2}{50}$ S	20 per day $\frac{1}{20}$ S
B Ships	2 per day 25 T	1 per day 20 T

Which country has the comparative advantage in producing toys and which country has the comparative advantage in producing ships?

a) Country A has the comparative advantage in producing both toys and ships.

b) Country B has the comparative advantage in producing both toys and ships.

c) Country A has the comparative advantage in producing toys and Country B has the comparative advantage in producing ships.

d) Country B has the comparative advantage in producing toys and Country A has the comparative advantage in producing ships.

e) need information on exchange rates to answer the question.

4. Using the information below to complete the following question.   Country A's production possibilities curve is represented by graph ___ and Country B's production possibilities curve is represented by graph ___.

	Country A	Country B
Autos	400 per day	500 per day
Airplanes	10 per day	5 per day

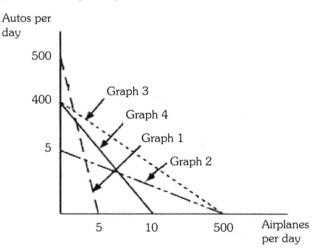

a) Graph 4; Graph 1.

b) Graph 2; Graph 1.

c) Graph 3; Graph 4.

d) Graph 4; Graph 3.

e) Graph 1; Graph 4.

5. Which one of the following statements is true?

a) an individual can have an absolute advantage in the production of both goods yet still be made better off by exchanging with an individual who does not have an absolute advantage in either.

b) the consumption possibilities curve will be above the production possibilities curve in the case where exchange makes individuals better off.

c) specialization and exchange result from differences in productivity.

d) Adam Smith claimed that specialization would increase productivity through the division of labor.

e) all of the above.

6. Which one of the following statements is NOT true?

a) repetition leads to increases in productivity. ✓

b) specialization leads to time-savings which enhances the productivity of a worker. ✓

c) specialization can foster innovation.

d) insurance makes starting up new ventures by entrepreneurs less likely.

e) contracts make markets work better.

7. Which one of the following characterizes a market economy?

a) people make decisions regarding production and consumption.

b) competition keeps prices lower than would otherwise be.

c) decisions regarding production and consumption are guided by prices in the market.

d) people act in their own interest.

e) all of the above.

8. In a centrally-planned economy:

a) entrepreneurs enter markets where they observe profits being earned.

b) an increase in the price of a good indicates that it is now more scarce.

c) the planning authority (government) decides what production techniques will be used.

d) the 'invisible hand' is at work.

e) losses in an industry will cause firms to exit from it.

9. A government's role in a market economy is to:

a) help overcome market failures.

b) establish rules (laws) of exchange.

c) enforce and protect property rights.

d) reduce economic uncertainty.

e) all of the above.

10. An example of rules of exchange is:

a) enforcement of laws.

b) product liability laws.

c) ads warning about potentially dangerous products.

d) patent laws.

e) all of the above.

VI. PRACTICE EXAM: ESSAY QUESTIONS

1. Use the information below to explain how international trade between Lithuania and Italy may alter the consumption possibilities of the Lithuania compared to when it is 'self-sufficient.' Discuss what might happen on the production side when international trade arises. What might the government do?

	Ore	Wine
Lithuania	2 tons/day	50 bottles/day
Italy	4 tons/day	60 bottles/day

2. Discuss how a market economy works, the importance of rules of exchange and the potential effects of economic uncertainty and how they can be overcome.

VII. ANSWER KEY: MULTIPLE CHOICE QUESTIONS

1. Correct answer: c.

Discussion: For Lena, the opportunity cost of producing one picture is the two brownies that must be given up (4 brownies/2 pictures) = (2 brownies/1 picture). For J. Martin, the opportunity cost of producing one picture is 1/2 brownie (5 brownies/10 pictures) = (1/2 brownie/1 picture). Since Lena must give up more brownies to produce one picture, the opportunity cost of producing pictures is higher for Lena than it is for J. Martin. This also means that for Lena, the opportunity cost of producing one brownie must be lower than it is for J. Martin. To see this, invert the ratios above. From this you'll see that so that for Lena, the opportunity cost of one brownie is 1/2 picture and for J. Martin, the opportunity cost of one brownie is two pictures. Since the opportunity cost of brownie production is lower for Lena than for J. Martin, Lena has a comparative advantage in brownie production. Statements a and b are wrong since these statements have the numbers reversed for Lena and J. Martin. Statement d is wrong since Lena's opportunity cost of pictures, not brownies, is greater than J. Martin's.

2.   Correct answer: e.

Discussion: Since Lena has a comparative advantage in making brownies (see answer 1, above) and J. Martin has a comparative advantage in painting pictures, Lena will specialize in baking brownies and J. Martin in painting pictures. None of the other statements are correct.

3.   Correct answer: c.

Discussion: Country A must give up 50 toys to produce 2 ships. On a per unit basis, Country A must give up 25 toys to produce 1 ship. On the other hand, Country B must give up 20 toys to produce 1 ship. Since Country B has to give up fewer toys to produce 1 ship, Country B incurs a smaller opportunity cost of building one more ship. That is, it is less costly to produce a ship in Country B than in country A.   So, Country B should produce ships, which means Country A should produce toys. The two countries will be able to acquire more of both goods by trading or exchanging toys for ships and vice-versa.

Statement a is not correct. It would be correct if the question had been "which country has an absolute advantage in toy production and which in ship production?" The table shows that Country A can produce more toys and more ships per day than can Country B. However, this is not the concept of comparative advantage. Statement b is not correct for similar reasons just mentioned. Statement d is not correct because it is the other way around -- Country A has a comparative advantage in toy production and Country B in ship building. Statement e is not correct because comparative advantage can be computed using the table of numbers given.

4.   Correct answer: a.

Discussion: Graph 4 represents Country A's production possibilities since it illustrates that Country A can produce 400 autos per day if it produces no airplanes and 10 airplanes per day if it produces no autos. Graph 1 represents Country B's production possibilities since it illustrates that Country B can produce 500 autos per day if it produces no airplanes and 5 airplanes per day if it produces no autos.

5.   Correct answer: e.

Discussion: All of the statements are true. It is especially important that you remember that statement a is true since many students tend to think that absolute advantage is the basis for deciding who produces what good.

6.   Correct answer: d.

Discussion: Statement d is not true. Insurance helps to reduce the uncertainty associated with new business ventures and therefore makes it more likely that an entrepreneur may be willing to start up a venture.

7.   Correct answer: e.

Discussion: A market economy functions largely through the actions of self-interested (rational) consumers and producers with prices providing information as to relative value of goods and services. In a market economy, the government plays much less of a role in determining what gets produced, how it gets produced, and who gets to buy it, and at what price. A market economy is also characterized by competition between businesses and one of the benefits of competition is that it helps keep prices down. A market economy is the opposite of a centrally-planned economy.

8.   Correct answer: c.

Discussion: A centrally-planned economy requires a planning authority to make decisions regarding not only what production techniques to use (as answer c indicates), but what goods are produced and at what price they will be sold.

Statement a characterizes a market economy since entrepreneurs play a key role in determining what gets produced and how. In a market economy, entrepreneurs are motivated to produce by the opportunity to profit from their ventures.   Statement b also characterizes a market economy where prices provide information about the relativity scarcity of a good. An increase in the price of a good provides information that it is in greater demand and/or lesser supply. Statement d offers a term introduced by Adam Smith that explains how a market economy works. There is no central planning authority but the outcomes are as if there is an 'invisible hand' guiding the outcomes. Statement e is also characteristic of a market economy. While profits motivate entry into an industry, losses can also cause entrepreneurs to exit the industry, as well.

9.   Correct answer: e.

Discussion: Statements a – d are all true of a government's role in a market economy.

10. Correct answer: e.

Discussion: Statements a – d all provide examples of rules of exchange. Rules of exchange ensure that both parties to a transaction (buyers and sellers) are treated 'fairly' and are protected from abuses by the other. In a sense, rules of exchange can provide a basis for trust between parties engaged in exchange.

VIII. ANSWER KEY: ESSAY QUESTIONS

1.   The information in the table reveals that the opportunity cost to Lithuania for 1 ton of ore per day is 25 bottles of wine per day. That is, Lithuania must give up producing 25 bottles of wine in order to produce 1 ton of ore. By contrast, the opportunity cost to Italy for 1 ton of ore per day is 15 bottles of wine. If Italy gives up producing 15 bottles of wine per day, she will be able to produce 1 ton of ore. The opportunity cost calculations show that it is less 'costly' for Italy to produce ore. This necessarily means that it is less costly for Lithuania to produce wine. Let's see if the numbers confirm this. For Lithuania to produce one bottle of wine, it must give up producing $1/25^{th}$ ton of ore.

For Italy, the opportunity cost of producing one bottle of wine is $1/15^{th}$ ton of ore. Since $1/25^{th}$ is less than $1/15^{th}$, the opportunity cost of producing wine in Lithuania is less than it is in Italy.

The production possibilities curve below illustrates the situation for Lithuania prior to engaging in exchange. Any point on the curve is also a consumption possibilities for Lithuania were she not to engage in trade.

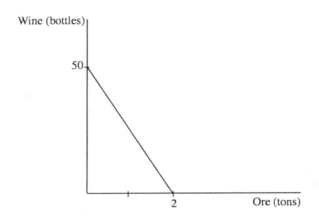

However, based on Lithuania's comparative advantage in wine production, Lithuania could devote all of its resources to producing wine (and Italy to ore). That is, Lithuania could specialize in wine production and Italy in ore production. Then, Lithuania and Italy could trade or 'exchange' with each other. Lithuania could exchange some bottles of wine for ore. The consumption possibilities for Lithuania will now be greater than were she to remain self-sufficient.

When Lithuania begins to trade with Italy, resources that were used in ore production will become idle. For example, workers that were producing ore in Lithuania may lose their jobs until they can be trained to work in the wine-making industry. The government may pay for programs that promote re-training of the workers. Alternatively, the government may restrict trade with Italy so that workers in the ore industry are 'protected' from job losses.

2. A market economy works when consumers and producers conduct transactions with each other to satisfy their mutual interests and there is little government involvement in the decisions regarding consumption and production. In a market economy, prices and relatedly, profits, provide information as to the relative scarcity of goods. In a market economy, an increase in the price of a good reflects that it is in greater demand or lesser supply. That is, it is relatively more scarce. The increase in the price of a good leads to higher profits. Higher profits prompt entrepreneurs to enter the industry. Their entry increases the availability of the good and thus relieves its relative scarcity. The opposite happens when prices decrease.

In a market economy, producers and consumers interact with each other within the rules of exchange. These rules include things like no stealing, paying for what you purchased, producing a good that is free of defects, being able to keep what you purchased, etc. These rules of exchange provide a basis for trust between consumers and producers and thereby increase the willingness to exchange. Exchange benefits all parties. To see why this is so, imagine a world with no Food and Drug Administration. That is, there is no agency to oversee the sale of anything from drugs to meat products. In this world, consider a consumer who does not trust the quality of meat sold at the local grocery store. Such a consumer may then forego purchasing any meat products even if he desired them. If there are rules and regulations that mandate the meat products pass a quality standard, then the rules and regulations can provide a basis for trust between the consumer and the grocery store. Thus, the consumer may now be willing to purchase meat products and satisfy his desire for a nice, juicy steak! So, rules of exchange benefit the consumer. They benefit the producer as well. With trust, more consumers enter the market, willing to purchase meat at the grocery store. The producer (grocery store) sees its revenue and profits rise. Thus, the grocery store benefits, too. The example illustrates how important rules of exchange can be in a market economy. Rules of exchange, thus, can help enhance trust and reduce uncertainty regarding product quality. There are other types of uncertainty that can impede transactions in a market economy. For entrepreneurs, uncertainty regarding the financial outcome of business ventures may cause them to be less willing to start up new ones. If the government can provide a safety net (perhaps through tax breaks, protection under bankruptcy proceedings, etc), more new businesses may be started up since entrepreneurs may view it as less risky to do so. Your book discusses several other safety net programs that reduce uncertainty in the face of natural disasters, accidents, or unforeseen hardship.

We invite you to visit the book's Companion Website at:
http://www.prenhall.com/osullivan/
for further exercises and practice quizzes.

CHAPTER 4
SUPPLY, DEMAND, AND MARKET EQUILIBRIUM

I. OVERVIEW

In this chapter, you will learn about two basic economic constructs: demand and supply. These two constructs can be used to answer questions like: what might happen to housing prices in a subdivision if a new mall is built near the subdivision? What might happen to the price of a share of a health services company when the government revamps the health care system? What might happen to the price of bread when former Soviet-block countries begin to trade with the U.S? What might happen to the price of tea when the price of coffee rises? Not only can demand and supply be used to guide your thinking about what will happen to prices, it can also be used to guide your thinking about whether more or less will be bought and sold. In this chapter, you will learn how to use graphs of demand and supply to determine what happens to a market price and the quantity bought and sold. Thus, in this chapter it is imperative that you familiarize yourself with shifts of a curve versus movements along a curve (see Chapter 1 of Practicum).

II. CHECKLIST

By the end of this chapter, you should be able to do the following:

✓ Explain the Law of Demand and the Law of Supply (for both price increases and price decreases).

✓ Understand what will cause a movement along a demand or supply curve and what will cause the curves to shift.

✓ Explain what happens to equilibrium price and equilibrium quantity when:

✓ demand increases (shifts right)

✓ demand decreases (shifts left)

✓ supply increases (shifts right)

✓ supply decreases (shifts left)

✓ List factors that will cause demand to shift (and in which direction).

✓ List factors that will cause supply to shift (and in which direction).

✓ Explain what happens to price, quantity demanded and quantity supplied when there is an excess demand and use a graph in your explanation.

✓ Explain what happens to price, quantity demanded and quantity supplied when there is an excess supply and use a graph in your explanation.

✓ Define a normal and inferior good and represent their response, using a demand curve, to an increase in income and to a decrease in income.

✓ Explain whether or not you can determine for certain what happens to equilibrium price and equilibrium quantity when demand and/or supply both shift.

✓ Infer whether demand or supply shifted and in which direction by having information on the direction in which the equilibrium price and quantity moved.

III. KEY TERMS

perfectly competitive market: A market with a very large number of firms, each of which produces the same standardized product in amounts so small that no individual firm can affect the market price.

demand schedule: A table of numbers that shows the relationship between price and quantity demanded by a consumer, ceteris paribus (everything else held fixed).

individual demand curve: A curve that shows the relationship between price and quantity demanded by an individual consumer, ceteris paribus (everything else held fixed).

quantity demanded: The amount of a good an individual consumer or consumers as a group are willing to buy

law of demand: The higher the price, the smaller the quantity demanded, ceteris paribus (everything else held fixed).

change in quantity demanded: A change in the amount of a good demanded resulting from a change in the price of the good; represented graphically by movement along the demand curve.

substitution effect: The change in consumption resulting from a change in the price of one good relative to the price of another good.

income effect: The change in consumption resulting from a change in the consumer's real income.

market demand curve: A curve showing the relationship between price and quantity demanded by all consumers together, ceteris paribus (everything else held fixed).

supply schedule: A table of numbers that shows the relationship between price and quantity supplied, ceteris paribus (everything else held fixed).

quantity supplied: The amount of a good an individual firm or firms as a group are willing to sell.

change in quantity supplied: A change in the quantity supplied resulting from a change in the price of the good; represented graphically by movement along the supply curve.

market supply curve: A curve showing the relationship between price and quantity supplied by all producers together, ceteris paribus (everything else held fixed).

market equilibrium: A situation in which the quantity of a product demanded equals the quantity supplied, so there is no pressure to change the price.

excess demand: A situation in which, at the prevailing price, consumers are willing to buy more than producers are willing to sell.

excess supply: A situation in which, at the prevailing price, producers are willing to sell more than consumers are willing to buy.

change in demand: A change in the amount of a good demanded resulting from a change in something other than the price of the good; represented graphically by a shift of the demand curve.

normal good: A good for which an increase in income increases demand.

substitutes: Two goods that are related in such a way that an increase in the price of one good increases the demand for the other good.

complements: Two goods that are related in such a way that an increase in the price of one good decreases the demand for the other good.

inferior good: A good for which an increase in income decreases demand.

change in supply: A change in the amount of a good supplied resulting from a change in something other than the price of the good; represented graphically by a shift of the supply curve.

IV. PERFORMANCE ENHANCING TIPS (PETS)

PET #1

Since price is a variable on the axis of a graph of the demand and supply of a particular good, a change in the price will NOT cause the demand or supply curve for that good to shift but will instead be represented by a movement along the demand and supply curves.

PET #2

When the price of good X rises (falls), the quantity demanded falls (rises). Do NOT say that the demand falls (rises) since this means the whole curve shifts left (right).

For example, suppose you read on the exam a statement that says, "What happens in the market for peanut butter when the price of peanut butter falls?" One of the test options might be "the demand for peanut butter increases." This is not the correct answer. A statement like "the demand for peanut butter increases" would be represented by shifting the whole demand curve out to the right. However, since the price of peanut butter has fallen and is a variable on the axis for which the demand and supply of peanut butter are drawn, the decline in the price of peanut butter will be represented by moving along the demand curve. As the price of peanut butter falls, the quantity of peanut butter demanded increases. This would be the correct answer.

PET #3

When the price of good X rises (falls), the quantity supplied rises (falls). Do NOT say that the supply rises (falls) since this means the whole supply curve shifts right (left).

For example, suppose you read on the exam a statement that says, "What happens in the market for jelly when the price of jelly falls?" One of the test options might be "the supply of jelly decreases." This is not the correct answer. A statement like "the supply of jelly decreases" would be represented by shifting the whole supply curve to the left. However, since the price of jelly has fallen and is a variable on the axis for which the demand and supply of jelly are drawn, the decline in the price of jelly will be represented by moving along the supply curve. As the price of jelly falls, the quantity of jelly supplied decreases. This would be the correct answer.

PET #4

A rightward shift in the demand curve can be expressed in the following ways:

a. *at every price, the quantity demanded that buyers want is now higher.*

b. *at every quantity demanded, the price buyers would be willing to pay is now higher.*

To see this, look at the two graphs below. Demand curve a corresponds to statement a because at every price, the quantity demand is now higher. Demand curve b corresponds to statement b because at every quantity demanded, the price buyers would be willing to pay is now higher. In both cases, the demand curve is further to the right after the shift than before.

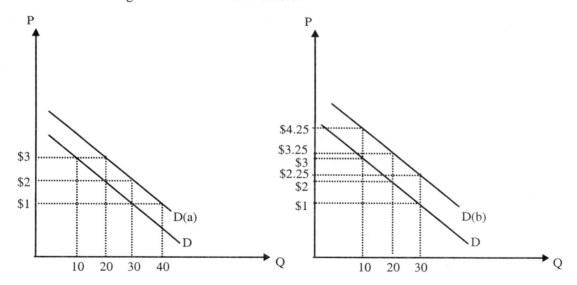

You should be able to re-write statements (a) and (b) for a leftward shift in demand.

PET #5

A rightward shift in the supply curve can be expressed in the following ways:

a. *at every price, the quantity that producers are willing to supply is now higher.*

b. *at every quantity supplied, the price at which producers would be willing to sell is now lower.*

To see this, look at the two graphs below. Supply curve a corresponds to statement a and supply curve b corresponds to statement b. In both cases, the supply curve is further to the right after the shift than before.

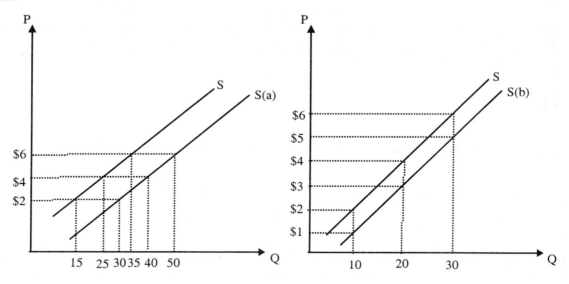

You should be able to re-write statements a and b for a leftward shift in supply.

PET #6

Factors other than a change in the price of good X may cause the demand and/or supply curves to shift to the right or left. These factors can be remembered with the simple mnemonic: P.I.N.T.E.O.

	For Demand	**For Supply**
P -	prices of related goods	prices of related goods
I -	income	input prices
N -	number of buyers (population)	number of producers
T -	tastes	technology
E -	expectations	expectations
O -	other (advertising, fads, etc.)	other (weather, strikes, taxes on producers, etc.)

While this mnemonic should help you if basic logic fails you during an exam (perhaps due to exam-induced stress), you should not simply memorize these lists. They should make sense to you. So, for example, if there is a technological improvement in producing computer chips, it should make sense that the technological improvement makes production of chips more efficient and less costly which you would represent by shifting the supply curve for computer chips to the right. That is, supply increases. Likewise, it should make sense to you than when the price of peanut butter goes up, the demand for jelly (a complement) will decrease which you would represent by shifting the demand curve for jelly to the left. You should work through different examples of each to ensure that your logic is correct.

PET #7

When you are asked to consider the effects of a shift in demand together with a shift in supply, you should first consider the directional effects on price and quantity of each shift individually. Then, you should assess whether the combined shifts move price in the opposite or the same direction and whether the combined shifts move quantity in the opposite or same direction. If the shifts move price (or quantity) in opposite directions, you will be unable to determine (without further information) the ultimate effect on price (or quantity).

To see why this is so, look at the table below and read the discussion following it. You may want to draw a graph of each shift listed below to assure yourself that the table is correct.

Shift	Effect on Price	Effect on Quantity
Demand increases (shifts right)	Price rises	Quantity rises
Demand decreases (shifts left)	Price falls	Quantity falls
Supply increases (shifts right)	Price falls	Quantity rises
Supply decreases (shifts left)	Price rises	Quantity falls

Suppose you are given a test question that asks what happens in the market for bicycles when rollerblading becomes the rage and when the price of aluminum used in making bicycles increases.

First, you must categorize the rollerblading rage as one of the four shift factors above and the increased price of aluminum as one of the four shift factors above. The rollerblading rage would be categorized as a leftward shift in the demand for bicycles and the increased price of aluminum as a leftward shift in the supply of bicycles. Since rollerblading and bicycling are substitutes, the increased rollerblading rage might decrease the demand for bicycles (leftward shift) which is to say that at every price, the quantity of bicycles demanded would now be lower. Since aluminum is an input into bicycles, the increased price of aluminum makes bicycle production more costly which is to say that at every quantity supplied, the price that producers would be willing to accept would be higher (to cover their costs). That is, the supply of bicycles decreases (shifts left).

Now, the decrease in demand for bicycles will lower both the equilibrium price and quantity of bicycles. The decrease in the supply of bicycles will raise the equilibrium price and lower the equilibrium quantity of bicycles. In this case, the two shifts together move price in the opposite direction but have the same directional effect on the equilibrium quantity. Therefore, you can only answer for sure what happens to the equilibrium quantity. (It falls). If you knew the magnitudes of the shifts in demand and supply, you would be able to answer what happens to the equilibrium price.

PET #8

Maximum prices (price ceilings) that are set below the equilibrium price create an excess demand where quantity demanded exceeds quantity supplied. A price ceiling set above the equilibrium price is ineffective.

To see this, compare the two graphs below. Graph A illustrates a maximum price (or price ceiling) set below the equilibrium price and graph B a price ceiling set above the equilibrium price. A maximum price is typically a government-controlled price above which the equilibrium price may not rise.

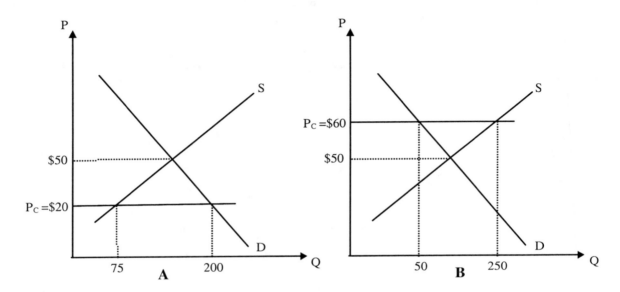

In Graph A, at a price of $20, the quantity demanded is 200 units and the quantity supplied is 75 units. Thus, there is an excess demand (or shortage) of 125 units. If the maximum price was removed, the price would rise to $50 and the excess demand would be eliminated as quantity demanded would decline and quantity supplied would increase (movements along the curves).

In Graph B, at a maximum price (or price ceiling) of $60, the quantity demanded is 50 units and the quantity supplied is 250 units. However, the equilibrium (or market-determined) price is $50. Thus, there is no tendency for the price to rise above the imposed price of $60 and so the price ceiling, in this case, is not effective.

PET #9

Minimum prices (price floors or price supports) that are set above the equilibrium price create an excess supply (or surplus) where quantity supplied exceeds quantity demanded. A price floor set below the equilibrium price is ineffective.

To see this, compare the two graphs below. Graph A illustrates a minimum price (or price floor) set above the equilibrium price and graph B a minimum price set below the equilibrium price. A minimum price is typically a government-controlled price below which the equilibrium price may not fall.

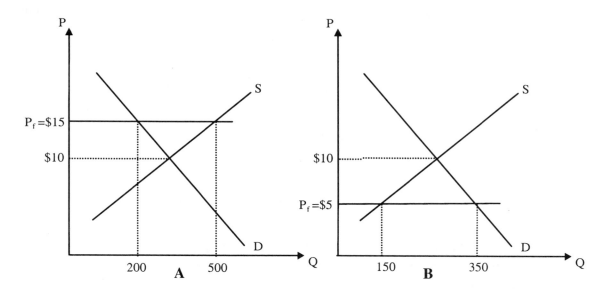

In Graph A, at a minimum price of $15, the quantity demanded is 200 units and the quantity supplied is 500 units. Thus, there is an excess supply (or surplus) of 300 units. If the minimum price was removed, the price would fall to $10 and the excess supply would be eliminated as quantity demanded would rise and quantity supplied would decrease (movements along the curves).

In Graph B, at a minimum price of $5, the quantity demanded is 350 units and the quantity supplied is 150 units. However, the equilibrium (or market-determined) price is $10. Thus, there is no tendency for the price to fall below $10 and so the minimum price of $5 is not effective.

V. PRACTICE EXAM: MULTIPLE CHOICE QUESTIONS

1. Which one of the following statements is correct about the Law of Demand?

a) as the price of oranges decreases, the demand for oranges increases.
b) as the price of oranges increases, the demand for oranges increases.
c) as the price of oranges decreases, the quantity of oranges demanded increases.
d) as the price of oranges increases, the quantity of oranges demanded increases.
e) as the price of oranges decreases, the demand for oranges shifts left.

2. A decrease in the demand for product X will:

a) cause the equilibrium price of product X to rise.
b) cause the equilibrium price of product X to fall.
c) cause the equilibrium quantity of product X to rise.
d) cause the equilibrium quantity of product X to fall.
e) (b) and (d).

3. Consider the market for flavored mineral water. If the price of soda (a substitute for flavored mineral water) increases, which one of the following might be an outcome?

a) the demand for soda will decrease.
b) the demand for mineral water will increase (shift right).
c) the price of mineral water will fall.
d) the equilibrium quantity of mineral water will fall.
e) (b) and (c).

4. Which one of the following statements is correct about the Law of Supply?

a) as the price of dog bones decreases, the supply of dog bones increases.
b) as the price of dog bones increases, the supply of dog bones increases.
c) as the price of dog bones decreases, the quantity of dog bones supplied decreases.
d) as the price of dog bones increases, the quantity of dog bones supplied decreases.
e) as the price of dog bones increases, the supply of dog bones shifts right.

5. Consider the market for mattresses. If the price of foam used in making mattresses declines, which one of the following might be an outcome?

a) the supply of mattresses will increase (shift right).
b) the demand for mattresses will increase.
c) the price of mattresses will rise.
d) there will be a shortage of mattresses. ✗
e) (a) and (b).

6. Which one of the following would NOT cause the supply of bananas to decrease?

a) a technological advance in banana production.
b) a decrease in the number of producers of bananas.
c) an increase in the price of a fertilizer used in growing bananas.
d) a severe rain shortage.
e) a tax placed on banana producers.

7. Which one of the following would NOT cause the demand for walking shoes to increase?

a) an advertising campaign that says walking is good for your health.

b) an increase in income.

c) a decrease in the price of rubber used in producing walking shoes.

d) an increased preference for walking rather than running.

e) all of the above will cause the demand for walking shoes to increase.

8. Consider the market for tulips depicted below.

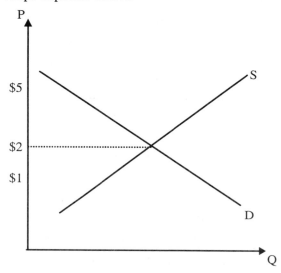

Which one of the following statements is correct based on the graph above?

a) if the price of tulips declines from $5 to $2, the demand for tulips will increase.

b) at a price of $1, there would be an excess demand for tulips.

c) at a price of $5, the quantity of tulips demanded exceeds the quantity supplied.

d) if the price of tulips increases from $1 to $2, the quantity of tulips demanded would increase.

e) none of the above.

9. Consider the market for chocolate candy. What is the effect on the equilibrium price and equilibrium quantity of a decrease in demand for and an increase in the supply of chocolate candy?

a) equilibrium price rises; equilibrium quantity falls.

b) equilibrium price falls; equilibrium quantity rises.

c) equilibrium price = ?; equilibrium quantity falls.

d) equilibrium price rises; equilibrium quantity rises.

e) equilibrium price falls; equilibrium quantity = ?.

10. Use the graph below to answer the following question.

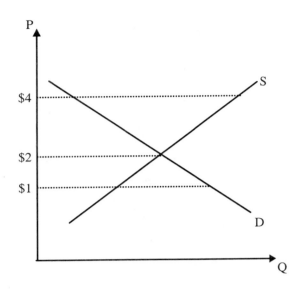

Which one of the following statements is true about the graph?

a)   there is an excess demand at a price of $4.
b)   there is an excess supply at a price of $4.
c)   at a current price of $1, there is pressure for the equilibrium price to fall.
d)   if the price fell from $4 to $2, quantity supplied would increase.
e)   if the price fell from $4 to $2, demand would shift right.

11. Pretend that you are an economic detective and are given the following clues about the market for wine: the price of wine rose and the equilibrium quantity of wine declined. In writing up your investigative report, which one of the following would you conclude might be responsible for the outcome?

a)   a decrease in the supply of wine.
b)   a decrease in the demand for wine.
c)   an increase in the demand for wine.
d)   an increase in the supply of wine.
e)   a decrease in the demand for wine and an increase in the supply of wine.

12. Suppose you hear reported in the news that the price of greeting cards declined at the same time the equilibrium quantity of greeting cards increased. Which one of the following would most likely be responsible?

a) a decrease in the price of paper used to make greeting cards.
b) a decrease in the demand for greeting cards. ✓
c) a decrease in supply and an increase in demand for greeting cards. ✗
d) an effective advertising campaign by the greeting card industry.
e) a decrease in the supply of greeting cards. ✗

13. The U.S. imports a lot of cars from Japan. Suppose that the price of steel that Japan uses in making cars declines. What effect might this have in the U.S. market for cars?

a) the supply of Japanese-made cars to the U.S. will decrease.
b) the price of Japanese-made cars sold in the U.S. will decrease.
c) the price of Japanese-made cars sold in the U.S. will increase.
d) the demand for Japanese-made cars will increase.
e) the quantity of Japanese-made cars sold in the U.S. will decrease.

14. Which one of the following statements would be true of an increase in demand for cameras?

a) equilibrium price rises and the supply of cameras increases.
b) equilibrium price rises and the supply of cameras decreases.
c) equilibrium price falls and the quantity of cameras supplied decreases.
d) equilibrium price rises and the quantity of cameras supplied increases.
e) equilibrium price falls and the supply of cameras falls.

15. Suppose you are given the following information about tattoos. (1) the Center for Disease Control reports that tattoos can cause liver and kidney problems; and (2) the price of dye used in tattooing has increased. Given this information, what can you say about the equilibrium price and quantity of tattoos?

a) equilibrium price will fall.
b) equilibrium price will rise and equilibrium quantity will fall.
c) equilibrium price will fall and equilibrium quantity will fall.
d) equilibrium quantity will fall.
e) equilibrium price will rise and effects on equilibrium quantity are uncertain.

16. Suppose income declines. What will be the effects on the equilibrium price and quantity of an inferior good like macaroni and cheese?

a) demand will increase and the price of macaroni and cheese will increase.

b) demand will decrease and the price of macaroni and cheese will decrease.

c) demand will increase and the price of macaroni and cheese will decrease.

d) demand will decrease and the price of macaroni and cheese will increase.

e) uncertain price effects.

VI.   PRACTICE EXAM: ESSAY QUESTIONS

1. Consider the market for athletic wear. Describe what happens to demand, supply, quantity demanded, quantity supplied, equilibrium price and equilibrium quantity when the price of spandex used in making athletic wear rises and at the same time a fitness craze sweeps the country, thanks in part, to Richard Simmons. Do not simply draw graphs. Write in complete sentences as you describe what happens.

2. Consider the market for American-made cheese. Suppose that the current equilibrium price is $1 per pound. Suppose that the French develop a preference for American-made cheese. Describe what would be true in the market if after this development, the price remained at $1. Would this be an equilibrium price? Why or why not? What would eventually happen in the market for American-made cheese?

VII.   ANSWER KEY: MULTIPLE CHOICE QUESTIONS

1. Correct Answer: c.

Discussion: The law of demand expresses an inverse or negative relationship between the price of a good and the quantity demanded (holding other factors constant). Thus, when the price of X rises, the quantity of X demanded falls and when the price of X falls, the quantity of X demanded rises.

Statement a is incorrect because demand does not increase (which would be represented by the demand curve shifting right). The law of demand is about a movement along a demand curve, not a shift in the curve. Statement b and e are incorrect for similar reasons. Statement d is incorrect because it infers a positive relationship between price and quantity demanded.

2. Correct answer: e.

Discussion: A decrease in demand is represented by a leftward shift of the demand curve (which you may want to draw out using a demand and supply graph with price on the vertical axis and quantity on the horizontal axis). A decrease in demand has the result of lowering the equilibrium price of a product and reducing the equilibrium quantity. Thus, statement e is correct since statements b and d are correct.

Statement a is not correct because a decrease in demand causes the equilibrium price to fall, not to rise. Statement c is not correct because a decrease in demand causes the equilibrium quantity to fall, not to rise.

3. Correct answer: b.

Discussion: Since mineral water and soda are substitutes, when the price of soda rises, consumers may switch to buying mineral water instead. Thus, the demand for mineral water increases, represented by a rightward shift in demand.

Statement a is incorrect because the price of soda is not a shift factor in the market for soda; a fall in the price of soda causes a movement along the demand curve for soda and thus causes the quantity of soda demanded (not the Demand) to decrease.

Statement c is not correct because when the demand for mineral water increases, the price of mineral water will rise. Statement d is not correct because when the demand for mineral water increases, the equilibrium quantity will rise. Statement e is not correct because statement a is not correct.

4. Correct answer: c.

Discussion: The Law of Supply states that there is a positive relationship between the price of X and the quantity of X supplied, holding other factors constant. This means that when the price of X increases, the quantity of X supplied increases and when the price of X decreases, the quantity of X supplied decreases. Statement c describes a positive relationship between the price of dog bones and the quantity of dog bones supplied.

Statements a, b and e are incorrect because a change in the price of dog bones will not cause the supply curve to shift in either direction but rather cause a movement along the supply curve (quantity supplied changes). Statement d is not correct because there is a positive relationship between the price and quantity supplied, not a negative relationship as implied in statement d.

5. Correct answer: a.

Discussion: Foam is an input into mattresses. When the price of foam decreases, it makes mattress production less costly. This would be represented by shifting the supply of mattresses to the right, i.e. supply increasing.

Statement b is not correct because the price of foam will not shift the demand for mattresses. What will happen, however, is that as the supply of mattresses increases, which will cause the price of mattresses to fall, the quantity of mattresses demanded will rise in response. Thus, b would have been correct if it had said "quantity demanded." Statement c is not correct because an increase in the supply of mattresses caused by the decrease in the price of foam will decrease the price of mattresses. Statement d is not correct because there is no reason given to think a shortage would occur. Statement e is not correct because statement b is not correct.

6. Correct answer: a.

Discussion: A technological advance in banana production would increase the supply of bananas, not decrease it.

Statements b, c, d, and e are all factors that would cause the supply of bananas to decrease. A decrease in the number of producers would obviously reduce the supply of bananas. An increase in the price of fertilizer raises the cost of producing bananas and would be represented by a leftward shift in supply, i.e. supply decreases. A severe rain shortage would obviously reduce the banana crop and thus decrease the supply of bananas. A tax on banana growers has the effect of raising the cost of doing business. This acts just like an increase in the price of fertilizer, i.e. the supply of bananas would shift left (decrease).

7. Correct answer: c.

Discussion: A decrease in the price of rubber used in producing walking shoes will lower the cost of producing walking shoes and cause the supply of walking shoes to increase, not the demand. However, quantity demanded would rise since the lower cost of production would translate to a lower price of walking shoes, which would raise the quantity of walking shoes demanded (movement along the demand curve).

Statements a, b, and d would lead to an increase in the demand for walking shoes. However, it may be worth noting that if walking shoes are considered inferior goods, then an increase in income would actually reduce the demand for walking shoes. Statement e is not correct because statement c should have been selected.

8. Correct answer: b.

Discussion: A price of $1 is below the equilibrium price of $2. As the price declines from $2 to $1, two things happen. First, quantity demanded increases based on the Law of Demand. Second, quantity supplied decreases based on the Law of Supply. Since quantity demanded has increased and quantity supplied has decreased, an excess demand (or shortage) is created at the $1 price. So, statement b is correct.

Statement a is not correct because it confuses what happens to quantity demanded with demand. A drop in the price of tulips will increase the quantity demanded, not demand. In other words, a decrease in the price of tulips will not shift the demand curve rightward. Statement c is not correct because at a price of $5, the quantity of tulips supplied will be greater than the quantity demanded. This happens because as the price of tulips rises, the quantity of tulips supplied increases (using the Law of Supply). Also, as the price of tulips rises, the quantity of tulips demanded decreases (using the Law of Demand). Thus, at a price of $5, which is above the equilibrium price, an excess supply will be created. Statement d is not correct, because as the price of tulips increases from $1 to $2 (or increases in general), the quantity of tulips demanded would decline, not increase. Statement e is not correct because statement b is a correct statement.

9. Correct answer: e.

Discussion: A decrease in demand for chocolate candy will lower the equilibrium price and lower the equilibrium quantity. An increase in the supply of chocolate candy will lower the equilibrium price and raise the equilibrium quantity. You can see these two cases by drawing graphs of them, separately. Since the demand and supply shift only push the price in the same direction, price will decline for sure. However, the demand and supply shifts push the equilibrium quantity in opposite directions so the effect is not known for certain.

10. Correct answer: b.

At a price of $4, the quantity supplied exceeds the quantity demanded which is the case of an excess supply or surplus. Just take the price of $4 and draw a line over to the demand and supply curves and then drop those points down to the quantity axis. You will see that the quantity supplied exceeds the quantity demanded.

Discussion: Statement a is not correct because there is not an excess demand (or shortage) but rather an excess supply (or surplus). Statement c is not correct because there would be pressure for the price to rise to the equilibrium price of $2. In fact, at a price of $1, there is a shortage. Statement d is not correct because if the price fell from $4 to $2, the quantity supplied would decrease. Statement e is not correct because if the price fell from $4 to $2, the quantity demanded would increase (not demand).

11. Correct answer: a.

Discussion: A decrease in the supply of wine is represented by shifting the supply curve to the left. A leftward shift in supply raises the equilibrium price and reduces the equilibrium quantity. You can see this by drawing a graph where supply shifts to the left and sketching out what happens to the equilibrium price and quantity.

Statement b is not correct because a decrease in demand would reduce the equilibrium price and reduce the equilibrium quantity. Statement c is not correct because an increase in demand would raise the equilibrium price and raise the equilibrium quantity. Statement d is not correct because an increase in supply would lower the equilibrium price and raise the equilibrium quantity. Statement e is not correct because the effects of these two shifts will have an uncertain effect on price but lower the equilibrium quantity for certain

12. Correct answer: a.

Discussion: A rightward shift in supply is a shift that will cause the price of a good to decline and the equilibrium quantity to rise. Thus, for the greeting card industry, there must have been an increase in supply. In this case, a decrease in the price of paper, which is an input into greeting cards, is the shift factor or cause for the increase in supply, and consequently for the decrease in equilibrium price and rise in equilibrium quantity.

Statement b is not correct because a decrease in demand for greeting cards (represented by a leftward shift in demand) will cause both the equilibrium price and equilibrium quantity to decline. Statement c is not correct because a decrease in supply and an increase in demand for greeting cards will raise the price of greeting cards and have uncertain effects on the equilibrium quantity. (See PET #7 for review). Statement d is not correct because an advertising campaign that is effective will increase the demand for greeting cards (represented by a rightward shift of demand) and thus raise the equilibrium price and quantity of greeting cards. Statement e is not correct because a decrease in the supply of greeting cards (represented by a leftward shift in supply) will cause the equilibrium price of greeting cards to rise and the equilibrium quantity to decline.

13. Correct answer: b.

Discussion: A decrease in the price of steel reduces the cost of manufacturing cars and thus increases the supply of Japanese-made cars. The increase in supply of Japanese-made cars will lower the price that American buyers pay for the cars. You can see this by drawing a graph where supply shifts to the right along the demand curve.

Statement a is not correct because the supply will increase, not decrease. Statement c is not correct because the price will decrease, not increase. Statement d is not correct because the event will not cause demand to shift; quantity demanded will however rise. Statement e is not correct because the quantity of cars sold in the U.S. will increase, not decrease.

14. Correct answer: d.

Discussion: An increase in the demand for cameras would be represented by shifting the demand curve to the right. The increase in demand raises the equilibrium price and quantity. As the equilibrium price rises, there is a movement along the supply curve which shows that the quantity supplied increases. You may wish to draw a graph to see this.

Statement a is not correct because the supply curve for cameras does not shift to the right; the quantity of cameras supplied increases. Statement b is not correct because the supply curve does not shift. Statement c is not correct because the equilibrium price rises, not falls, and the quantity of cameras increases not decreases. Statement e is not correct because the price of cameras rises and because the supply curve does not shift.

15. Correct answer: d.

Discussion: The report by the Center for Disease Control noting the health hazards associated with getting a tattoo should cause the demand for tattoos to decline. By itself, the decline in demand (represented by a leftward shift in demand) will cause the equilibrium price of tattoos to decline and the equilibrium quantity to decline, too. The effect of a rise in the price of dye used in tattooing causes the supply of tattoos to decline. This is represented by a leftward shift in the supply of tattoos. By itself, the reduction in supply of tattoos will raise the equilibrium price of tattoos and reduced the equilibrium quantity. When these two events are combined, you can see that the directional effects of the two events is the same on equilibrium quantity (it declines) but not on the equilibrium price. Therefore, without further information, you can only say that the equilibrium quantity of tattoos has fallen. Thus, statement d is correct and none of the other options can be correct.

16. Correct answer: a.

Discussion: An inferior good is a good for which demand increases when income decreases. Thus, a decline in income will have the effect of increasing the demand for macaroni and cheese. This would be represented by a rightward shift in demand. The increase in demand will have the effect of raising the equilibrium price of macaroni and cheese and increase the equilibrium quantity. Thus, statement a is correct.

Statements b and d are not correct since a decrease in income will increase the demand for an inferior good like macaroni and cheese. Statement c is not correct because while demand increases, the price of macaroni and cheese will increase, not decrease. Statement e is not correct since the directional effect on price is certain.

VIII. ANSWER KEY: ESSAY QUESTIONS

1. I will analyze the two events of an increase in the price of spandex and the fitness craze separately for their effect on the equilibrium price and quantity of athletic wear. Then, I will consider the combined effect of the two events on price and quantity. First, the increase in the price of spandex used in making athletic wear is an increase in an input price. As such, the increased input price raises the cost of producing athletic wear at every quantity supplied. This can be represented by shifting the supply curve of athletic wear to the left. The shift reflects that at every quantity supplied, the price that producers would be willing to accept in order to produce various amounts of athletic wear is now higher. By itself, this raises the equilibrium price of athletic wear and lowers the equilibrium quantity. (Notice that the price increase caused by supply shifting left will cause a movement along the demand curve which means that the quantity of athletic wear demanded will decrease). The fitness craze spawned in part by Richard Simmons will increase the demand for athletic wear. That is, at every price, the quantity demanded will now be higher than before. An increase in demand is represented by shifting the demand curve for athletic wear to the right. By itself, the rightward shift raises the price of athletic wear and increases the equilibrium quantity. (Notice that the price increase caused by demand shifting right will cause a movement along the supply curve which means that the quantity of athletic wear supplied will increase).

    When the effects of the shifts in demand and supply are combined, we know for certain that the equilibrium price will increase since both events cause price to increase. However, we do not know for sure what the effect is on the equilibrium quantity since in the first case, the equilibrium quantity declines but in the second case, the equilibrium quantity rises.

2. An increased preference by the French for American-made cheese would mean that there would be an increase in the demand for American-made cheese. This would be represented by shifting the demand curve for American-made cheese to the right, as the graph below shows. At every price, the quantity demanded is now higher (or at every quantity, the price that buyers would be willing to pay is now higher). If the price remained at $1 (rather than rising as it should), there would be a shortage of American-made cheese. That is, if the price remained at $1, the new quantity demanded would now exceed the quantity supplied at a price of $1. This would not be an equilibrium price any more. The shortage should not persist for too long because the shortage creates upward pressure on the price of cheese. Eventually, the price of cheese will rise to a new equilibrium price which is above $1. As the price rises, two things happen to eliminate the shortage. (1) As the price rises, the quantity supplied increases as the arrows along the supply curve indicate (Law of Supply; movement along

supply curve); this helps eliminate the shortage.   (2) As the price rises, the quantity demanded decreases as the arrows along the demand curve indicate (Law of Demand; movement along demand curve); this too helps eliminate the shortage.   Eventually, a new equilibrium price will be reached where the new quantity supplied is equal to the new quantity demanded.

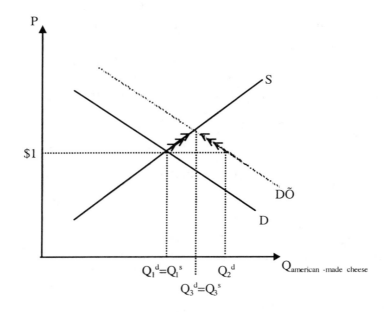

PART 2: A CLOSER LOOK AT SUPPLY AND DEMAND

CHAPTER 5
ELASTICITY: A MEASURE OF RESPONSIVENESS

I. OVERVIEW

In this chapter, you will learn about the price elasticity of demand and the price elasticity of supply. Price elasticities can be used to compute by how much, in percentage terms, quantity demanded and quantity supplied of a good will change in response to an X% change in the price of that good. You will also learn that the elasticity of demand can be used to figure out what will happen to the total revenue of a firm when it lowers or raises the price of one of its products or services by X%. You will learn that the elasticity of demand and supply can be used to determine by what percentage the equilibrium price of a good will change when either demand or supply shifts. You will learn why the elasticity of demand for some products is very high and for others very low and you will learn what factors affect the elasticity of demand. You will learn that the concept of elasticity has important applications for business decision-making or policymaking. You will also learn about other elasticities. You will learn about income elasticity and cross elasticity. Since you will be using formulas that require that you compute percentage changes, you may wish to review appendix 1 of the text and the Basic Algebra chapter of the practicum.

II. CHECKLIST

By the end of this chapter, you should be able to:

✓ Explain in words what the elasticity of demand and supply are.
✓ Use formulas to compute the elasticity of demand and supply.
✓ Explain in words the differences between inelastic, elastic, and unitary elastic demand.
✓ Discuss factors that affect the price elasticity of demand.
✓ Use formulas to compute the income elasticity of demand and the cross elasticity of demand.
✓ Use the elasticity of demand and supply to figure out the percentage price change for a given percentage quantity change.
✓ Use the elasticity of demand and supply to figure out the percentage quantity change for a given percentage price change.
✓ Use the elasticity of demand to determine what happens to the total revenue of a firm when it raises or lowers the price of one of its products.
✓ Use the elasticity of demand to determine whether a particular policy enacted by the government will have the desired effects.

✓ Use the elasticity of demand and supply to determine what happens to the equilibrium price when demand or supply shifts.

III. KEY TERMS

price elasticity of demand: A measure of the responsiveness of the quantity demanded to changes in price; computed by dividing the percentage change in quantity demanded by the percentage change in price.

price elasticity of supply: A measure of the responsiveness of the quantity supplied to changes in price; computed by dividing the percentage change in quantity supplied by the percentage change in price.

elastic demand: The price elasticity of demand is greater than one.

Inelastic demand: The price elasticity of demand is less than one.

Unitary elastic: The price elasticity demand equals one.

perfectly inelastic demand: Price elasticity of demand equals zero.

perfectly elastic demand: Price elasticity of demand is infinite.

income elasticity of demand: A measure of the responsiveness of the quantity demanded to changes in consumer income; computed by dividing the percentage change in the quantity demanded by the percentage change in income.

cross elasticity of demand: A measure of the responsiveness of the quantity demanded to changes in the price of a related good; computed by dividing the percentage change in the quantity demanded of one good (X) by the percentage change in the price of another good (Y).

perfectly inelastic supply: Price elasticity of supply equals zero.

perfectly elastic supply: Price elasticity of supply is infinite.

price-change formula: A formula that shows the percentage change in equilibrium price resulting from a change in demand or supply, given values for the price elasticity of supply and the price elasticity of demand.

midpoint method: A method of computing a percentage change by dividing the change in the variable by the average value of the variable, or the midpoint between the old value and the new one.

IV. PERFORMANCE ENHANCING TIPS (PETS)

PET #1

Elasticities are quoted on a "per unit basis."

Maybe this statement doesn't make sense quite yet, but it will after you look at the following example. Suppose you are told that the elasticity of demand is 2. What does that mean? You know that the elasticity of demand (E_d) for good X is given by the formula $\%\Delta Q^d_x/\%\Delta P_x$. You may think that when you are given the number 2, all you have is the number in the numerator. Since, 2 is equal to 2/1, you do have a number for the numerator and denominator of the elasticity of demand formula. The number in the denominator is 1. Thus, an elasticity of demand of 2 means that a 1% increase in the price of good X leads to a 2% decline in the quantity of good X demanded. Once you know the elasticity of demand on a per unit basis, you can also scale up or down the percentage changes in price and quantity but keeping the proportion equal to 2. For example, you could say that with an elasticity of demand of 2, a 10% increase in the price of good X leads to a 20% decline in the quantity of good X demanded.

PET #2

For any formula, if you are given two of three missing components, you can always figure out the third component. Likewise for three of four, four of five, and so on.

This performance enhancing tip will prove useful in this chapter as you apply it to elasticities and will also prove useful in other chapters of this textbook.

Let's see how this works by applying it to the elasticity of demand. Suppose you are told that the elasticity of demand is 0.5 and that a firm is considering reducing the price of one of its products by 10%. Can you determine by how much quantity demanded would change? All you have to do is plug the numbers that you are given into the formula:

$$E_d = \%\Delta Q^d_x/\%\Delta P_x$$
$$0.5 = \%\Delta Q^d_x/10$$
$$0.5 \times 10 = \%\Delta Q^d_x$$
$$5 = \%\Delta Q^d_x$$

Thus, a 10% reduction in the price of the product will lead to a 5% increase in the quantity of the good demanded.

Let's try another example. Suppose you are told that the elasticity of demand is 4 and that a firm wants to increase the quantity it sells by 20%. By how much must it lower price in order to generate a 20% increase in the quantity it sells? The elasticity formula could be re-written to solve for $\%\Delta P_x$ as:

$$\%\Delta P_X = \%\Delta Q^d_X/E_d$$

$$\%\Delta P_X = 20/4$$

$$\%\Delta P_X = 5$$

Thus, the firm would have to lower the price of the product by 5% in order to generate a 20% increase in quantity demanded.

PET #3

Lowering the price of a good does not always lower the total revenue that a firm will earn nor does raising the price of a good always increase the total revenue that a firm will earn.

Let's see why the statement above is true. First, total revenue is computed as price X quantity demanded. In order to understand the effect on total revenue of a given percentage price change, you must also know by how much the quantity demanded will change in percentage terms. Obviously, a lower price will reduce total revenue but only if the quantity demanded does not increase but instead remains the same (no change). Likewise, a higher price will raise total revenue but only if the quantity demanded does not decrease but remains the same (no change). However, it is usually the case that when the price of a good is lowered, the quantity demanded increases and when the price of a good is raised, the quantity demanded declines. In the case of a lower price, the lower price by itself reduces total revenue but since quantity demanded will increase, this will tend to raise total revenue. In the case of a price increase, the higher price will by itself raise total revenue but since quantity demanded will fall, this will tend to decrease total revenue. Thus, the combined effects on price and quantity must be determined.

Suppose you are told that the elasticity of demand is 2 and that a firm is going to raise the price of its product by 5%. What will be the effect on total revenue? With an elasticity of demand of 2, the percentage change in quantity demanded can be figured out. It will decrease by 10% (See PET #2). The net effect on revenue is based on a comparison of the percentage change in price to the percentage change in quantity demanded. A 5% increase in the price by itself would raise total revenue by 5%. A 10% decrease in the quantity demanded would by itself reduce total revenue by 10%. The combined effect depends on which one dominates. Since the 10% reduction is bigger in magnitude than the 5% increase, total revenue will decline.

PET #4

A unitary price elasticity of demand ($E_d = 1$) will occur when the percentage change in quantity demanded is equal to the percentage change in price. An "elastic" demand ($E_d > 1$) will occur when the percentage change in quantity demanded is greater than the percentage change in price. An "inelastic" demand ($E_d < 1$) will occur when the percentage change in quantity demanded is less than the percentage change in price.

You can best understand this PET by an example. Suppose the percentage change in quantity demanded = 4% and the percentage change in price = 4%. Obviously, the elasticity of demand would be 4%/4% = 1. Thus, you can infer that for a unitary elasticity, the percentage change in quantity demanded and price will be equal.

Now, suppose the percentage change in quantity demanded is 4% and the percentage change in price is 2%. Here, the elasticity of demand would be 2 (= 4%/2%) which is characterized as "elastic" since it is a number greater than 1. Notice that in this case, the percentage change in quantity demanded exceeds the percentage change in price. Thus, based on that information alone, without calculating a number for the elasticity, you could infer that the elasticity of demand would be greater than 1 and thus "elastic."

Now, suppose the percentage change in quantity demanded is 4% and the percentage change in price is 8%. Here, the elasticity of demand would be 0.5 (= 4%/8%) which is characterized as "inelastic" since it is a number less than 1. Notice that in this case, the percentage change in quantity demanded is less than the percentage change in price. Thus, based on that information alone, without calculating a number for the elasticity, you could infer that the elasticity of demand would be less than 1 and thus "inelastic."

V. PRACTICE EXAM: MULTIPLE CHOICE QUESTIONS

1. Which one of the following is the correct formula for the elasticity of demand?

a) $\Delta P_X / \Delta Q^d_X$

b) $\%\Delta Q^d_X / \%\Delta P_X$

c) $\Delta Q^d_X / \Delta P_X$

d) $\%\Delta P_X / \%\Delta Q^d_X + \%Q^s_X$

e) $\%\Delta P_X / \%\Delta Q^d_X$

2. Suppose the elasticity of demand for bowling is 1.5 and the manager of the bowling alley decides to raise the price of a game by 5%. By what percentage will quantity demanded change?

a) decline by 7.5%.
b) rise by 7.5%.
c) decline by 3%.
d) rise by 3%.
e) not enough information to answer the question.

3. Suppose the government wants to reduce teenage smoking by 50%. Suppose further that the government knows that the teenage elasticity of demand for a pack of cigarettes is 2. By what percentage would the government have to increase the price of a pack of cigarettes (through a tax) in order to cut teenage smoking by 50%?

a) 100%.
b) 25%.
c) 50%.
d) 250%.
e) 20%.

4. Which one of the following defines an inelastic demand?

a) $E_d > 1$

b) $E_d = 1$

c) $E_d < 1$

d) $E_d > 0$

e) $E_d < 0$

5. Which one of the following factors would reduce the elasticity of demand for a particular product?

a) more time to shop around.
b) no close substitutes.
c) big part of budget.
d) luxury item.
e) all of the above reduce the elasticity of demand.

6. Which one of the following goods would you characterize as being the most elastic?

a) insulin.
b) coffee.
c) cigarettes.
d) gasoline.
e) cookies.

7. Suppose product X's price is reduced by 5% and the quantity demanded increases by 2%. Based on this information, demand for product X would be:

a) unitary elastic.

b) inelastic.

c) elastic.

d) tertiary.

e) second-order elastic.

8. Suppose the elasticity of demand for flowers at a local florist is estimated to be 4, as computed by a savvy economics student. If the florist raises the price of flowers by 5%, then:

a) the revenue earned by the florist will decline.

b) the quantity of flowers sold by the florist will decline by 1.25%.

c) the quantity of flowers sold by the florist will decline by 0.2%.

d) the quantity of flowers sold by the florist will decline by 20%.

e) (a) and (d).

9. Suppose a dentist wants to increase her client base by 30%. Suppose further that the elasticity of demand for dental services is 5. By what percentage would the dentist have to reduce her dental fees in order to increase her client base by 30%?

a) 60%.

b) 6%.

c) 15%.

d) 150%.

e) 16.7%.

10. Total revenue _____ when the price of a good increases and its demand is inelastic. Total revenue _____ when the price of a good decreases and its demand is elastic.

a) increases/increases.

b) increases/decreases.

c) increases/does not change.

d) decreases/decreases.

e) decreases/increases.

11. What is the elasticity of the supply of cows if the price of a cow increases from $500 to $550 and the quantity supplied rises from 100,000 to 130,000? (Do not use the midpoint formula).

a) 3.33.
b) 3.0.
c) 5.0.
d) 6.0.
e) cannot be determined without information on percentages.

12. Suppose that the supply of tweed jackets increases by 20%. Further, suppose that the elasticity of demand for tweed jackets is 1 and the elasticity of supply is 4. What will happen to the equilibrium price of tweed jackets?

a) rise by 8%.
b) fall by 8%.
c) rise by 4%.
d) fall by 4%.
e) fall by 5%.

13. Suppose a men's clothing store estimates that the income of its consumer base has increased by 24%. Further, suppose it has calculated the income elasticity of demand to be 1.2. By how much should the quantity of ties demanded change based on this information?

a) increase by 12%.
b) increase by 28.8%.
c) increase by 20%.
d) decrease by 28.8%.
e) increase by 5%.

14. Suppose you observe an increase in the price of product J by 10%. At the same time, you observe a decrease in the quantity demanded of product L by 2%. Which one of the following statements is correct using this information?

a) J and L are substitutes and the cross elasticity of demand is 5.
b) J and L are complements and the cross elasticity of demand is 0.2.
c) J and L are substitutes and the cross elasticity of demand is 0.2.
d) J and L are complements and the cross elasticity of demand is 5.
e) J and L are substitutes and more information is needed to calculate the cross elasticity.

15. Suppose you are given the following information:

1999: average income = $50,000; quantity demanded = 20,000 units.
2000: average income = $55,000; quantity demanded = 16,000 units.

All other factors over 1999-2000 are held constant. What is the income elasticity of demand and is the good a normal good or an inferior good?

a) 10; inferior good.
b) 2; normal good.
c) 20; inferior good.
d) 2; inferior good.
e) 1/2; normal good.

16. Suppose a business lowers the price of a product it sells from $10 to $8 and that the amount sold increases from 1,000 units to 1,500 units. Use the midpoint formula to calculate the elasticity of demand based on the following information.

a) 2.5
b) 2.0
c) 1.82
d) 1.50
e) 1.33

17. Which one of the following statements is true about a perfectly elastic demand curve?

a) it is vertical.
b) the elasticity of demand must be 0.
c) its elasticity is calculated as percentage change in price divided by percentage change in quantity demanded.
d) it shows that any increase in price of a product will cause the quantity demanded to fall to 0.
e) none of the above.

18. Which one of the following statements is NOT true about a perfectly inelastic supply curve?

a) it is vertical.
b) it has an elasticity of that is 0.
c) it shows that the percentage change in quantity supplied is always 0, no matter what the price change.
d) shifts in demand along the perfectly inelastic supply curve will lead to changes in price only.
e) its elasticity is calculated as the percentage change in price divided by the percentage change in quantity supplied.

VI. PRACTICE EXAM: ESSAY QUESTIONS

1. Discuss the short and long run effects of a government policy of imposing a tax that would raise the price of oil and gasoline by 20% assuming that the elasticity of demand for oil is currently estimated to be 0.5 and the elasticity of demand for gasoline to be 1.2. Be sure to address what factors might alter the elasticity numbers over time.

2. Suppose that you are an economic consultant for a large company that produces and sells lollipops that are shaped as the faces of Hollywood celebrities. The company has shops in the major cities around the country and also sells by mail order catalog. As an economic consultant, you have estimated the elasticity of demand for store-bought lollipops to be 0.75 and the elasticity of demand for mail order lollipops to be 3. What advice would you give to the president of the company if she wanted to increase revenue from the shops and through mail orders? Now, suppose that the price of sugar increases causing a 20% reduction in the supply of celebrity lollipops. What information would you need to compute the effect of the reduction in supply on the equilibrium price?

VII. ANSWER KEY: MULTIPLE CHOICE QUESTIONS

1. Correct answer: b.

Discussion: The elasticity of demand is the percentage change in the quantity of good X demanded by the percentage change in its price.

Statement a is not correct because it is not expressed in percentage changes (but rather absolute changes) and has the numerator and denominator reversed. Statement c is not correct because it is expressed in absolute changes. Statement d is not correct because the elasticity of supply does not enter the formula. Statement e is not correct because the numerator and denominator should be reversed.

2. Correct answer: a.

Discussion: A rise in the price will always reduce the quantity demanded so, first you must look for an answer that has quantity demanded declining. The percentage change in quantity demanded is computed by multiplying E_d times $\%\Delta P = 1.5 \times 5 = 7.5$.

Statement b is not correct because the quantity demanded will decline, not increase, when the price rises. Statements c and d are wrong based on the formula. Statement e is not correct because there is enough information to answer the question.

3. Correct answer: b.

Discussion: Since you are given the elasticity of demand and a desired percentage change in the quantity demanded, you can figure out the percentage change in price as $\%\Delta P_x = \%\Delta Q^d_x/E_d$. Thus, $\%\Delta P_x = 50\%/2 = 25\%$.

Statement a is not correct because the two numbers should not be multiplied. Statement c would only be correct if the elasticity of demand was 1. Statement d is not correct; it is off by a factor of 10. Statement e is also not correct.

4. Correct answer: c.

Discussion: An inelastic demand is defined as one for which E_d is less than 1 which means that a 1% increase in price reduces the quantity demanded by less than 1% (and vice-versa for a price decrease).

Statement a defines an elastic demand. Statement b defines a unitary elastic demand. Statements d and e are not correct because elasticity is defined with respect to 1, not zero.

5. Correct answer: b.

Discussion: When there are no close substitutes for a product that makes the demand for it more inelastic. That is, the price of the good can be raised by a big percentage but quantity demanded will not respond by very much because there are not close substitutes consumers could switch their purchases to. This describes a good that has an inelastic demand.

If consumers have more time to shop around, they are more likely to compare prices. This means that consumers will be more sensitive to price changes, i.e. demand will be more elastic. If a good is a big part of a consumer's budget, a small change in the price will have a bigger impact on their budget. Thus, consumers will be more likely to greatly reduce their purchases of the good even if its price goes up a little bit. This defines demand to be more elastic. (You may want to think about the effects on budget and spending if the price of a pen goes up by 10% to the price of housing going up by 10%). Luxury items, because they are not necessities, tend to have a more elastic demand. Since a, c, and d are likely to raise the elasticity of demand, (make it more elastic), statement e cannot be correct.

6. Correct answer: e.

Discussion: Cookies are the only good that are not a "necessity." Goods that are not a necessity tend to have a more elastic demand.

Insulin is a necessary good to a diabetic; no matter how much the price of insulin increases, the purchases of insulin will not drop. In this case, the elasticity of demand for insulin is likely to be zero. The same, to a lesser degree, is true of gasoline. People must have transportation to their jobs, the grocery store, etc. Thus, gasoline is more of a necessity than cookies. A similar story can be told for coffee. Most people cannot seem to get through the day without at least one cup of coffee which makes coffee more of a necessity than cookies. Cigarettes have an addictive property which means that price increases will have less of an effect of reducing consumption than for a non-addictive good. Thus, cookies are likely to have a higher elasticity of demand than cigarettes.

7.   Correct answer: b.

Discussion: The elasticity of demand is calculated as the percentage change in quantity demanded divided by the percentage change in price. (See PET #2). Thus, the elasticity of demand would be 2/5 = 0.4. Since the elasticity of demand is less than 1.0, demand is said to be "inelastic." You should also be aware that if the percentage change in quantity demanded is less than the percentage change in price, demand for the product will be inelastic. In this case, the percentage change in quantity demanded is 2 while the percentage change in price is 5 and so demand must be inelastic.

Statement a is not correct. Unitary elasticity occurs when the elasticity of demand is 1.0. This happens when the percentage change in quantity demanded is exactly equal (in absolute value) to the percentage change in price. Statement c is not correct. An elastic demand occurs when the elasticity of demand is greater than 1.0. This will happen whenever the percentage change in quantity demanded (in absolute value) is greater than the percentage change in price. Statements d and e are made-up terms.

8.   Correct answer: e.

Discussion: When the elasticity of demand is greater than 1, an X% price change will cause a greater than X% change in quantity demanded. In this case, the florist has chosen to raise, not lower, the price of flowers. With an elasticity of demand of 4, the 5% point increase in the price will lead to a 20% point decline in the quantity of flowers sold. Thus, statement d is correct. At the same time, since the percentage change in the price increase is swamped by the percentage reduction in the quantity of flowers sold, the revenue earned by the florist will drop. Thus, statement a is correct, too.

Statement b is not correct; the effect on quantity is not determined by dividing 5 by 4 but instead multiplying the two numbers. Statement c is not correct because it is off by a factor of 10.

9.   Correct answer: b.

Discussion: The percentage change in quantity demanded (i.e. client base) desired by the dentist is an increase of 30%. The dentist also knows the elasticity of demand for dental services to be 5. The formula for the elasticity of demand can be used to solve for the percentage change in the price of dental services that would generate the 30% increase in the client base. (See PET #2). Using the elasticity of demand formula: 5 = 30%/percentage change in price. So, percentage change in price = 30%/5 = 6%. Since the dentist wants the client base to increase (not decrease), dental fees must decline by 6%.

Based on the above, none of the other statements are correct.

10. Correct answer: a.

Discussion: With an inelastic demand, the percentage rise (in this case) in the price of the good is greater than the percentage reduction in the quantity demanded which means that on net, total revenue (p X q) will increase. With an elastic demand, the percentage drop (in this case) will be less than the percentage increase in the quantity of the good demanded. (Remember price and quantity demanded move in opposite directions). Thus, on net, total revenue will rise.

Statement b is not correct; it would have been correct if the second part of the question asked what happened to total revenue when the price of a good with an elastic demand was increased. Statement c is not correct; only a unitary elasticity of demand leads to no change in total revenue when price is raised or lowered. Statement d is not correct; it would have been correct if the question had asked what happens to total revenue when price is decreased and demand is inelastic and what happens to total revenue when price is increased and demand is elastic. Statement e is not correct; it would have been correct if the first part of the question had asked what happens to total revenue when price is decreased and demand is inelastic.

11. Correct answer: b.

Discussion: The percentage change in the price of a cow is 10% [($550-500)/500] X 100 and the percentage change in the quantity of cows supplied is 30% [(130,000-100,000)/100,000] X 100. The elasticity of supply is computed as the percentage change in the quantity supplied divided by the percentage change in the price which is 30%/10% = 3.

For the reasoning just mentioned, statements a, c, and d are not correct. Statement e is not correct because you are given information that allows you to compute percentage changes.

12. Correct answer: d.

Discussion: Since the supply of tweed jackets has increased, you should be looking for an answer that has the price of tweed jackets declining. The formula used to compute the percentage change in the equilibrium price is to take the percentage shift in supply (or demand, if that had been the question) and divide it by the sum of the elasticity of supply and demand. Thus, the percentage change in the equilibrium price will be 20%/(1 + 4) = 20%/5 = 4%.

Statements a and c cannot be correct because a supply increase causes a drop in the equilibrium price (see Chapter 4 for review if you don't remember this). Statements b and e are not correct because the formula gives an answer of 4%.

13. Correct answer: b.

Discussion: Since income has increased, you should be looking for an answer that says the quantity demand has increased. Thus, statement d can be ruled out right away. The income elasticity of demand formula is income elasticity of demand = percentage change in quantity demanded/percentage change in income. Since you know the income elasticity of demand is 1.2 and the percentage change in income is 24%, you can plug the numbers in and solve for the percentage change in quantity demanded. Thus, 1.2 = percentage change in quantity demanded/24%. Using a little algebra to solve for the answer gives (1.2 X 24%) = percentage change in quantity demanded. Thus, the correct answer is 28.8%. You may have incorrectly arrived at the answer of 20% if you had carelessly divided 24% by 1.2.

Based on the discussion above, none of the other options are correct.

14. Correct answer: b.

Discussion: Complements are goods for which the price change in one good leads to a change in quantity demanded of another good in the opposite direction of the price change. For example, when the price of peanut butter increases, the quantity of jelly demanded decreases because the two goods are complements. They are used together so that when the cost of one of the goods rises (peanut butter), it causes the price of the finished good (peanut butter and jelly sandwich) to rise and thus quantity of peanut butter and jelly sandwiches to decline which in turn indirectly reduces the quantity of jelly demanded. The cross-elasticity of demand is computed as the percentage change in quantity demanded of product Y/percentage change in the price of product X. Using the information from the question, the cross elasticity of demand is 2%/10% = 0.2. Thus, statement b is correct.

Since J and L are complements, statements a, c, and e are not correct. Statement d is not correct because the cross-elasticity is calculated as 2%/10% and not 10%/2%.

15. Correct answer: d.

Discussion: The income elasticity of demand is the percentage change in quantity demanded divided by the percentage change in price. In this case, the percentage change in quantity demanded is -20% = (16,000 - 20,000)/20,000. The percentage change in average income is +10% ($55,000 - $50,000)/$50,000. Thus, the income elasticity of demand, expressed in absolute terms (i.e. without the negative sign) is 20%/10% = 2. However, since you are told that quantity demanded has decreased while income has increased, you should infer (based on Chapter 4) that this is an inferior good. Inferior goods are goods for which increases in income cause demand to decline and so to, the equilibrium quantity. (vice-versa for decreases in income). Thus, statement d is correct.

Based on the discussion above, statements a, b, c, and e are incorrect.

16. Correct answer: c.

Discussion: Using the midpoint formula, the percentage change in the price is ($10 - $8)/ [(10 + 8)/2] = $2/$9 = 0.22. The percentage change in quantity demanded is (1,000 – 1,500)/ [(1,500 + 1,000)/2] = -500/1,250 = -0.4. The elasticity of demand is the absolute value of the percentage change in quantity demanded divided by the percentage change in price, so it would be (0.4/0.22) = 1.82.

None of the other answers are correct using the midpoint formula above.

17. Correct answer: d.

Discussion: Statement d is correct because a horizontal supply curve shows that any movement off of the established price will result in a quantity demanded of zero.

Statement a is not true. A perfectly elastic demand curve is horizontal. Statement b is not true. A perfectly elastic demand curve has an elasticity that is infinite. Statement c is not true. The elasticity of demand is always calculated as percentage change in quantity demanded divided by percentage change in price, not the other way around. Statement e cannot be true since statement d is true.

18. Correct answer: e.

Discussion: Statement e is not true. The elasticity of supply is always calculated as percentage change in quantity supplied divided by percentage change in price, not the other way around. All the other statements are true of the elasticity of supply.

VIII. ANSWER KEY: ESSAY QUESTIONS

1. Since the currently estimated elasticity of demand for oil is 0.5, a 20% increase in the price of oil will reduce the quantity demanded by 10% (0.5 X 20%), at least in the short run. The tax revenue collected by the government on oil will, however, increase. The tax revenue will increase because the percentage increase in the price of oil dominates the percentage decrease in the quantity demanded. For gasoline, a 20% increase in its price will reduce the quantity demanded by 24% (1.2 X 20%), at least in the short run. In the short run, the 20% increase in the price of gasoline is much more effective at reducing consumer use of gasoline than is the 20% increase in the price of oil at reducing consumer use of oil (compare 10% to 24%). However, the tax revenue collected on gasoline sales will actually decline because the percentage decrease in the quantity demanded outweighs the percentage increase in the price. Thus, on balance, tax revenue collected by the government on gasoline will decline. While in the short run, it may be difficult to find substitutes for oil or gasoline, in the long run, consumers may be able to modify their spending behavior. They may find substitutes for oil or gasoline (perhaps because innovative companies will invent products like methanol or battery-run automobiles). Thus, in the long run, the estimated elasticities may increase. In fact, if the elasticity for oil increased above 1, then the tax increase of 20% would end up lowering the tax revenue collected by the government on oil consumption.

2. The advice I would give to the president of the celebrity lollipop company is this: raise the price of lollipops purchased in shops throughout the country and lower the price of lollipops purchased through mail order catalogs. However, be aware that eventually, when consumers become aware of the price difference, you may eventually see your revenue from the stores decline (rather than rise after you have raised the price) but your revenue from mail orders may eventually increase by more than originally estimated. This may happen because customers from the store-bought shops may begin to purchase by mail order. That is, they will have found an almost identical substitute for the store-bought lollipops.

If the price of sugar rises, the supply of celebrity lollipops will decrease (shift left). The decreased supply will raise the price of a store-bought and mail order lollipops. In order to know by how much the equilibrium prices would rise, you would need information on the elasticity of supply of store-bought and mail order lollipops (in addition to the elasticity of demand) as well as on the percentage reduction in the supply of each type of lollipop. For example, if the supply of mail order lollipops dropped by 40% and the elasticity of supply is 1 and you are given that the elasticity of demand is 3, then the equilibrium price will change by 40%/(1+3) = 40%/4 = 10%.

We invite you to visit the book's Companion Website at:
http://www.prenhall.com/osullivan/
for further exercises and practice quizzes.

CHAPTER 6
CONSUMER CHOICE

I. OVERVIEW

In this chapter, you will learn about factors that affect an individual's decision about how much of a particular product or products to consume (or buy). You will see that an individual attempts to get the most satisfaction (i.e. utility) from the products purchased subject to the amount of money or income they have to spend. So, you will see that an individual's income imposes a constraint on the amounts and combinations of products a consumer can purchase. You will see a more graphical depiction of consumer choice. You will use budget lines and indifference curves which are just ways of representing income constraints for given prices of goods and services and preferences. You will re-encounter the principle of opportunity cost, the marginal principle, and the real-nominal principle. You will learn about utility and marginal utility (economists' way of measuring the satisfaction that consumers receive from the consumption of goods). You will learn about the law of diminishing marginal utility and the utility-maximizing rule. You will also consider an individual demand curve (instead of a market demand curve as in Chapters 4 and 5).

II. CHECK LIST

By the end of the chapter, you should be able to:

✓ Explain how a consumer's income (or budget) and the prices of products force the consumer to make tradeoffs in consumption choices.

✓ Apply the principle of opportunity cost to consumption decisions.

✓ Draw a budget line assuming different prices for the goods under consideration.

✓ Define the slope of the budget line and explain why it is equal to the price of the good on the horizontal axis divided by the price of the good on the vertical axis.

✓ Define an indifference curve and explain the relationship of an indifference curve to one above it and one below it.

✓ Define the marginal rate of substitution.

✓ Explain why the indifference curve becomes flatter as you move down along the curve.

✓ Draw a graph of a budget line and indifference curve and find the utility-maximizing point.

✓ Explain why the utility-maximizing point is the point of tangency between the budget line and the indifference curve and why non-tangency points are not utility maximizing.

✓ Derive a demand curve by changing the slope of the budget line and finding new utility-maximizing points.

✓ Explain the law of diminishing marginal utility and represent it with a graph.

✓ Explain why consumers are willing to pay a higher price for consuming the first unit of a good than for any subsequent units.

✓ Explain why each point on an individual demand curve represents a point at which the marginal benefit of consuming (using) a good equals the marginal cost to the consumer.

✓ Explain how changes in prices, income, and tastes might affect consumer choice.

✓ Explain why a doubling of prices and income will leave a consumer's choice unchanged.

✓ Use the equimarginal rule (utility-maximizing rule) to explain consumer choice.

✓ Use the equimarginal rule (utility-maximizing rule) to decide whether a consumer should increase or decrease the consumption of one good and decrease or increase the consumption of another.

III. KEY TERMS

budget set: A set of points that includes all the combinations of goods that a consumer can afford, given the consumer's income and the prices of the goods.

budget line: The line connecting all the combinations of two goods that exhaust a consumer's budget.

Price ration: The ratio of the price of one good to the price of a second good; the market trade-off.

Indifference curve: the set of combinations of two goods that generate the same level of utility or satisfaction.

util: A unit of utility.

utility: The satisfaction the consumer gets from a product.

Marginal rate of substitution (MRS): the rate at which a consumer is willing to substitute one good for another.

Indifference map: A set of indifference curves, each with a different level of utility.

total utility: The utility (measured in utils) from a particular quantity of a product.

marginal utility: The change in total utility from one additional unit of a good.

law of diminishing marginal utility: As the consumption of a particular good increases, marginal utility decreases.

utility-maximizing rule: Pick the affordable combination that makes the marginal utility per dollar spent on one good equal to the marginal utility per dollar spent on a second good.

IV. PERFORMANCE ENHANCING TIPS (PETS)

PET #1

The slope of the budget line is the ratio of the price of good X (good on the horizontal axis) to the price of good Y (good on the vertical axis) which is also equal to the ratio of the change in good Y divided by the change in good X.

Suppose the price of a single-serving pizza is $4 and the price of a deli sandwich is $2. Further, suppose a consumer has a budget/income of $200. The budget line representing this scenario is:

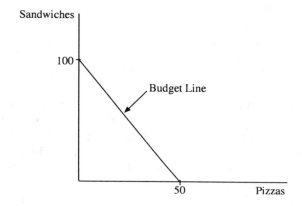

If the consumer buys 20 pizzas, she will spend $80 and have $120 remaining to spend on sandwiches. Thus, she could buy 60 sandwiches. If the consumer decides to buy 30 pizzas, she will spend $120 and have $80 remaining to spend on sandwiches. Thus, she could buy 40 sandwiches. The change in the quantity of pizzas is +10 and the change in the quantity of deli sandwiches is -20.

Notice that the ratio of the price of a pizza to a sandwich is ($4/pizza)/ ($2/sandwich) = 2 sandwiches/1 pizza. Also, notice that based on the numbers above, the change in the quantity of sandwiches divided by the change in the quantity of pizzas is 20/10 = 2 sandwiches/1 pizza (allowing for a negative sign since the consumer must trade off sandwiches for pizzas).

PET #2

When you see the term "marginal," you should always think of computing the change in a variable. Computing the change requires that you have some numeric value before the change and some numeric value after the change. The difference between the two is the change in the variable.

You have seen this PET in Chapter 2 but it is repeated again here because you will use it in this chapter to compute marginal utility.

Marginal utility is the change in utility or utils from increasing consumption (or cutting back on consumption) by one more unit of a good. The change in utility or utils is a way of measuring the change in satisfaction or benefits or "happiness" that consumers receive from consuming that one more unit of the good.

Use the table below to fill in the marginal utility reaped from buying potato chips.

Bags of Potato Chips	Utility	Marginal Utility
1	50 utils	
2	90 utils	
3	120 utils	
4	140 utils	
5	150 utils	
6	120 utils	

The marginal utility (change in utility) associated with consuming the first bag of potato chips is 50 utils since 0 bags of potato chips yields 0 utility. The total utility associated with consuming two bags of potato chips is 90 utils which means that the change in utility (marginal utility) from consuming the second bag of potato chips is 40 utils. The marginal utility for the third bag is computed similarly as 30 utils; 20 utils for the fourth bag, and 10 utils for the fifth bag. However, the sixth bag actually reduces total utility from 150 to 120 so the marginal utility is negative = -30. A rational consumer obviously would not consume any more than 5 bags of potato chips since that would reduce his overall level of satisfaction.

PET #3

The ratio of two variables can increase because the variable in the numerator gets bigger or because the variable in the denominator gets smaller. The ratio of two variables can decrease because the variable in the numerator gets smaller or because the variable in the denominator gets bigger.

For example, suppose the ratio of the marginal utility of good X to the marginal utility of good Y (MU_x/MU_y) is 4. That is, the marginal rate of substitution is 4. Now, suppose a consumer consumes more of good X. Based on the law of diminishing marginal utility, the marginal utility of good X will decline. This means that the ratio, (MU_x/MU_y), will decrease from the value of 4. Suppose instead that the consumer consumes less of good Y. Based on the law of diminishing marginal utility (in reverse now because the consumer is consuming less, not more), the marginal utility of good Y will increase. This too, means that the ratio, (MU_x/MU_y), will decrease.

PET #4

Diminishing marginal utility means that the utility (or satisfaction) from consuming more and more of a good increases but at a decreasing rate. Just because the term "diminishing" is used does NOT mean that the level of utility (satisfaction) decreases or diminishes.

In chapter 2, you encountered the principle of diminishing marginal returns or diminishing marginal output. In this chapter, the principle is applied to utility. In fact, if you look at the table above, assuming you've now filled in the correct numbers, you will see that the numbers in the table reflect diminishing marginal utility. The marginal utility declines from 50 to 40 to 30 to 20 to 10 utils. The numbers are just a way of expressing that an individual gets less and less satisfaction from eating more and more bags of potato chips.

PET #5

The equimarginal rule (or rule of utility-maximization) is a marginal benefit-marginal cost comparison. If there is not an equality in the expression, then a consumer can re-arrange his consumption choices and be better off (get more utility).

The equimarginal rule (or rule of utility-maximization) can be expressed two ways:

  i.   [Marginal Utility of Good X/Price of X]=[Marginal Utility of Good Y/Price of Y]

which can be re-arranged as:

  ii. [Marginal Utility of Good X/Marginal Utility of Good Y]=[Price of Good X/Price of Good Y].

The first expression compares the marginal utility per unit price paid of good X to good Y. It says that the marginal utility (or marginal benefit) per unit of cost to the consumer of good X is equal to the marginal utility (or marginal benefit) per unit of cost to the consumer of good Y. If the equality sign was replaced with a > sign, then the marginal utility per unit price paid for good X would be greater than the marginal utility per unit price paid for good Y. Thus, a consumer could be better off (receive more utility) by re-arranging his budget to consume more of good X and less of good Y. (vice-versa if the equality sign were replaced with a < sign).

The second expression compares the relative marginal utility of good X to good Y to the relative price paid for good X to good Y. Remember that to the consumer, the price paid for one unit of a good represents the marginal cost to the consumer. The second expression says that the relative marginal utility (or marginal benefit) of good X to good Y is equal to the relative marginal cost to the consumer of good X to good Y. If the equality sign was replaced with a > sign, then the marginal utility of good X relative to good Y would be greater than the relative marginal cost of good X to good Y. Since the relative marginal benefit of good X is greater than the relative marginal cost of good X, a consumer could be better of by re-arranging his budget to consume more of good X and less of good Y (vice-versa if the equality sign were replaced with a < sign).

PET #6

The equimarginal rule (or utility-maximizing rule) is based on a consumer having a given budget (income) and facing fixed prices of the goods. A bigger budget (income) or changes in the price of the goods the consumer typically purchases could alter the quantities that a consumer would select based on the utility-maximizing rule.

Suppose based on the utility-maximizing rule, you decide to buy one chicken-salad sandwich and three sodas a day.   Suppose that the price of a chicken salad sandwich is $2.00 and the price of a soda is $0.50. Furthermore, the marginal utility you receive from the one and only chicken salad sandwich is 8 utils and the marginal utility you receive from the additional third soda is 2 utils. Are you maximizing your total utility? Let's see:

Using (i) from PET #5 above:

> 8 utils/$2.00 = 2 utils/$0.50
> 4 = 4

Using (ii) from PET #5 above:

> 8 utils/2 utils = $2.00/$0.50
> 4 = 4.

Thus, you are maximizing your total utility (for the given prices and your given income) by consuming one sandwich and three sodas since the two ratios are equal.

Now, suppose the price of a soda goes up to $1 but you continue to consume one chicken salad sandwich and three sodas. What would happen to the conditions above? Let's see:

Using (i) from PET #5 above:
> 8 utils/$2.00 = 4 utils/$1.00
> 4 > 2.

This means that the marginal benefit per unit cost of one more chicken salad sandwich is greater than the marginal benefit per unit cost of one more soda. Thus, the consumer could be better off by increasing his consumption of chicken salad sandwiches and reducing his consumption of sodas.

Using (ii) from PET #5 above:
> 8 utils/2 utils = $2.00/$1.00
> 4 > 2.

This means that the marginal utility of chicken salad sandwiches relative to sodas is greater than the marginal cost of chicken salad sandwiches relative to sodas. Thus, the consumer could be better off by increasing his consumption of chicken salad sandwiches and reducing his consumption of sodas since he receives relatively more benefits than costs from chicken salad sandwiches.

Both of these examples illustrate what you probably already know: an increase in the price of a good (relative to others) will lead to a reduction in the amount consumed, for a given income, tastes, etc.

Now, suppose that rather than the price of the goods changing, the income of the consumer changes. Let's suppose that the consumer gets an increase in his income. What will happen? Without any price changes, the ratio of prices will still be 4. However, since the consumer now has more income, he can consume more of both goods. When he does this, what will happen to the marginal utility of the goods? They will decline. Diminishing marginal utility tells you that as more of a good is consumed, the addition to utility (marginal utility) of consuming one more unit of that good declines. Thus, for example, a consumer may now consume 3 chicken salad sandwiches and 6 sodas a day. The third chicken salad sandwich may now yield a marginal utility of 4 utils and the sixth soda may now yield a marginal utility of 1 util. However, it is no accident that the ratio of marginal utilities remains at 4. The equimarginal rule (utility-maximizing rule) dictates that the consumer consumes chicken salad sandwiches and sodas until the ratio of marginal utilities is equal to the ratio of the prices. Since the ratio of prices hasn't changed, the ratio of the marginal utilities must still be 4 even though the quantities consumed (and the respective marginal utilities) have changed.

V. PRACTICE EXAM: MULTIPLE CHOICE QUESTIONS

1. Suppose you are given a monthly income of $200 to spend on food while at college. Further, suppose the price of a single-serving pizza is $4 and the price of a deli-sandwich is $2. Which one of the following consumption combinations is possible given these prices and income?

a) 40 pizzas, 50 sandwiches.

b) 15 pizzas, 80 sandwiches.

c) 20 pizzas, 60 sandwiches.

d) 10 pizzas, 100 sandwiches.

e) 50 pizzas, 20 sandwiches.

2. In consumer choice theory:

a) a consumer compares total costs to total benefits in making a purchase decision.

b) a consumer compares marginal costs to marginal benefits in making a purchase decision.

c) consumers prefer to buy only low price goods. ✓

d) consumers face the law of increasing marginal utility.

e) consumers are assumed to all have identical tastes. ✗

3. Which one of the following terms is used in economics to describe the satisfaction that individuals receive from their consumption of goods and services?

a) utility.

b) opportunity cost.

c) totality.

d) plaisir.

e) hedonity.

4. Which one of the following statements is correct?

a) as a consumer consumes more of a good, marginal utility increases.
b) marginal utility is always positive.
c) consumer choice is limited by income.
d) consumer choice depends on the relative price of goods.
e) (c) and (d).

5. Which one of the following is true of indifference curves?

a) they represent the combination of two goods that generate the same level of income.
b) combinations of goods above the indifference curve generate more satisfaction.
c) a lower point along an indifference curve yields less satisfaction than a higher point.
d) the slope of the indifference curve gets bigger (steeper) as you move down the indifference curve.
e) (b) and (c).

6. Which one of the following statements is true assuming the marginal rate of substitution between good G and good H is equal to 3?

a) an increase in the consumption of good G and a decrease in the consumption of good H will increase the marginal rate of substitution.
b) if the ratio of the price of good G to the price of good H is 4, then a consumer is maximizing his utility.
c) an increase in the consumption of good G and an increase in the consumption of good H will increase the marginal rate of substitution.
d) a decrease in the consumption of good G and an increase in the consumption of good H will increase the marginal rate of substitution.
e) a decrease in income will reduce the marginal rate of substitution.

7. Which one of the points in the graph below is associated with utility-maximization?

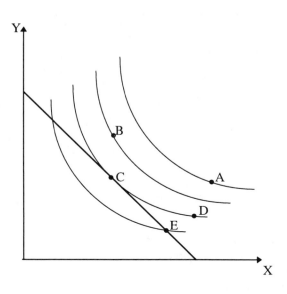

a) point A.
b) point B.
c) point C.
d) point D.
e) point E.

8. Suppose you are given the following information:

marginal utility of 1 cup coffee = 20 utils.
marginal utility of 1 can soda = 10 utils.
price of 1 cup of coffee = $1.00.

What would the price of one can of soda have to be in order for the consumer to maximize his utility?

a) $0.50.
b) $2.00.
c) $5.00.
d) $200.
e) cannot be answered without information on consumer's income/budget.

9. Which one of the statements based on the following table is true?

Number of Sweaters Purchased	Total Utility
1	25 utils
2	40 utils
3	50 utils
4	55 utils
5	58 utils

a) the marginal utility of the fifth sweater is 33 utils (58-25).

b) total utility is diminishing.

c) total utility is increasing but at a decreasing rate.

d) marginal utility is negative.

e) marginal utility cannot be computed without more information.

10. The marginal cost of consuming one more unit of item X is:

a) the loss of utils associated with consuming the last unit of some other good, Y.

b) the marginal utility of consuming the last unit of good Y multiplied by the units of good Y that must be sacrificed to obtain one unit of good X.

c) the market price paid for good X.

d) necessarily negative.

e) (b) and (d).

11. Which one of the following statements is NOT correct?

a) the smaller the amount of a good consumed, the higher the marginal utility derived from consuming it.

b) the marginal cost of consuming one more unit of good X is higher when the amount of good Y consumed is lower.

c) at a price ratio of $4 per sandwich to $2 per iced tea, two iced teas must be sacrificed in order to obtain one more sandwich, assuming all income is currently being spent.

d) points along a rational individual's demand curve are points where the marginal benefit of consuming a good is greater than the marginal cost of consuming it.

e) all of the above are correct statements.

12. Use the following information to compute the marginal cost (in terms of utils) from obtaining a fourth ice cream cone. Assume the consumer's budget is $20, the price of an ice cream cone is $2 and the price of cookies is $1. Also, assume the consumer has purchased 12 cookies and the marginal utility of the twelfth cookie is 4 utils.

a) 4 utils.

b) 0.25 utils.

c) 8 utils.

d) 2 utils.

e) 1 util.

13. Use the equimarginal rule (utility-maximizing rule) and the information below to determine the correct answer.

Marginal utility of 1 shrimp = 10

Marginal utility of 1 strawberry = 5

Price of 1 shrimp = $0.25

Price of 1 strawberry = $0.10.

Based on this information, a consumer:

a) is maximizing their utility.

b) should eat more strawberries and fewer shrimp.

c) should eat more shrimp and fewer strawberries.

d) is minimizing their utility.

e) (b) and (d).

14. Suppose you are given the following information:

price of an ice cream cone = $1.50

price of french fries = $0.75.

Which one of the following statements is true given the information above?

a) If a consumer is maximizing utility, then the marginal utility of an ice cream cone/marginal utility of french fries = 0.50.

b) If a consumer is maximizing utility, then the marginal utility of an ice cream cone/marginal utility of french fries = 2.00.

c) A consumer will maximize utility by eating 2 bags of french fries for every one ice cream cone.

d) With an income of $600 a month, a consumer could eat 200 ice cream cones and 400 bags of french fries.

e) (b) and (d).

15. Fred currently buys 6 CDs and 40 lottery tickets and spends his entire income of $100 per week. The CDs cost $10 each and the lottery tickets are $1 each. The marginal utility of the next lottery ticket is 6 utils and the marginal utility of the next CD is 60 utils. If the price of CDs rise to $20 each, the price of lottery tickets rise to $2 each, and Fred's income increases to $200 per week, then which of the following is true?

   a) Fred will buy more CDs and less CDs

   b) Fred will buy more lottery tickets and more CDs

   c) Fred will buy less CDs and less lottery tickets

   d) Fred will buy the same number of lottery tickets and CDs as before.

   e) Fred will buy more lottery tickets and CDs

VI. PRACTICE EXAM: ESSAY QUESTIONS

1. Given the following information, draw a budget line for the consumer. Be sure to label the axes and provide a number for the vertical and horizontal intercepts.

   Income = $1000/month.
   Price of 1 pound of steak = $4.00
   Price of 1 pound of potatoes = $0.50

   Now, draw several indifference curves into the picture, being sure to draw one that represents utility-maximization. Describe what is true at the utility-maximizing point. Describe why points on the other indifference curves do not represent utility-maximization.

2. Using the equimarginal rule (utility-maximizing rule), explain how a consumer's utility (satisfaction) could be increased based on the following information:
   Income = $1,000 per week
   Price of a suit = $200
   Price of a pair of shoes = $50
   Marginal Utility of the third suit = 300 utils
   Marginal Utility of the eighth pair of shoes = 100 utils.

3. Suppose that you are a member of a book club for which you have paid an annual subscription fee of $30. As a member, you may purchase books for $1 a book and no more than 12 books per year. Using economic principles, explain how you might decide how many books to buy.

VII. ANSWER KEY: MULTIPLE CHOICE

1.   Correct answer: c.

Discussion: The cost of 20 pizzas is $80 and the cost of 60 sandwiches is $120. The sum of these equals the monthly income of $200.

Statements a, b, d, and e are all combinations of pizza and sandwiches that require more than $200.

2.   Correct answer: b.

Discussion: In economics, a consumer computes the marginal benefits and marginal costs associated with making a purchase decision. So, statement b is correct.

Statement a is not correct because a consumer uses marginal analysis, not an analysis based on total benefits and total costs in making a purchase decision. Statement c is not correct. Consumer choice theory tells us consumers will buy goods based on their preferences or tastes compared to price and not just based on the price alone. Statement d is not correct because consumers face the law of *diminishing* marginal utility. Statement e is not correct. Consumer choice theory accommodates differences in preferences in explaining consumer choice.

3.   Correct answer: a.

Discussion: Utility is the term used to describe the satisfaction or enjoyment individuals receive from the consumption of goods and services.

While opportunity cost is an economic concept, it is not the term used to describe satisfaction from consumption. Totality, plaisir (French for pleasure), and hedonity are not correct.

4.   Correct answer: e.

Discussion: Consumer choice (how much an individual buys) is limited by income as any student can attest. In addition, the relative amounts of goods purchased are influenced by the prices of goods and services relative to each other since relative prices establish the tradeoff within a budget at which more of one good can be consumed by reducing consumption of another. Thus, since statements c and d are correct, statement e must be correct.

Statement a is not correct. As a consumer consumes more of a good, marginal utility declines, not increases. Statement b is not correct since it is possible for marginal utility to be negative. For example, eating one, then two, then three slices of pizza may increase total utility from 10 utils to 15 utils to 18 utils while eating a fourth and fifth slice may actually decrease utility to 16 utils, then to 12 utils. That is the marginal utility of the first, second, and third slice is positive (at 10 utils, 5 utils (15-10), 3 utils (18-15) while the marginal utility of the fourth and fifth slice are negative (at -2 utils (16-18), -4 utils (12-16)).

5. Correct answer: b.

Discussion: An indifference curve that is further to the right than another represents a higher level of satisfaction. The reason is that a curve that is further to the right shows that more of good X can be had for every level of good Y or alternatively, that more of good Y can be had for every level of good X. (See PET #3 of Chapter 1 of Practicum).

Statement a is not correct; it would be correct if "income" was replaced with "utility" or "satisfaction." Statement c is not correct because a point on the same indifference curve, whether it is higher or lower, yields the same level of satisfaction.   Statement d is not correct because the slope of the indifference curve gets flatter as you move down the indifference curve. This happens because as you move down the indifference curve, more of good X (the good on the horizontal axis) is being consumed and less of good Y (the good on the vertical axis) is being consumed. Thus, the marginal utility (addition to utility) of good X is declining and that of good Y is increasing. Since the slope of the indifference curve is MU_x/MU_y, the slope is getting smaller or flatter.

6. Correct answer: d.

Discussion: A decrease in the consumption of good G will increase the marginal utility of good G (law of diminishing marginal utility in reverse because consumption of good G is decreasing, not increasing). An increase in the consumption of good H will decrease the marginal utility of good H. Since the question asks about MU_G/MU_H, this number will increase.

Statement a is not correct because the marginal rate of substitution would decrease. Statement b is not correct; for utility-maximization the price ratio would have to be 3. Statement c is not correct because the marginal rate of substitution is defined with respect to trade-offs in consumption of one good relative to another. Statement c allows for an increase in the consumption of both goods. Statement e is not correct because income does not affect the marginal rate of substitution (which is the slope of the indifference curve).

7. Correct answer: c.

Discussion: At point c, the indifference curve is tangent to the budget line. The tangency means that the marginal rate of substitution between good X and good Y is equal to the price ratio of good X to good Y.

Points A, B, D, and E are not tangencies. Points A and B are unattainable given the current income of the consumer. Point D is on the same indifference curve as point C but is not the tangency point. Point E is on a lower indifference curve than point C and thus cannot be utility-maximizing given the consumer's current income.

8. Correct answer: a.

Discussion: The marginal utility of 1 cup of coffee/marginal utility of 1 can of soda is 2 (20/10). Thus, the price of 1 cup of coffee/price of 1 can of soda must also be 2. Since the price of 1 cup of coffee is $1, a can of soda must cost $0.50 for utility-maximization to prevail.

Based on the above, statements b, c, and d cannot be correct. Statement e is not correct because you do not need information on the consumer's budget to determine the condition for utility maximization.

9. Correct answer: c.

Discussion: This question requires that you compute the marginal utility associated with each sweater purchased. Thus, the marginal utility from the first sweater is 25 utils. The marginal utility or addition to utility from the second sweater is 15 utils (40-25); from the third sweater is 10 utils (50-40); from the fourth sweater is 5 utils (55-50); and from the fifth sweater is 3 utils (58-55). Thus, while total utility is increasing (from 25 to 58), it is increasing at a decreasing rate. Marginal utility is diminishing.

Statement a is not correct because the marginal utility from the fifth sweater is measured by asking what the addition to utility is from buying the fifth sweater. Thus, the correct answer would be 3 utils. Statement b is not correct because total utility is increasing; marginal utility is diminishing. Statement d is not correct because in no case is marginal utility computed to be negative. Statement e is not correct because you can compute marginal utility from the table.

10. Correct answer: b.

Discussion: The marginal cost associated with consuming one more unit of good X is what must be given up in order to consume that one more unit. In consumer theory, where consumers are operating within a budget, the marginal cost associated with consuming one more unit of good X is measured by the opportunity cost of what must be given up in order to be able to have one more unit of good X. In this case, let's say consumption of good Y must be cut back. But, by how much? It depends on the prices of good X and good Y which establish the rate at which the consumption of one good can be cut back and that of another good increased. Let's suppose the price of good X is $25 and the price of good Y is $5. In this case, 5 units of good Y must be given up in order to get back (i.e. have the income to purchase) one unit of good X. And vice-versa. If one unit of good X is given up, 5 units of good Y can be obtained. The tradeoff must then be translated into utils given up. So, if the consumer wants one more unit of good X, 5 units of good Y must be given up. Corresponding to the reduction in consumption of good Y comes a loss in utility which is based on what the marginal utility of consuming the last unit of good Y was. Let's say it was 11 utils. In this case, the marginal cost of consuming one more unit of good X would be - 11 utils per unit X multiplied by 5 units of Y/1 unit of X = -55 utils per one unit of X.

Statement a is not correct, although it's close. Statement a is not correct because the loss of utils associated with cutting back consumption of good Y must be converted to the rate at which good Y must be given up in order to have one more unit of good X. See discussion above. Statement c is not correct since the marginal cost must also take into account the opportunity cost in terms of lost utility from decreasing consumption of the other good. Statement d is not correct since marginal cost is not necessarily negative and is in the analysis done in this text, positive. Statement e is not correct since statement d is not correct.

11. Correct answer: d.

Discussion: Statement d is not a true statement since points along an individual's demand curve represent points where the marginal benefit of consumption equals the marginal cost of consumption.

Statements a, b, and c are true statements.

12. Correct answer: c.

Discussion: Since ice cream cones are twice as expensive as cookies, two cookies must be given up in the consumer's budget if one more ice cream cone is desired for consumption. Furthermore, since the twelfth cookie is providing 4 utils of satisfaction and given that two must be given up in order to free up the income to purchase one more ice cream cone, then the loss in (cookie) utility is 8 utils for being able to eat one more ice cream cone.

Statements a, b, d, and e are not correct based on the discussion above.

13. Correct answer: b.

Discussion: The ratio of the marginal utility of 1 shrimp to the price of 1 shrimp is 40 and the ratio of the marginal utility of one strawberry to the price of one strawberry is 50. Since the marginal utility per unit cost to the consumer of a strawberry is greater than for shrimp, the consumer could be made better off by consuming more strawberries and fewer shrimp.

Statement a is not correct. For the consumer to be maximizing utility, the ratios mentioned above would have to be equal to each other. (See PET #4). Statement c is not correct since it should be the other way around. Statement d is not correct; while we know the consumer is not maximizing his utility, we can't say (without other information) whether the consumer is minimizing his utility. Statement e is not correct because statement d is not correct.

14. Correct answer: e.

Discussion: Statement b is correct because the ratio of the price of an ice cream cone/price of french fries is 2. Thus, the ratio of the marginal utility of an ice cream cone/marginal utility of french fries must be equal to 2. (See PET #4). Statement d is also correct because if the consumer buys 200 ice cream cones at a price of $1.50 per cone, he spends $300 and has $300 remaining to spend on french fries. At a price of $0.75 per bag of french fries, the consumer can by 400 bags of fries with the remaining $300 from his income.

Statement a is not correct because the ratio is 2/1 not 1/2 (= 0.50). Statement c is not correct because the utility-maximizing rule only tells you about the ratio of the marginal utilities, not about the ratio at which ice cream cones and french fries would be eaten to maximize utility. For example, a 2/1 ratio of marginal utilities might correspond to 100 ice cream cones and 600 french fries which is a ratio of 6 bags of french fries/1 ice cream cone.

15. Correct answer: d.

Discussion: Statement d is correct because inflation does not effect Fred's consumer decision.   If consumer prices double, and Fred's income doubles, then Fred's budget set does not change. He will choose the same quantities of lottery tickets and CDs as before.

Statements a, b c, and e are not correct because the budget set doesn't change so Fred's choice does not change. What matters to Fred is real income.

VIII. ANSWER KEY: ESSAY QUESTIONS

1. My drawing puts potatoes on the vertical axis and steak on the horizontal axis. With an income of $1000, 2000 pounds of potatoes could be purchased in one month if no steak was purchased. With an income of $1000, 250 pounds of steak could be purchased in one month if no potatoes were purchased. Thus, the vertical intercept if 2000 pounds of potatoes and the horizontal intercept is 250 pounds of steak. The slope of the budget line is given by the ratio of the price of steak to the price of potatoes. Thus, the slope of the budget line is 8 pounds of potatoes/1 pound steak. You can also figure out the slope of the budget line by taking two points (end points since you have information on them) and calculating the change in pounds of potatoes consumed and pound of steak consumed. The change in pounds of potatoes consumed is (2000 - 0) and the change in pounds of steak consumed is (250 - 0). Using the formula for a slope of rise/run, the slope of the budget line would be 8 pounds of potatoes/1 pound of steak.

The utility-maximizing point is found where the slope of the indifference curve is tangent to the budget line. This occurs at point A. At this point, the marginal utility of steak/marginal utility of potatoes = price of steak/price of potatoes. A consumer cannot get to a higher indifference curve, like point B, since his income does not allow him to afford that combination of goods. A point like point C is on a lower indifference curve than point A and thus not one that achieves the highest level of utility (satisfaction).

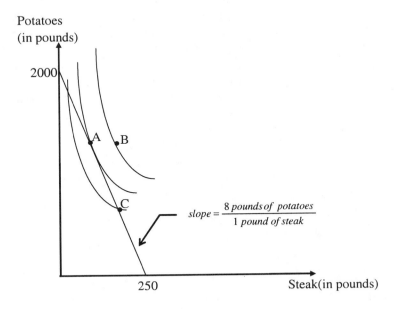

2. I would first calculate the ratios of marginal utility to price for suits and for shoes. If utility is being maximized, these two ratios will be equal to each other. This is an application of the equimarginal rule (or utility-maximizing rule).   If the two ratios are not equal to each other, then utility can be improved by altering the consumption bundle of shoes and suits.

(marginal utility of suits/price of suits) > = < (marginal utility of shoes/price of shoes)?

By substituting in from the information given:

(300 utils per suit/$200 per suit) > = <

(400 utils per pair of shoes/$50 per pair of shoes)?

which reduces to:

(1.5 utils/$1)   <   (2 utils/$1)

(suits)   (shoes)

Since I get more utils per dollar from shoes, I can increase shoe purchases and cut back on suit purchases (in order to stay within my budget) and increase my utility. Let's see how. Since suits are four times more expensive than a pair of shoes, when I cut back on suit purchases by one, I free up $200 of my income to spend on shoes. At $50 a pair, I will now be able to buy four more pairs of shoes. However, when I cut back on purchasing suits, I lose utility. In this case, since I reduce my suit purchases by one, I lose 300 utils of satisfaction. But, I compensate for the loss in utility with the four new pairs of shoes which also bring me satisfaction. In terms of utils, each pair of shoes delivers 100 utils of satisfaction. Since I've purchased four, my utility will increase by 400 utils. On net, my total utility will rise by 100 utils since my increase in utility (400 utils) was bigger than my loss of utils (-300). Thus, I have increased my overall level of satisfaction by buying one less suit and four more pairs of shoes.

3. In order to decide how many books to buy, I would have to compute the marginal utility (addition to utility) I received from buying successively more and more books. I would also consider, in my mind, the opportunity cost of buying a book. The opportunity cost might be that I am able to buy fewer and fewer classical music tapes. I would then translate that opportunity cost into a loss of marginal utility. I would have to know how much marginal utility I would lose by giving up the purchase of classical music tapes. I would also have to know what the price of a classical music tape was. For example, suppose I received 15 utils from the third book and correspondingly given that I purchased three books, I am able to purchase twenty classical music tapes where the twentieth classical music tape yields 10 utils. Further, suppose that the price of a classical music tape is $5. In this case, the marginal utility of the fifth book/price of book = 5 = (5/$1) and the marginal utility of twentieth tape/price of tape = 2 (= 10/$5). Thus, I would benefit by buying more books and fewer tapes since I will receive a relatively bigger addition to utility (per unit price paid) from more books than I will lose from cutting back on my purchases of classical music tapes.

We invite you to visit the book's Companion Website at:
http://www.prenhall.com/osullivan/
for further exercises and practice quizzes.

CHAPTER 7
MARKET EFFICIENCY AND GOVERNMENT INTERVENTION

I. OVERVIEW

In this chapter, you will re-visit the principle of voluntary exchange in understanding market equilibrium. You will be introduced to the concepts of "consumer surplus" and "producer surplus." These concepts will be used to guide your understanding about whether market outcomes based on the interaction of consumers and producers will be efficient or inefficient. You will also learn what happens when a government intervenes in a market and what effects it may create. You will examine the effects of government price setting policies such as rent control and dairy price supports on equilibrium price, quantities, consumer and producer surplus, and efficiency. You will also examine the effects of government restrictions on quantity such as import quotas, voluntary export restraints, and licensing agreements. You will see that quantity restrictions affect equilibrium price, quantity, consumer and producer surplus, and efficiency. You will learn that there are always winners and losers of price setting and quantity-restricting policies.

II. CHECKLIST

By the end of this chapter, you should be able to:

✓ Explain what an efficient market outcome is and what an inefficient market outcome is.

✓ Use a graph of demand and supply to show the area that measures consumer surplus and show how consumer surplus changes when price changes.

✓ Use a graph of demand and supply to show the area that measures producer surplus and show how producer surplus changes when price changes.

✓ Use a graph of demand and supply to show the area that measures total surplus – consumer plus producer surplus.

✓ Explain what a maximum price (price ceiling) policy is and the effects it creates on price, quantity demanded and quantity supplied.

✓ Show the effect on total surplus, dead weight loss, and efficiency of raising (lowering) the price above (below) the equilibrium price.

✓ Explain the effect of the invisible hand on the market and how it affects total surplus, dead weight loss, and efficiency.

✓ List some real world examples of maximum prices.

✓ Explain what a minimum price (price floor or price support) policy is and the effects it creates on price, quantity demanded and quantity supplied.

✓ List some real world examples of minimum prices.

✓ List some real world examples of quantity restrictions and illustrate their effects with a demand and supply graph.

✓ List some real world examples of taxes and illustrate their effects with a demand and supply graph.

✓ Use a graph of demand and supply to show the deadweight loss (decline in total surplus) that arises when a government enacts a minimum or maximum price, restricts quantity, or imposes a tax.

✓ Identify who "wins" and who "loses" under different government policies.

✓ Explain what a quantity restriction (licensing or import restraint) policy is and the effects it creates on price, quantity demanded, quantity supplied, total surplus, dead weight loss, and efficiency.

✓ Explain the concept of tax shifting.

III. KEY TERMS

willingness to pay: The maximum amount a consumer is willing to pay for a product.

consumer surplus: The difference between a consumer's willingness to pay for a product and the price that he or she pays for the product.

willingness to accept: The minimum amount a producer is willing to accept as payment for a product; equal to the marginal cost of production.

producer surplus: The difference between the price a producer receives for a product and the producer's willingness to accept for the product.

total surplus: The sum of consumer surplus and producer surplus.

market failure: A situation in which a market fails to be efficient because of external benefits, external costs, imperfect information, or imperfect competition.

deadweight loss: The decrease in the total surplus of the market.

deadweight loss from taxation: The difference between the total burden of a tax and the amount of revenue collected by the government.

excess burden of a tax: Another name for deadweight loss.

IV. PERFORMANCE ENHANCING TIPS (PETS)

PET #1

Consumer surplus is the area above a given price and below the demand curve ranging out to the quantity that would arise at the given price. Producer surplus is the area below a given price and above the supply curve ranging out to the quantity that would arise at the given price.

Below are three graphs – the first graph is based on a price that is the 'market equilibrium' price; the second and third graphs are based on prices that are different from the market equilibrium price. The first graph shows the consumer and producer surplus areas when the price is the equilibrium price given as P_{eq}. At P_{eq}, the quantity that would arise is given by Q_{eq}. The second graph shows the consumer and producer surplus areas that would arise were price below the equilibrium price, such as at P_0, as in the case where a maximum price is imposed. At a price below the equilibrium price, quantity is restricted by how much is supplied and so consumer and producer surplus areas will range out to Q_0. The third graph shows the consumer and producer surplus areas that would arise were price above the equilibrium price, such as at P_1, as in the case of where a minimum price is imposed. At a price above the equilibrium price, quantity is restricted by how much is demanded and so consumer and producer surplus areas will range out to Q_1.

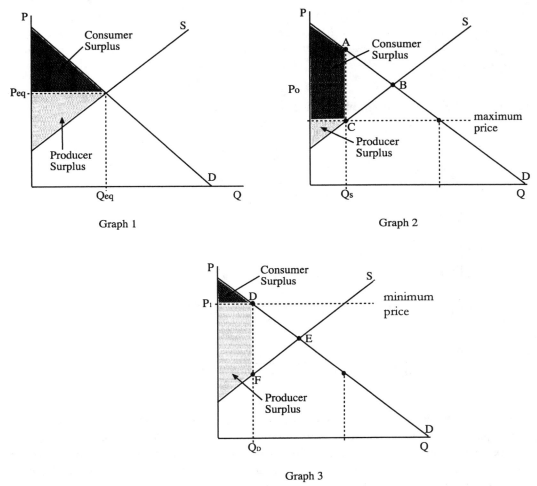

Graph 1

Graph 2

Graph 3

PET #2

*Deadweight loss is the total loss in consumer surplus **plus** producer surplus from a market equilibrium that occurs when a government sets a maximum or minimum price, restricts the quantity, or imposes a tax. To calculate 'deadweight loss', shade in the areas corresponding to consumer and producer surplus before and after the government enacts a policy. Then, compare the difference.*

The graphs from PET #1 can be used to illustrate the deadweight loss going from a market equilibrium to a non-market equilibrium outcome. Non-market equilibrium outcomes arise for prices below the equilibrium price and prices above the equilibrium. A comparison of Graph 1 to Graph 2 illustrates that the loss in consumer plus producer surplus (total surplus) is the area given by the triangle ABC when a price is set below the equilibrium price. A comparison of Graph 1 to Graph 3 illustrates that the loss in total surplus from imposing a price above the equilibrium price is the area given by the triangle DEF.

PET #3

With a maximum price, consumer surplus is an area bounded by the quantity that would be supplied at the maximum price, under the demand curve, and above the maximum price line. Producer surplus is an area bounded by the quantity that would be supplied at the maximum price, above the supply curve, and below the maximum price line.

To see this, look at the graph below which establishes a maximum price for gasoline at $1 per gallon.

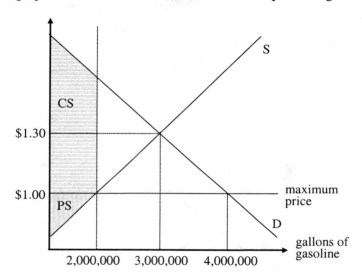

At $1 per gallon, the quantity supplied is 2 million gallons. Consumer surplus is bounded by the 2 million gallon quantity as the area above the maximum price line drawn at $1 and below the demand curve. This area is labeled CS for consumer surplus. Producer surplus is also bounded by the 2 million gallon quantity as the area below the maximum price line but above the supply curve. The graph below has this area labeled as PS for producer surplus.

PET #4

With a minimum price, consumer surplus is an area bounded by the quantity that would be demanded at the minimum price, under the demand curve, and above the minimum price line. Producer surplus is an area bounded by the quantity that would be demanded at the minimum price, above the supply curve, and below the minimum price line.

To see this, look at the graph below which establishes a minimum price for gasoline at $4 per gallon.

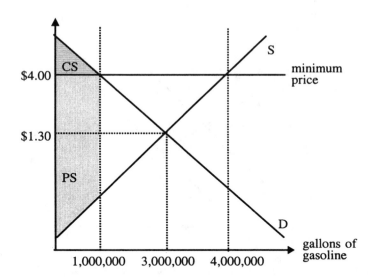

At $4 per gallon, the quantity demanded (which determines how much can be sold) is 1 million gallons. Consumer surplus is bounded by the 1 million gallon quantity as the area above the minimum price line drawn at $4 and below the demand curve. This area is labeled CS for consumer surplus. Producer surplus is also bounded by the 1 million gallon quantity as the area below the minimum price line but above the supply curve. The graph below has this area labeled as PS for producer surplus.

PET #5

Review PETS #8 and #9 from Chapter 4 to revisit the effects of maximum and minimum prices on quantity demanded and supplied.

PET #6

The market demand and supply curves of goods with external costs or benefits do not depict the efficient equilibrium outcome.

This means that in the presence of external costs or benefits, the equilibrium price and quantity represented by the intersection of market demand and supply curves is not "efficient." This means that the price and quantity outcome does not take into account those consumers (or producers) that receive benefits or incur costs but are not directly using the good.

PET #7

A tax on a good or service is represented by shifting the supply curve to the left. The rise in the equilibrium price depends on how flat or steep (elastic) the demand curve is.

To see this, look at the graph below.

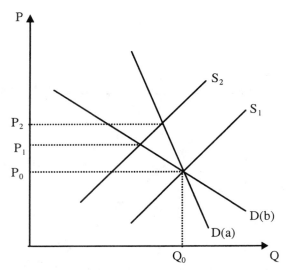

The steeper demand curve, D(a), is the less elastic demand curve; the flatter demand curve, D(b), is the more elastic demand curve. The shift in the supply curve from S1 to S2 is caused by a tax on the good. As you can see, the equilibrium price rises by more along the less elastic demand curve, D(a), and rises by less along the more elastic demand curve. Thus, more of the tax is shifted forward to consumers with a less elastic demand curve than with a more elastic demand curve. Consequently, when demand is less elastic and thus price rises more to consumers so that more of the tax is paid for by them, less of the tax is shifted backward to input suppliers. This means that with a less elastic demand curve, input suppliers bear less of the burden of the tax than when demand is more elastic.

PET #8

A tax on the supply of a good shifts the supply of the good to the left, reduces the equilibrium quantity sold, and thus reduces the demand for inputs used in producing the good and thus the price of inputs.

You should know from Chapter 4 of the textbook and the practicum that a leftward shift in the supply of good X reduces the equilibrium quantity (and raises the price of the good) of good X. From this, you should be able to logically infer that if industry X is selling fewer units of output, it will need fewer units of inputs. In economics terms, this means that the demand for inputs will decline. You should know from Chapter 4 of your textbook and the practicum that a decrease in the demand for any good (represented by a leftward shift in demand) will reduce the equilibrium price (and reduce the equilibrium quantity) of the good. In this case, the good is inputs into good X.

One input into the production of most goods is labor. Thus, a tax on good X may not only raise the price of good X, it may also reduce the demand for labor (and other inputs) used in making good X. When the demand for labor declines, the equilibrium price (in this case, wage) of labor and the equilibrium quantity will decline (that is, some workers will lose their jobs).

V. PRACTICE EXAM: MULTIPLE CHOICE QUESTIONS

1. An efficient market outcome is one in which:

a) consumer surplus is greater than producer surplus.

b) there are external benefits but no external costs.

c) consumer and producer surplus are equal.

d) a third party can benefit from a transaction.

e) no buyer, seller, or third party can benefit from any further transactions.

2. Consider the graph below depicting the market for guitars.

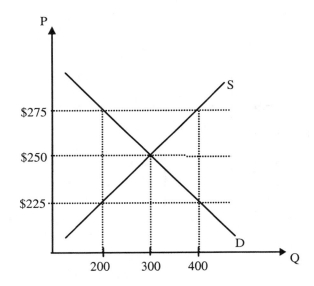

Which one of the following statements is true?

a) The price a customer would be willing to pay for the 400th guitar is greater than the marginal cost of producing the 400th guitar.

b) producer surplus is the area below the supply curve at the equilibrium price.

c) If the price was $225 per guitar, there would be an excess supply of guitars.

d) One more consumer could be better off if 299 guitars were produced instead of 300.

e) none of the above.

3.   Who is responsible for the metaphor of the "invisible hand"?

a)   Adam Smith.

b)   Art O'Sullivan.

c)   John Maynard Keynes

d)   Milton Friedman.

e)   Steven Sheffrin.

4.   Use the graph below to answer the following question.

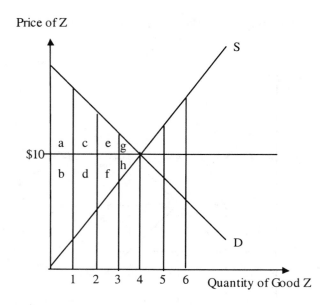

Which one of the following statements is correct?

a)   at the equilibrium price and quantity, total surplus is equal to a + c + e + g.

b)   at the equilibrium price and quantity, total surplus is equal to b + d + f + h.

c)   for the second customer, consumer surplus is equal to c + d.

d)   for the fourth customer, no consumer surplus is generated and so this must be an efficient outcome.

e)   surplus arising from the sale of the first unit of good Z is a + b.

5.   At the equilibrium price and quantity, consumer surplus is measured as the area:

a)   above the demand curve.

b)   below the demand curve.

c)   below the demand curve but above the equilibrium price line.

d)   above the demand curve out to the equilibrium quantity.

e)   below the demand curve and above the supply curve.

6.   Which one of the following statements is correct about the graph below?

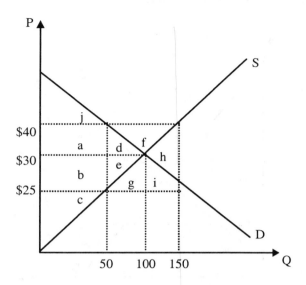

a)   at a price of $30, consumer surplus is area f and producer surplus is area g + i.

b)   at a price of $25, consumer surplus is area a + b + d + e and producer surplus is area c.

c)   at a price of $40, consumer surplus is area a + b + c and producer surplus is area j.

d)   at a price of $25, consumer surplus is area a + b + j and producer surplus is area c.

e)   at a price of $40, consumer surplus is area a + d and producer surplus is area b + e.

7.   Suppose the government sets a maximum price (price ceiling) for pacemakers (a medical device that monitors the beats per minute of the heart). The maximum price is set at $1299 and the equilibrium price is $1750. Which one of the following would NOT be a likely result?

a)   consumers may bribe their doctors for pacemakers or be willing to pay special hook-up fees.

b)   an excess supply (surplus) would develop.

c)   the quality of pacemakers may decline.

d)   the quantity of pacemakers supplied may decline in the long run.

e)   all of the above would be likely to develop.

8. Suppose the government sets a minimum price (price floor) for cheese of $1.25 per pound. Based on the diagram below, which one of the following statements is correct?

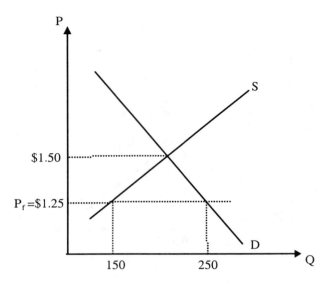

a) there will be an excess supply (surplus) of 100 pounds of cheese.
b) there will be an excess demand (shortage) of 100 pounds of cheese.
c) at $1.25, consumer surplus is less than at a price of $1.50.
d) the price floor is ineffective.
e) supply will decrease.

9. Which one of the following is an effect of a minimum price (price floor) that is set above the equilibrium price?

a) quantity supplied increases.
b) quantity demanded decreases.
c) an inefficient outcome is produced.
d) suppliers win and consumers lose.
e) all of the above are effects of a minimum price.

10. Which one of the following is NOT an example of a quantity restriction (control)?

a) a quota on aircraft imports.
b) a voluntary export restraint on automobiles.
c) subsidized housing.
d) licensing liquor stores.
e) a ban on oil imports.

11. Which one of the following would be an effect of the U.S. government imposing a quota on imports of say, automobiles?

a) the price of imported automobiles will increase.

b) the quantity of automobiles supplied by the foreign source will increase. ✓

c) the quantity of automobiles demanded will increase.

d) employment in the U.S. automobile industry will decrease. ✗

e) a surplus of foreign-made automobiles will be created in the U.S. ✗

12. Suppose a licensing scheme is used in the market depicted below. The scheme has the effect of reducing the quantity supplied to 300 units. Use the graph to complete the following statement:

Before the licensing scheme, consumer surplus was _____ and after the licensing scheme, consumer surplus is _____.

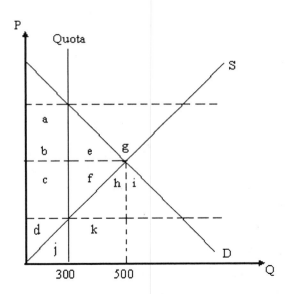

a) a + b + e; a.

b) a + b + e; a + b.

c) a + b + e; e.

d) g; e.

e) b + e; a.

13. Using the graph from question 12, complete the following statement:

Before the licensing scheme, producer surplus was _____ and after the licensing scheme, producer surplus is _____.

a) c + d + f; d.
b) c + d + f; d.
c) c + d + f; b + c + d.
d) c + d; b + c + f.
e) c + f; b.

14. Using the graph from question 12, complete the following statement:

The loss in total surplus or deadweight loss is _____.

a) g + h + i.
b) e + f.
c) b + c + e + f.
d) e + f + g + h + i.
e) h + i + j + k.

15. Suppose the government imposes a tax on the sale of new refrigerators. The government collects the tax from appliance centers and other outlets that sell the refrigerators. Who pays for the tax assuming market demand is negatively sloped and supply is a horizontal?

a) consumers.
b) consumers and refrigerator input suppliers.
c) appliance centers and other outlets.
d) consumers and appliance centers.
e) refrigerator input suppliers.

16. Which one of the following statements is true of a tax that is collected from producers in a perfectly competitive market?

a) it shifts the demand curve to the left.
b) the demand for inputs will decline and thus so will the price of inputs.
c) in the long run, producers' profits will decline.
d) the price of output will decline.
e) it shifts the supply curve to the right.

17. Consider the market for yachts. A tax on yachts collected by the government from yacht producers will:

a) shift more of the tax forward to consumers if demand is inelastic than if it is elastic.

b) put the tax burden on consumers and yacht input suppliers, including workers in the yachting industry.

c) reduce the price of yacht inputs by more if input supply is inelastic rather than elastic.

d) reduce the equilibrium quantity of yachts sold.

e) all of the above.

18. Use the graph below to determine the deadweight loss (excess burden) of a tax placed on gasoline.

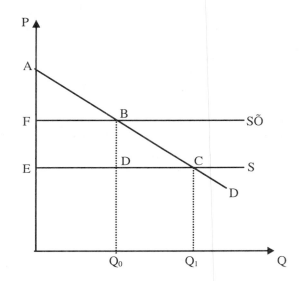

a) area ABF.

b) area BCD.

c) area FBCE.

d) area FBED.

e) area ABC.

VI.   PRACTICE EXAM: ESSAY QUESTIONS

1. Suppose that you are an economist for the textile industry and are ardently seeking a ban on all textile imports. Assume the textile industry is perfectly competitive and has no external benefits or costs associated with it. Discuss the effects of the ban on the textile industry (producers). Explain your answer using graphs.

2. Suppose that you are a consumer advocate for the textile industry and are fighting to keep the import ban from being placed on the textile industry. Assume the industry is perfectly competitive and has

no external benefits or costs associated with it. Discuss the effects of the ban on consumers. Explain your answering using graphs.

3. Use demand and supply diagrams to discuss and illustrate the effects of a tax on peanut butter, consumers of peanut butter, and peanut growers. Be sure to discuss the extent of forward and backward shifting and the deadweight loss caused by the tax.

VII. ANSWER KEY: MULTIPLE CHOICE QUESTIONS

1. Correct answer: e.

Discussion: Statement e is correct because it is the only statement that points out that no further transactions can make anybody else better off. This defines an efficient outcome.

Statement a is not correct. An efficient outcome is simply one in which the sum of consumer and producer surplus is maximized or as big as possible. Statement b is not correct because external benefits lead to inefficient outcomes, just as do external costs. Statement c is not correct because efficiency does not necessarily imply anything about the equality of consumer and producer surplus.   Statement d is not correct because if a third party can benefit from a transaction, the outcome must not currently be the efficient one.

2. Correct answer: e.

Discussion: None of the above statements is correct.

Statement a is not correct because the price a consumer is willing to pay for the 400th guitar is $225; this is greater than the marginal cost to produce that 400th guitar which is $275. Statement b is not correct because producer surplus is the area above the supply curve and below the price line.   Statement c is not correct because a price of $225 leads to an excess demand (shortage), not an excess supply (surplus). At a price of $225, quantity demanded is 400 guitars and quantity supplied is 200 guitars. Statement d is not correct because the equilibrium quantity of 300 guitars is the efficient outcome and so nobody could be made better off by producing fewer (or even more) guitars. Statement e is not correct because statement c is not correct.

3. Correct answer: a.

Discussion: Adam Smith, who wrote the Wealth of Nations is responsible for the metaphor of the "invisible hand" which is just that people acting in their own self-interest can frequently lead to outcomes in which all participating parties benefit.

None of the other statements are correct. In fact O'Sullivan and Sheffrin are the authors of your textbook.

4. Correct answer: e.

Discussion: Total surplus is the sum of consumer plus producer surplus. Consumer surplus for a customer is the area under the price the customer would be willing to pay for a unit of output (measured off of the demand curve) and the market or equilibrium price he or she actually has to pay. Thus, for the first consumer, he or she would be willing to pay a price higher than $10 for q = 1 unit but only has to pay $10. Consumer surplus for this customer is the area a. Producer surplus for a producer is the difference between his or her cost of production for a unit of output (measured off of the supply curve) and the market or equilibrium price he or she will receive from selling that unit of output. Thus, for the first producer, the price received at $10 is greater than the marginal cost of producing that first unit of output. Producer surplus for the first unit sold is the area b. Thus, total surplus is area a + b.

Statement a is not correct. Area a + c + e + g measures consumer surplus. Statement b is not correct because area b + d + f + h measures producer surplus. Statement c is not correct because consumer surplus for the second customer would be area c. Statement d is not correct because consumer surplus for the fourth customer is the area g.

5. Correct answer: c.

Discussion: Consumer surplus is the area measured under the demand curve and above the price line assuming the consumer surplus is being measured in reference to an equilibrium price. If maximum or minimum prices are imposed, or any form of quantity-restriction, consumer surplus will be measured differently (and will be less than consumer surplus based on an equilibrium price). See PETS #1-#4 for review.

6. Correct answer: d.

Discussion: With a price of $25 and an equilibrium price of $30, you can infer that $25 is a maximum price. At the maximum price of $25, only 50 units will be supplied and thus able to be purchased by consumers. Consumer surplus is thus limited by the quantity supplied (at 50 units) and based on a price of $25. In this case, consumer surplus is the area a + b + j which is the area below the demand curve and above the maximum price line but restricted by the quantity supplied (See PET #3). Producer surplus is area c. It is also affected by the maximum price and the quantity that would be supplied. With a maximum price, producer surplus is the area above the supply curve and below the maximum price line but restricted by the quantity supplied.

Statement a is not correct because consumer surplus at a price of $30 would be a + d + j and producer surplus would be b + c + e. Statement b is not correct since statement d is correct. Statements c and e are not correct because at a price of $40 (which would be a minimum price), consumer surplus would be area j and producer surplus would be area a + b + c.

7. Correct answer: b.

Discussion: A maximum price that is set below the equilibrium price creates an excess demand (shortage), not an excess supply (surplus).

Since a maximum price set below the equilibrium price creates an excess demand, several consequences emerge. One is that people may bribe their doctors with monetary or non-monetary gifts so that they can be one of the recipients of the limited supply of pacemakers. Second, the quality of pacemakers may decline because the shortage or excess demand for pacemakers doesn't give an incentive to the producers to produce a better product. They know that they can sell what they produce because if one buyer makes demands on them, another buyer will be ready to pay the $1,299 for the pacemaker. Third, the quantity of pacemakers supplied may decline in the long run as pacemaker manufacturers decide that it is not as profitable to produce pacemakers (because of the governmentally-imposed price) and so they may decide to produce other medical devices or get out of the business altogether.

8.   Correct answer: d.

Discussion: Since the price floor is set below the equilibrium price, it is ineffective. Remember that a price floor is a governmentally-imposed price below which the price may not drop. By market forces, the price will naturally rest at $1.50.

Statements a and b are not correct because the price floor is ineffective and so neither an excess supply (surplus) nor an excess demand (shortage) will emerge. An equilibrium where quantity demanded = quantity supplied at a price of $1.50 will emerge. Statement c is not correct because consumer surplus without any price of quantity restrictions is always greater than consumer surplus when there is some form of restriction imposed. Statement e is not correct because an ineffective price floor does not have the effect of decreasing supply (supply shifting left).

9.   Correct answer: e.

Discussion: A minimum price set above the equilibrium price creates a surplus. It does so by raising the price above the equilibrium. As the price is increased, quantity supplied increases (movement along the supply curve, Law of Supply) and quantity demanded decreases (movement along the demand curve, Law of Demand). An inefficient outcome is produced because we are no longer at the equilibrium level of output which is where marginal benefit equals marginal cost. Suppliers win because they get a higher price for their product but consumers lose because they have to pay a higher price for it.

10. Correct answer: c.

Discussion: Subsidized housing is housing that is provided to people at a price below the market price.

Quotas, voluntary export restraints, licenses, and bans all restrict or limit the quantity of a good to various degrees.

11. Correct answer: a.

Discussion: A quota restricts the supply of imports and thus reduces the overall supply of automobiles in the U.S. market. This raises the price of automobiles.

Statement b is not correct because the quota reduces the quantity of automobiles supplied by the foreign source, not increases it. Statement c is not correct because as the price increases, the quantity of automobiles demanded will decrease not increase. Statement d is not correct because employment in the U.S. automobile industry will increase as they increase production to make up for the reduction from the foreign source. Statement e is not correct because a shortage of foreign-made automobiles will be created in the U.S.

12. Correct answer: a.

Discussion: Before the quota, consumer surplus is based on the equilibrium price and quantity which is found where the demand and supply curves intersect. In this case, consumer surplus is the area below the demand curve but above the equilibrium price line (and out to the equilibrium quantity). This is the area a + b + e. After the quota, quantity is restricted to 300 units and so price increases. The rise in price and reduced quantity will affect consumer surplus. Now, consumer surplus is the area below the demand curve, above the quota-restricted price line and out to the quota-quantity. This is the area a. Consumer surplus declines because consumers pay a higher price and are able to purchase less of the good.

13. Correct answer: c.

Discussion: Before the quota, producer surplus is based on the equilibrium price and quantity which is found where the demand and supply curves intersect. In this case, producer surplus is the area above the supply curve but below the equilibrium price line (and out to the equilibrium quantity). This is the area c + d + f. After the quota, quantity is restricted to 300 units and so price increases. The rise in price and reduced quantity will affect producer surplus. Now, producer surplus is the area above the supply curve, below the quota-restricted price line and out to the quota-quantity. This is the area b + c + d. Producer surplus may increase or decrease since area f is lost due to the quota restriction but area b is gained.

14. Correct answer: b.

Discussion: Surplus that is lost due to the quota restriction is area e + f. Before the quota, total surplus was the area a + b + e + c + d + f. Area a + b + e was consumer surplus -- see answer to #12. Area c + d + f was producer surplus -- see answer to #13. The sum of these is total surplus. After the quota, consumer surplus is the area a and producer surplus is the area b + c + d. This makes total surplus under the quota, a + b + c + d. The loss in total surplus which is the deadweight loss is thus e + f. Area e is the loss in consumer surplus and area f is the loss in producer surplus.

15. Correct answer: b.

Discussion: A tax leads to "forward shifting" -- i.e. consumers pay some of the tax, and "backward shifting" -- i.e. input suppliers pay some of the tax (in the form of receiving a lower price for the inputs they provide). While the appliance center may write and send the check to the government, the tax dollars paid by the appliance center are, in effect, collected from the consumers and input suppliers. As an aside, if the demand for refrigerators was vertical (perfectly inelastic), consumers would pay for the entire tax.

16. Correct answer: b.

Discussion: A tax collected from producers is represented by shifting the supply curve to the left. Thus, statement a and e are not true. As the supply curve shifts to the left, the price of output will rise. Thus, statement d is not true. Statement c is not true because, as your textbook points out, producers profits remain at zero in the long run. Statement b is true because when the supply curve shifts to the left, not only does the price rise, but the equilibrium quantity falls. Suppose the good in question is furniture. As the equilibrium quantity of furniture sold declines, the demand for inputs used in making furniture, like labor and wood, will decline. As the demand for these inputs declines, the price of the inputs declines. (See PET #8 for review).

17. Correct answer: e.

Discussion: A tax on yachts will shift the supply of yachts to the left. If demand for yachts is inelastic (steeper), the price paid by consumers will rise by more than if the demand for yachts was elastic (see PET #7 for review). As just discussed in the answer to question (9), consumers and input suppliers of yachts both bear the burden of the tax. Since the demand for inputs will decline, there will be a drop in the price of yacht inputs. The price drop will be bigger the more inelastic is the supply of the inputs.

18. Correct answer: b.

Discussion: The deadweight loss is the loss in the area of consumer surplus that is not covered by the gain in tax revenue collected by the government. In this case, the initial consumer surplus area is area ACE. After the tax, when the price goes up, the consumer surplus area is ABF. The loss in consumer surplus is thus FBCE. However, the gain in tax revenue is the amount of the tax times the equilibrium quantity. This is measured by the area FBDE. Thus, the deadweight loss is the difference between the area FBCE and FBDE which is BCD.

VIII. ANSWER KEY: ESSAY QUESTIONS

1. The ban on textile imports serves to eliminate all textile imports. Thus, the supply of textiles to a country, say the United States, will be reduced since supply will now come from domestic (U.S) producers only. The ban is represented in the graph below as a leftward shift in supply from the supply based on domestic and foreign producers to a supply now based only on domestic producers.

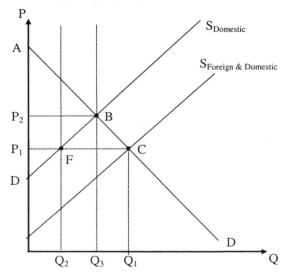

The graph shows that the price of textiles will rise from P_1 to P_2 as is expected with a reduction in supply. The equilibrium quantity also declines from Q_1 to Q_3. Producer surplus for domestic producers will be affected in a few ways. Prior to the ban, producer surplus for domestic producers is based on price P_1. At price P_1, domestic producers were willing to supply the quantity Q_2 (which is read off of the domestic supply curve at that price). Producer surplus was thus the triangle DFP_1. After the ban on foreign producers, the price rises to P_2 and encourages domestic producers to produce more than prior to the ban. Thus, quantity produced by domestic producers increases from Q_2 to Q_3. (Note, however, that the ban has restricted the total quantity supplied from Q_1 to Q_3). Producer surplus for domestic producers is now the triangle DBP_2. As far as domestic production goes, the increase in production may generate an increase in employment in the textile industry, possibly at the expense of employment in some other industry. Profits in the textile industry may also rise. The graph shows that in economic terms, producer surplus for domestic producers increases. It has increased by the area P_2BFP_1.

2. The ban on textile imports affects consumers by raising the price paid for textiles like material, yarn, threads, etc. (and goods for which textiles are an input, e.g. clothing). The ban also reduces the quantity available for purchase. Thus, consumers will be negatively affected by the ban on foreign imports. The graph above shows that prior to the ban, consumer surplus was the triangle ACP_1. After the ban, consumer surplus becomes ABP_2. The loss in consumer surplus from the ban is P_2BCP_1. The loss in consumer surplus and the corresponding higher prices and reduced availability may not be the only effect. Since the threat of competition from foreign producers is reduced or eliminated, the quality of textiles may decline. Domestic producers may not feel they need to be as vigilant about the quality of their product when they do not have to compete with foreign producers.

3. A tax on peanut butter is represented by a leftward shift in the supply curve. The supply curve of peanut butter is drawn horizontally to reflect that in the long run, this industry is a constant-cost industry. Thus, the leftward shift in the supply curve, with it drawn horizontally, appears as an upward shift showing that at every quantity supplied the price that suppliers would now be willing to produce at would be higher. This is because part of the money they receive on the sales of peanut butter will have to be paid in taxes to the government. The leftward shift in the supply curve does two things: (1) the equilibrium price of peanut butter rises; and (2) the equilibrium quantity of peanut butter falls. The graph below shows this.

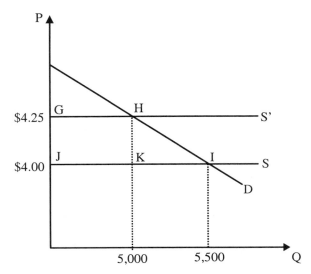

108   Chapter 7

The rise in the price of peanut butter means that consumers will now pay more for peanut butter. That is, some of the tax is shifted forward to consumers. The equilibrium price rises but not by the full $0.50. The extent of the price increase to consumers depends on how elastic the demand for peanut butter is. If the demand for peanut butter is very elastic (perhaps because there are a lot of close substitutes like cream cheese, butter, jelly, etc), the price rise will not be very great -- certainly not the full $0.50. Suppose the equilibrium price rises from $4.00 a jar to $4.25. Suppliers must still pay $0.50 per jar in taxes to the government which means the supplier will be left with $3.75. The price that they receive per jar of peanut butter has effectively dropped from $4.00 to $3.75. Will their profits decrease? Perhaps in the short run but in the long run, the costs of peanut butter production will fall so that in the end the producer will still be earning $4.00 per jar of peanut butter. The reason the cost of peanut butter production will fall is that the equilibrium quantity of peanut butter sold drops. Peanut butter producers thus need less peanut butter to bring to the market. This in turn means that peanut butter producers will not need to buy as many peanuts. So, the demand for peanuts will decrease and this will bring down the price of peanuts, an input into the production of peanut butter. Thus, peanut growers in effect bear some of the burden of the tax because they receive a lower price for their output. This is the backward shifting nature of the tax. In the long run, with a tax of $0.50, peanut growers will receive $0.25 less for their peanuts which means that the cost of production to the peanut butter producers will decline. That's why the peanut butter producer is still, in a way, receiving $4.00 per jar of peanut butter. Or, you could say the profit per jar of peanut butter will be unchanged before and after the tax.

As for the tax revenue, the government collects $0.50 per jar of peanut butter. The new equilibrium quantity (let's say it is 5,000 jars per week) times the tax per jar gives the government $2,500 in tax revenue per week.

As for consumers, they pay a higher price for peanut butter and purchase a smaller equilibrium quantity so their consumer surplus declines. The graph shows that the decline in consumer surplus (area GHIJ) exceeds the gain in tax revenue (area GHKJ) so that on net there is a deadweight loss to society equal to area HIK.

We invite you to visit the book's Companion Website at:
http://www.prenhall.com/osullivan/
for further exercises and practice quizzes.

PART 3: INFORMATION AND EXTERNALITIES

CHAPTER 8
IMPERFECT INFORMATION: ADVERSE SELECTION AND MORAL HAZARD

I. OVERVIEW

In this chapter, you will learn about the effect of imperfect information on buyers and sellers and the price at which they strike deals. You will learn that markets with imperfect information are typically "mixed markets" meaning that the quality of goods sold in a particular market is not uniform and that it is difficult for buyers to know whether the quality of the good that they are purchasing is of high or low quality. That is, there is a chance that a buyer will purchase a high-quality good and a chance that a buyer will end up purchasing a low quality version of the same good. You will learn that imperfect information arises when one side of the market (either buyers or sellers) has more information about the good in question than the other side of the market. You will learn that this situation is referred to as an information asymmetry and that it arises most commonly in the market for used goods and insurance. You will learn about the adverse selection problem. You will also learn what a thin market is and why they occur. You will use probabilities to compute expected amounts that uninformed buyers may be willing to pay.   You will learn about some methods used to overcome the asymmetric information problem. You will also learn about applications of asymmetric information to the market for used cars, baseball pitchers, auto insurance, and health insurance. You will learn about moral hazard and why it is that insurance may actually encourage risky behavior.

II. CHECKLIST

By the end of this chapter, you should be able to:

✓ Define asymmetric information.

✓ Explain the effects of asymmetric information on the price, quality, and volume of a good sold in a market.

✓ Use probabilities to compute expected prices.

✓ Convert ratios into probabilities.

✓ Apply the asymmetric information problem to a market for used goods or insurance.

✓ Explain why asymmetric information typically raises the cost of insurance and lowers the price of used goods.

✓ Explain why the actually probability of a buyer purchasing a lemon (low quality good) in a used market is greater than the probability that may be casually assumed.

✓ Define the adverse selection problem and explain what gives rise to it.

✓ Define a thin market and explain what gives rise to it.

✓ Explain some methods used by buyers and sellers for overcoming the asymmetric information problem and increasing the probability that they are dealing with a high-quality good as opposed to a low-quality good.

✓ Describe two outcomes predicted to occur under markets with asymmetric information.

✓ Explain the difference between community and experience ratings used by the health insurance industry.

✓ Define moral hazard and discuss instances in which moral hazard might arise.

III. KEY TERMS

asymmetric information: A situation in which one side of the market—either buyers or sellers—has better information about the good than the other.

mixed market: A market in which products of different qualities are sold for the same price.

adverse-selection problem: A situation in which the uninformed side of the market must choose from an undesirable or adverse selection of goods.

thin market: A market in which some high-quality goods are sold but fewer than would be sold in a market with perfect information.

experience rating: A situation in which each firm pays a different price for medical insurance, depending on the past medical bills of its employees

moral hazard problem: Insurance encourages risky behavior

IV. PERFORMANCE ENHANCING TIPS (PETS)

PET #1

The expected (or average) amount that a buyer is willing to pay for a good of unknown quality is computed using the probabilities associated with whether the good is high or low quality (we'll assume only two categories of qualities) and what the corresponding prices would be for a good of a certain quality.

Let's suppose that you are considering buying a used computer. Further, you are aware that more lemon computers are likely to be sold in the used market than not. Suppose the probability of getting a faulty computer is 75% and thus the probability of buying a good computer is 25%. If the going price for a good, used computer were $1,000 and the going price for a faulty, used computer were $200, what is the expected price at which used computers will sell in the mixed market of good and faulty computers?

To answer the question, use the following formula:

(probability of high-quality good/100) X price of high-quality good + (probability of low-quality good/100) X price of low quality good.

Thus, your answer to the question should be:

(25/100) X ($1,000) + (75/100) X $200) = 0.25 X $1,000 + 0.75 X 200 = 250 + 150 = $400.

PET #2

The probability of a low (or high) quality good in the market can be determined by dividing the observations of a low (or high) quality good by the total number of goods (i.e. sum of low plus high quality goods).

Suppose you have done some research on the market for used evening gowns and determined that in your town, 30 used evening gowns are typically for sale each month. Further, you've determined that typically, 20 of the used evening gowns are very high quality and that 10 of the evening gowns are low quality. What is the probability in any given month that you or somebody that you may give advice to will buy a low quality evening gown?

The probability of purchasing a low quality evening gown is (10/30) X 100 = 33.3%

Thus, the probability of buying a high quality evening gown must be 66.7% (100% - 33.3%).

V. PRACTICE EXAM: MULTIPLE CHOICE QUESTIONS

1. A mixed market is one in which:

a) consumers can be buyers and sellers and producers can be sellers and buyers.

b) there are different qualities of a good being sold in the market and there is imperfect information about the quality of each good.

c) a seller of a good requires that the purchase of one good be tied to the purchase of another.

d) demand is positively sloped and supply is negatively sloped.

e) none of the above.

2. In a market for used goods,

a) the seller has more information than the buyer about the quality of the good.

b) the buyer has more information than the seller about the quality of the good.

c) there are no high-quality used goods for sale.

d) low quality used goods will be under-priced.

e) the quality of used goods sold in the market will typically rise over time.

3. Which one of the following is an example of asymmetric information?

a) a grocery store selling cookies that are stale.

b) a builder building a house with 2" instead of 4" studs.

c) a company hiring an employee that has an addiction to sleeping pills.

d) a seller at a flea market selling stolen goods.

e) all of the above.

4. Which one of the following is true of a used market, e.g. used market for cars?

a) a consumer typically overestimates the probability of getting a lemon (low quality car).

b) the more pessimistic buyers become that their chance of buying a high quality car is high, the lower will the price of all (low and high quality) used cars become.

c) there is an adverse information problem.

d) the willingness to pay and the willingness to accept are equal.

e) (b) and (d).

5. The adverse selection problem is that:

a) the informed side of the market pays more for a good than the less informed side of the market.

b) a seller does not inform a buyer of all of the add-on fees that will be incurred upon the purchase of a good.

c) product differentiation makes it difficult to decide which product to buy.

d) the uninformed side of the market must choose from an undesirable selection of goods.

e) all of the above.

6. Which one of the following is an equilibrium?

a) buyers assume a 40% chance of getting a lemon and 8 lemons and 2 plums are supplied.

b) buyers assume a 60% chance of getting a lemon and 6 lemons and 4 plums are supplied.

c) buyers assume a 40% chance of getting a lemon and 4 lemons and 4 plums are supplied.

d) buyers assume an 80% chance of getting a lemon and 2 lemons and 8 plums are supplied.

e) buyers assume a 75% chance of getting a lemon and 7 lemons and 3 plums are supplied.

7. Which one of the following is NOT true of a thin market?

a) it may be caused by asymmetric information.

b) there are relatively few high-quality goods sold.

c) in a thin market, there may be some sellers of high-quality goods because of extenuating circumstances (moving out of the country; increased family size, etc.)

d) the price of a high quality good will be higher than if the market was thick.

e) all of the above.

8. A mixed market is:

a) dominated by low-quality goods.

b) one in which there is asymmetric information.

c) one where buyers encounter an adverse selection problem.

d) typical of used goods and insurance.

e) all of the above.

9. Use the following information to complete the sentence below:

Average cost of settling a lawsuit of a careful plastic surgeon = $6,000.

Average cost of settling a lawsuit of a reckless plastic surgeon = $36,000.

Probability that a careful doctor will want insurance = 25%

Probability that a reckless doctor will want insurance = 75%

Assuming insurance companies cannot distinguish between careful and reckless plastic surgeons, an insurance company will charge $_____ for malpractice insurance and a careful plastic surgeon would be inclined to _____ insurance.

a) $28,500; not buy.

b) $21,000; not buy.

c) $36,000; not buy.

d) $21,000; buy.

e) $42,000; not buy.

10. The use of "experience rating" of health insurance has resulted in:

a) lower costs of insurance for all firms.

b) lower costs of insurance for firms with a history of lower medical bills of its employees.

c) higher costs of insurance for all firms.

d) firms investing in safety and health programs for their employees.

e) (b) and (d).

11. Which one of the following is an example where the problem of moral hazard would be likely to occur?

a) insurance against theft.

b) high and low quality used computers being sold by the same store.

c) commercial dating services.

d) a real estate company providing homeowner's warranties on appliances and plumbing for each "used" house it sells.

e) the national blood supply.

12. Suppose the probability of buying a lemon was .9 or 90% and the cost of a lemon was $4000. Suppose the probability of buying a plum was .1 or 10% and the cost of a plum was $10,000. Suppose consumers know that more lemons are likely to be sold in the market. What is the expected price of a car in this market?

a) $14,000

b) $7,000.

c) $4,000.

d) $4,600.

e) $5,000.

VI. PRACTICE EXAM: ESSAY QUESTIONS

1. Suppose you are a college admissions director and every year you receive 5,000 applications for admission to your school while your school only has 1,000 slots open. Your school is prestigious and has a reputation for producing some of the best and brightest college graduates on the national market. What problems might you encounter as the admission director? How might you handle them?

2. Explain the effects of asymmetric information on the price, quality, and volume of used computers sold in a market.

VII. ANSWER KEY: MULTIPLE CHOICE QUESTIONS

1. Correct answer: b.

Discussion: In a mixed market, there are different qualities of a good being sold and unfortunately the buyer or seller of the good may not know for sure (has imperfect information) what the quality of the good is. The market for used goods is typically a mixed market as is the market for insurance.

All of the other statements are bogus.

2. Correct answer: a.

Discussion: A used market is a market for which there is asymmetric information — in this case, the information is asymmetric because the seller knows more about the true quality of the good than does the buyer.

Based on the above, statement b is not true. Statement c is generally not true (only in extreme cases would no high quality used goods be for sale) because a used market is also one that is "mixed" in that high and low quality versions of the same good will be offered for sale. Statement d is not true because the price of low quality used goods is based on the price at which a high and low quality version of the good would be priced. This leads to a higher price for a low quality good than reflects its true value. Statement e is not true because there is a tendency for the quality of goods sold in a used market to decrease over time.

3. Correct answer: e.

Discussion: While asymmetric information typically arises in a market for used goods, it can occur elsewhere. All of the above examples are cases in which one party (the buyer or the seller) has more information about the product than the other party.

4. Correct answer: b.

Discussion: When buyers become more pessimistic that their chance of buying a high quality car is high, they will attach a lower probability to the price they would be willing to pay for a high quality car and thus a higher probability to the price they would be willing to pay for a low quality car. This necessarily lowers the price that a buyer would be willing to pay for a car about which they have no information as to its quality.

You may wish to review PET #1 and attach different probabilities to that associated with buying a good computer and a faulty one and then see what happens to the expected price of the computer.

Statement a is not true; consumers typically underestimate the probability of purchasing a lemon. Statement c is not correct because the term is "adverse selection" not "adverse information." Statement d is not true because there are typically differences in the willingness to pay and accept (which is why buyers and sellers bargain with each other). Statement e is not true because statement d is not true.

5.   Correct answer: d.

Discussion: The adverse selection problem arises in a mixed market because the quality of every good being sold in a particular market is not known to the buyer. That is, the uninformed side of the market must choose which good to buy knowing that some of the selection is of poor quality but not knowing which of the goods are poor quality.

6.   Correct answer: b.

Discussion: An equilibrium will be reached in the market when the assumed (or perceived) chance of purchasing a lemon is equal to the actual chance. In statement b, the actual chance is $(6/10) \times 100 = 60\%$. (See PET #2 for review).

Statement a is not correct because the actual chance is 80%. Statement c is not true because the actual chance is 50%. Statement d is not true because the actual chance of getting a lemon is 20%. Statement e is not true because the actual chance of getting a lemon is 70%.

7.   Correct answer: d.

Discussion: A thin market is a market in which there are relatively few high quality goods but an abundance of low quality goods being offered for sale. This drives down, not up, the price of the good in a thin market.   If the market were thicker, the price of the good would be higher than in a thin market. Thus, in a thin market, where both qualities of good are being sold at the same price, it will generally be the case that low quality goods are overpriced (relative to their true value) and high quality goods under-priced (relative to their true value).

A thin market, in part, exists because of asymmetric information. Asymmetric information leads to a lower price for the high quality good and thus induces many of the sellers of the high quality good not to sell.

However, there will be some high quality goods being sold perhaps because sellers find themselves in extenuating circumstances where they are forced to sell their good.

8.   Correct answer: e.

Discussion: Your book stresses that all of the above are true of a mixed market and hopefully so too will your instructor because then you'll be prepared for a question like this!

9. Correct answer: c.

Discussion: In this example, insurance companies face an adverse selection problem about plastic surgeons because they do not have as much information about how careful or reckless a plastic surgeon is while the plastic surgeon knows more about him or herself than the insurance company.   Faced with the adverse selection problem, insurance companies protect themselves against it by charging a price that is equal to the average settlement that the reckless plastic surgeon pays. In this example, that price is $36,000. However, since careful doctors know that they are careful and that their average settlement is $6,000, they find it less costly to settle than to pay for malpractice insurance. Thus, careful doctors will not buy the insurance.

Based on the above reasoning, statements a, b, d, and e are not correct.

10. Correct answer: e.

Discussion: Health insurance that is experience rated charges a price to its customers that is based on the history of medical bills that the insurance company must cover for its customer. Customers with high medical bills will see the premiums that they must pay to have health insurance increase. Thus, a firm that pays the health insurance premiums of its employees has an incentive to keep its employees healthy and safe on and off the job. This explains why firms invest in health and safety programs for their employees. While these programs cost the firm money, the firm expects to save more money through having lower health insurance premiums to pay.

Statements a and c are not correct because experience rating raises the cost of insurance to those firms with a history of high medical bills and lowers the cost to those firms with a history of low medical bills.

11. Correct answer: a.

Discussion: The problem of moral hazard is that the provision of insurance leads to riskier behavior than would otherwise occur without the insurance. When insurance companies provide insurance coverage for valuables that are stolen, people knowing that they will be monetarily reimbursed for the stolen items may not be as vigilant about where they leave their valuables and about who may have access to their valuables. People may not be as vigilant about locking their car doors or doors to their houses or about keeping their valuables hidden. Thus, by having insurance against theft, individuals take riskier behavior with respect to the care of their valuables than they would if they had no insurance at all.

Statements b-e are examples of mixed markets where adverse selection, asymmetric information, and a thin market may prevail.

12. Correct answer: d.

Discussion: Use the following formula for expected price:

(probability of high-quality good/100) X price of high-quality good + (probability of low-quality good/100) X price of low quality good.

Thus, your answer to the question should be:

$$(10/100) \times (\$10,000) + (90/100) \times \$400 = 0.1 \times \$10,000 + 0.9 \times \$4,000 = 1,000 + 3,600 = \$4,600.$$
See Pet #1.

Statements a, b, c and e are incorrect given the formula above.

VIII. ANSWER KEY: ESSAY QUESTIONS

1. As the admissions director and having read Chapter 16 of my textbook, I would recognize that I am facing an adverse selection problem that arises because of asymmetric information. There is asymmetric information because the students (the sellers of their talents and aptitude) have more information about themselves (the product they are selling) than I might have about their true abilities. Students vary a good deal in quality and their high school academic record may not always be the best reflection of the quality of a student. That is, some students may have shining academic records but in fact be very poor students. In the language of the used car market, some students are "lemons." In fact, the pool of students applying to the school represents a mixed market — there are high quality and low quality students in the pool together. As the admissions director, I would like to avoid the problem of admitting lemons, particularly because the admittance of such students could ultimately harm the prestigious reputation of the college.

So, as admissions director, I may not only use high school transcripts and SAT or ACT scores to determine who should be admitted, but I may also require a written essay, personal interviews, letters of reference, and evidence of extracurricular activity involvement. The additional information may help reduce the probability that I will admit lemons to my college. In a way, you could say that essays, interviews, and the like are the school's form of insurance against admitting a poor student.

2. In a market with asymmetric information, the price of a used good is typically lower than it would otherwise be. The reason is that a used market is a mixed market where high and low quality goods are being sold without obvious information on which of the goods are high quality and which are low quality. In such a market, the seller has more information about the quality of the good being sold than the buyer has. Thus, buyers attach a probability to the possibility that they will end up buying (unbeknownst to them) a low quality good rather than a high quality good. Since buyers are not willing to pay very much for a low quality good, the probability that they will end up buying one is factored into the price that they will offer to pay. This means that high quality used goods will also have to be sold at a lower price. For example, a buyer may be willing to pay $1,000 for a high quality, used computer but only $200 for a low quality used computer. Thus, the price they are willing to offer will range between $200 and $1,000 and will depend on how likely the buyer thinks he may end up getting a low quality computer. That is, the equilibrium price for used computers (regardless of their quality) will range between $200 and $1,000. The higher the probability that buyers attach to getting a low quality computer, the lower will be the equilibrium price at which used computers sell.

Since the equilibrium price of used computers (both high and low quality) will be lower than otherwise, the quality of used computers offered for sale will be lower than otherwise, too. This is because sellers with high-quality computers will not, unless extraordinary circumstances dictate, be willing to part with their computers for such a low price. This means that in the used market for computers, there will be a lot more low quality computers for sale than one might expect had they not taken account of how the price feeds into determining the quality of used computers offered for sale. The market may also end up being a "thin" market in the sense that there will be fewer high quality computers for sale in because the sellers of the high quality computers have elected not to sell at the low price.

We invite you to visit the book's Companion Website at:
http://www.prenhall.com/osullivan/
for further exercises and practice quizzes.

CHAPTER 9
ENVIRONMENTAL POLICY

I. OVERVIEW

In this chapter, you will learn about the economic consequences and policy surrounding environmental problems. You will learn how a public policy such as a tax on polluters both leads to firms taking steps to cut the pollution that they create when they produce output and because the tax also reduces the amount of output that polluters produce. You will also learn that the government can use regulation to reduce the amount of pollution that producers may be generating. You will learn about the traditional form of pollution regulation which is command and control based, and the modern form of pollution regulation which is market-based. You will learn which policy is most efficient from an economic standpoint. You will learn about global warming and urban smog and how public policy has been devised to reduce these problems.

II. CHECKLIST

By the end of this chapter, you should be able to:

✓ Explain the two ways in which a pollution tax reduces the level of pollution.
✓ Explain the effects of a tax on pollution using demand and supply.
✓ Use the marginal principle to determine how much abatement a firm would undertake in response to a pollution tax.
✓ Discuss how command and control regulations work to reduce pollution.
✓ Compare the efficiency of command and control regulations to a tax.
✓ Explain the effects of pollution regulation using demand and supply.
✓ Discuss how market-based pollution permits work to reduce pollution.
✓ Compare the efficiency of pollution permits to a tax and regulations.
✓ Explain when pollution permits will be traded -- who will buy and who will sell them.
✓ Compare the effects of marketable versus non-marketable permits in reducing the amount of pollution.
✓ Discuss some of the shortcomings of a pollution permits.
✓ Discuss the type of regulation currently used to control ozone pollution (smog) and suggest some alternative policies.

III. KEY TERMS

pollution tax: A tax or charge equal to the external cost per unit of waste.

uniform abatement policy: A policy under which each polluter is required to reduce pollution by the same amount.

command-and-control policy: A policy under which the government commands each firm to produce no more than a certain volume of pollution and specifies the pollution-control technology used.

marketable pollution permits: A system under which the government picks a target pollution level for a particular area, issues just enough pollution permits to meet the pollution target, and allows firms to buy and sell the permits; also known as a cap-and-trade system.

carbon tax: A tax based on a fuel's carbon content.

private cost of production: The production cost borne by a firm, which typically includes the costs of labor, capital, and materials

external cost of production: A cost incurred by people outside the firm.

social cost of production: Private cost plus external cost.

pollution offset: A credit received for supporting a project that either reduces the pollution emissions of another firm or organization or results in the absorption of pollutants; also known as a reduction credit.

IV. PERFORMANCE ENHANCING TIPS (PETS)

PET #1

Production of a good with external costs (such as pollution) imposes a cost that producers do not explicitly pay for unless they are forced to by the government.

Consider a firm that produces chemicals. A by-product of the production process is that some emissions are released into the air. The emissions create pollution which creates health hazards for which people ultimately pay. The chemical producer generates an external cost by polluting the air and creating costs for other members of society. Because air is free, the chemical producer does not have to explicitly pay for the "use of the air." A tax on the chemical producer, in effect, forces it to pay for the cost of the air (and indirectly, assuming the tax revenues are used to help clean up the air, for the health costs that are imposed on society).

PET #2

"Abatement" is the term used for "pollution clean-up."

When a firm undertakes an abatement project, it is cleaning up (or at least, reducing) the amount of pollution that it creates.

You should also know that the marginal cost of pollution clean-up increases. That is, the cost of reducing pollution by one unit, and then by one more, and then by one more, increases. This, means, in effect, that the cost of doing more and more clean-up for the same one ton of output increases.

PET #3

A tax imposed on polluters raises their cost of production and hence the price at which they sell their output. This is represented by a leftward shift in supply. The equilibrium quantity of output the producer sells will decline. The tax thus works to reduce the amount of pollution by (1) reducing the amount of production the firm undertakes (and consequently the pollution that results); and (2) by motivating the firm to devise abatement methods so as to avoid having to pay the tax. Thus, new and improved methods of abatement may emerge.

PET #4

An sale of a pollution permit from one firm to another will occur if two conditions are satisfied: (1) the seller receives more money from the sale of the permit than is his marginal cost of having to abate and the buyer pays less for the permit than is his marginal cost of having to abate; and (2) the buyer is willing to pay an amount equal to or more to the seller than the seller is willing to sell the permit for.

Condition (1) can be explained in the following way. A seller of a permit gives up some of his right to pollute. Without the right to pollute, the seller must abate (do pollution clean-up). If the seller can receive, say $500,000 for his permit but must pay $400,000 to devise a clean-up method, the seller will sell the permit. A buyer of a permit buys the right to pollute more than they are currently polluting. With the right, the seller doesn't have to clean up as much and so the cost of abatement (pollution clean-up) declines. If the buyer can pay, say $500,000 for a permit to pollute and thus avoids $600,000 in abatement costs, the buyer will purchase the permit. This is just an application of the marginal principle.

Condition (2) is just a way of saying that the buyer's willingness to pay is greater than or equal to the seller's willingness to accept. To put it in more practical terms, suppose you would like to buy a used t.v. for your apartment or dorm room and the amount you would be willing to pay is $100. If the seller is willing to accept $75, then a deal could be struck. You may buy the television for $85. In the example above, if the seller of the permit was willing to sell at $500,000 and the buyer was willing to pay at $600,000, a deal could be struck.

V. PRACTICE EXAM: MULTIPLE CHOICE QUESTIONS

1. The optimal level of pollution is:

a) always zero.
b) depends on the marginal benefits to society from reducing the amount of pollution.
c) depends on the marginal costs associated with reducing the amount of pollution.
d) may be different for different societies (or countries).
e) (b), (c), and (d).

2. Which one of the following is NOT a public policy for reducing pollution?

a) a tax on polluters.
b) marketable permits for pollution.
c) non-marketable permits for pollution.
d) government regulation.
e) subsidies to polluters.

3. In economics, pollution:

a) is an external cost.
b) is a private good.
c) generates diminishing returns.
d) is really a cost of production.
e) (a) and (d).

4. Which one of the following is an effect of a pollution tax on paper production?

a) the price of paper will decline.
b) paper producers will have an incentive to abate.
c) the quantity of paper produced will rise.
d) the marginal cost of paper production will decline.
e) none of the above.

5. Use the table below to decide how many gallons of water per ton of output produced a firm will decide to emit.

Waste per ton	Clean-up Cost per ton	Tax Cost per ton
20 gallons	$100	$60
19 gallons	$102	$57
18	$106	$54
17	$112	$51
16	$120	$48

a) 20 gallons.
b) 19 gallons.
c) 18 gallons.
d) 17 gallons.
e) 16 gallons.

6. Which one of the following is true of traditional pollution regulation (command and control policy)?

a) the policy imposes that a single abatement technology (method of clean-up) be used.
b) it creates an incentive to pollute.
c) it encourages innovation in new and less costly methods of abatement.
d) it is less costly than imposing a tax on polluters.
e) all of the above are true.

7. Which one of the following is true of a comparison between a pollution tax and traditional pollution regulation?

a) regulation raises the price of the output of the polluter more than would a pollution tax.
b) firms produce and sell less output under regulation than a tax.
c) pollution is reduced by less with a regulation than with a tax.
d) regulation does not produce any tax revenue that can be used to fund other clean-up projects.
e) all of the above.

8. Marketable pollution permits:

a) make it hard to predict how much pollution abatement will actually take place.

b) can only be bought and sold by polluters.

c) may lead to severe pollution in some areas.

d) lead to the high-abatement cost firms selling the permits and the low-abatement cost firms buying the permits.

e) are not as effective as non-marketable permits at reducing the amount of pollution.

9. Which one of the following would explain why a firm might not sell its marketable pollution permit?

a) the cost to the firm of reducing pollution is greater than the price the firm will get for selling the permit.

b) the cost to the firm of reducing pollution is less than the price the firm will get for selling the permit.

c) the cost to the firm of increasing pollution is greater than the price the firm will get for selling the permit.

d) the cost to the firm of increasing pollution is less than the price the firm will get for selling the permit.

e) none of the above.

10. Which one of the following is NOT true of global warming?

a) it is due to an accumulation of carbon dioxide in the atmosphere.

b) there is uncertainty about how much the earth's temperature will actually rise.

c) total rainfall is expected to decrease.

d) a carbon tax (a tax on the burning of fossil fuels like oil, coal, and gasoline) is one solution aimed at reducing the pace of global warming.

e) sea levels are expected to increase.

11. Which one of the following is expected to be an effect of the ban on production of CFCs (chlorofluorocarbons)?

a) a slower pace of ozone depletion.

b) innovation of products that achieve the same purpose as CFCs.

c) short run increase in the price of refrigerators.

d) innovation in products that have previously used CFCs.

e) all of the above.

12. Which one of the following statements is true?

a)   a recent study of global warming suggests that crop production may fall substantially.

b)   the state of Arizona helps pay for abatement associated with global warming effects that are produced in other countries.

c)   a ban on the production of CFCs has been in place since 1985.

d)   the government currently uses non-marketable permits to control the amount of urban smog.

e)   all of the above are true.

VI.   PRACTICE EXAM: ESSAY QUESTIONS

1.   Explain how a tax on polluters works to help reduce the amount of pollution.

2.   Explain how a system of marketable permits to pollute works to reduce the amount of pollution. Be sure to discuss who will buy and sell the permits and why some communities do not like the system.

VII. ANSWER KEY: MULTIPLE CHOICE QUESTIONS

1.   Correct answer: e.

Discussion: The optimal level of pollution (as with the optimal level of just about anything else) depends on the marginal (additional) benefits and marginal (additional) costs associated with altering the level of pollution. Thus, statements (b) and (c) are correct. It is also the case that the marginal benefits and costs associated with reducing the amount of pollution will be different for different societies (or countries). That is, not all societies will evaluate the benefits and costs of pollution abatement (reduction) the same. Thus, statement (d) is also correct. The optimal level of pollution is not necessarily always zero for any and every society – as the discussion before shows – the optimal level of pollution for a society depends on their evaluation of the marginal benefits and costs associated with reducing pollution.

2.   Correct answer: e.

Discussion: A subsidy to a polluter may not discourage them from polluting. All of the other public policies are discussed in your textbook as ways in which the government attempts to reduce the amount of pollution.

3.   Correct answer: e.

Discussion: Pollution is an external cost of production because it imposes costs on other segments of society that bear the cost of pollution such as health costs, inability to use a river to fish or a lake to swim, etc. Pollution should also rightly be considered a cost of production because a firm that pollutes a river or the air is using the river or the air in the production process. Thus, it should be treated as a cost just like the use of labor and raw materials is considered a cost of production.

Statement b is not correct because pollution is a public good (that is, in fact, bad).   Statement c is not correct because the reduction of pollution entails increasing marginal costs.

4. Correct answer: b.

Discussion: A tax forces the polluting firm to bear some of the cost of polluting in production. Since the tax imposes a cost on the firm, the firm has an incentive to avoid it by finding methods of abatement.

Statement a is not correct because the price of paper will rise. Statement c is not correct because the quantity of paper produced will decline. Statement d is not correct because the marginal cost of abatement will increase. Statement e cannot be correct because statement b is true.

5. Correct answer: b.

Discussion: The marginal cost of reducing pollution from 20 gallons to 19 gallons per ton is $2 whereas if the polluter did not clean up, the tax cost would be $3. (The government forces the polluter to pay $3 more dollars to pollute 20 gallons instead of 19 gallons). Thus, the marginal cost of abatement is less than the tax cost so the firm should abate.

The marginal cost of reducing pollution from 19 gallons to 18 gallons per ton is $4 whereas if the polluter did not clean up that one more gallon of waste, the tax cost would be $3. Since the tax cost of polluting by one more gallon is less than the cost of cleaning up, the polluter will not clean up and instead pay the tax cost. The same reasoning applies to the 17th and 16th gallons.

6. Correct answer: a.

Discussion: A command and control pollution policy imposed by regulators forces all firms in the same industry to use the same method of abatement.

Statement b is not true; regulation does not create the incentive to pollute but rather forces the polluter not to pollute. Statement c is not true because the policy discourages innovation in pollution abatement by dictating that all firms use the same method of clean-up. Statement d is not true because command and control regulation is more costly to polluters than a tax. Statement e is not true because statement a is true.

7. Correct answer: e.

Discussion: A pollution tax is more efficient than traditional pollution regulation. All of the statements above are reasons why it is more efficient.

8.   Correct answer: c.

Discussion: Marketable pollution permits mean that a firm that buys the permit has the right to pollute more than the target level set by the government. Thus, some firms with high costs of abatement will buy up a lot of permits and pollute a lot. If the firm resides in your community, your community will experience a lot of pollution.

Statement a is not true because marketable pollution permits make it easy to predict how much pollution will be emitted by firms, collectively. While the government cannot predict how much each firm will emit individually, the government can predict how much firms will in total (collectively) emit. Statement b is not true because marketable pollution permits can be purchased by environmental groups, as well. Statement d is not true; it is the reverse -- low abatement cost firms sell their permits to high abatement cost firms. Statement e is not true because marketable permits are more effective than non-marketable permits in reducing the amount of pollution.

9.   Correct answer: a.

Discussion: If the firm sells its permit, it will not have the right to pollute as much and thus will have to do more clean-up. The clean-up means that the firm will incur a cost. If the cost of clean-up is more than the firm can receive from the sale of its permit, it will choose to hold onto the permit and thereby avoid the cost of clean-up. If it chose to sell its permit, it would not receive enough money to cover the clean-up costs that it would incur as a result of not having a permit to pollute. Thus, based on the marginal principle, it makes sense not to sell the permit.

Based on the above reasoning, statements b, c, d and e cannot be true. In fact, statement b suggests that the firm would sell the permit. This is because the price the firm would receive from selling the permit is greater than the costs of clean-up it will incur without having the permit.

10. Correct answer: c.

Discussion: Global warming is expected to increase, not decrease, the amount of rainfall. All of the other statements are true.

11. Correct answer: e.

Discussion: The ban on CFCs has been established for the purpose of reducing the pace of ozone depletion (and thus the amount, too). The ban on CFCs will inspire innovation in products that previously used CFCs as well as in finding a replacement for CFCs.   Because refrigerators (air conditioners, hairspray, etc.) used CFCs in the past and must now find another technology that achieves the same purpose as CFCs, the cost of producing a refrigerator will rise, at least in the short run.

12. Correct answer: b.

Discussion: Since air circulates around the world, an oil refinery in Houston contributes to global warming just as much as an oil refinery in Bogotá. Thus, firms in the U.S. have been mandated to help reduce the problem of global warming that occurs anywhere in the world. This means that they can pay for abatement in cities and countries different from where they are located.

A recent study of global warming suggests that crop production may not fall by as much as previously predicted, in part because farmers will find new ways of growing crops just as efficiently as before in a "globally-warmed" climate. The ban on CFCs has been in place since 1996. The government currently uses a traditional command and control regulatory policy to control urban smog.

VIII. ANSWER KEY: ESSAY QUESTIONS

1. A tax on polluters implicitly raises their cost of production as they must pay for the tax or adopt methods of abatement to avoid the tax. Abatement, of course, is a cost to the firm. However, since the tax creates the incentive to adopt methods of abatement, pollution will be reduced by the abatement actions of the firms. Secondly, a pollution tax raises the cost of output that the polluter produces. (This is represented by a leftward shift in supply). A higher cost of production is, in part, passed on to consumers through a higher consumer price. The higher price reduces the equilibrium quantity of the output demanded. Firms respond by producing less of the output which means they, in turn, end up polluting less. It may also happen that firms invent a similar product that has a manufacturing process that does not pollute or pollutes by much less.

2. A system of marketable permits is a new form of regulation aimed at reducing the amount of pollution. Under such a system, the government sets a target limit of pollution that they desire to achieve. They then give firms permits to pollute, but only by a specified amount. The innovation is that firms can buy and sell the permits so that they are not constrained to pollute only up to the amount allotted in the permit. However, in total, the target amount of pollution desired by the government is maintained. For example, suppose there are only two firms that pollute and the government issues permits to each of them allowing them to emit 30 tons of waste per year. The government's target level of pollution is thus 60 tons of waste per year. If one firm sells its permit to the other, the selling firm can no longer emit any waste (it must completely abate) and the buying firm is now permitted to emit up to 60 tons of waste per year. Thus, the target level of waste per year is achieved while each individual firm's emission level may vary.

    A firm for which it is very expensive to abate (clean up) will be a buyer of a permit if the price they have to pay for the permit (the right to pollute) is less costly than having to clean up. A firm for which it is not very expensive to abate will be a seller of a permit if the price they can sell their permit for is greater than the cost of having to clean up. In this case, the money they receive for the permit would pay for the firm's clean-up and leave them with extra money that they could use elsewhere. For a deal to be struck, the buyer's willingness to pay must be equal to or greater than the seller's willingness to accept. For example, if the buyer was willing to pay $200,000 for a permit and the seller was willing to accept $175,000, then the two could likely reach a price at which an exchange of the permit for money would take place.

    Some citizens do not like the system of marketable permits because they may end up getting a lot more pollution in their community, especially if they have a high-cost-of-abatement firm in their town. The high-cost-of-abatement firm is much more likely to be a buyer of permits and thus will acquire the right to pollute more rather than less under the policy.

We invite you to visit the book's Companion Website at:
http://www.prenhall.com/osullivan/
for further exercises and practice quizzes.

CHAPTER 10
PUBLIC GOODS AND PUBLIC CHOICE

I. OVERVIEW

In this chapter, you will learn about public goods -- goods that benefit society but are so expensive to pay for that no individual can pay for it by him or herself. You will learn that government policy, including the tax system, can be used to ensure that worthwhile public goods are provided to society. You will learn what distinguishes public goods from private goods and learn of the special challenges that public goods create in a market economy. You will learn about the different levels of government and what roles they play in your community. You will learn about a branch of economics called "public choice" which studies the way in which governments operate and how they make decisions.

II. CHECKLIST

By the end of this chapter, you should be able to:

✓ Define a public good and the characteristics of a public good.

✓ Compare and contrast public and private goods.

✓ List some real world examples of public goods and private goods with external benefits.

✓ Explain what external benefits are and give some examples.

✓ Explain the free rider problem and why voluntary contributions will generally not lead to the provision of a public good.

✓ Discuss some ways in which organizations can increase the voluntary contributions that they receive.

✓ Discuss the three levels of government and the main services each provides.

✓ Explain the three views on how a government makes decisions.

✓ Explain the median voter rule.

III. KEY TERMS

median-voter rule: A rule suggesting that the choices made by government will reflect the preferences of the median voter.

deadweight loss from taxation: The difference between the total burden of a tax and the amount of revenue collected by the government.

excess burden of a tax: Another name for deadweight loss.

public choice economics: A field of economics that explores how governments actually operate.

public good: A good that is available for everyone to consume, regardless of who pays and who doesn't.

private good: A good that is consumed by a single person or household.

free-rider problem: A problem that occurs when people try to benefit from a public good without paying for it.

IV. PERFORMANCE ENHANCING TIPS (PETS)

PET #1

A subsidy is a transfer of money from the government to private citizens; a tax is a transfer of money from private citizens to the government.

Since a subsidy is the reverse of a tax, it is sometimes referred to as a "negative tax." It should be pointed out, however, that the ability of the government to extend subsidies to certain private citizens or groups of private citizens comes from the taxes that private citizens (households and businesses) pay to the government. Thus, your tax dollars are used to pay for government subsidies. Thus, indirectly, your tax dollars are transferred to other citizens in society.

V. PRACTICE EXAM: MULTIPLE CHOICE QUESTIONS

1.   Which one of the following describes a public good?

a)   it is rival in consumption and excludable.
b)   it is non-rival in consumption and excludable.
c)   it is rival in consumption and non-excludable.
d)   it is non-rival in consumption and non-excludable.
e)   none of the above.

2.   Which pair of the following is an example of a private good and a public good?

a)   preservation of endangered species/space exploration.
b)   public housing/free concert in a city park.
c)   highways/ice cream.
d)   newspapers/golf courses.
e)   law enforcement/national defense.

3.   Which one of the following statements is NOT true?

a)   the government spends money only on public goods, not private goods.
b)   public and private goods can both generate external benefits.
c)   the market for a good which generates external benefits is not efficient.
d)   education is likely to generate a workplace externality.
e)   a government subsidy for a good with an external benefit can lead to a more efficient outcome.

4.   Which one of the following statements is NOT true of a subsidy?

a)   subsidies are often given in the case of private goods that carry external benefits.
b)   subsidies internalize an external benefit.
c)   subsidies are ultimately paid for by taxpayers.
d)   a subsidy for education might come in the form of federal grants for financial aid.
e)   all of the above are true of subsidies.

5.   Which one of the following is NOT an example of a private good with an external benefit?

a)   education.
b)   on-the-job training.
c)   the space program.
d)   preventative health care.
e)   research at private universities.

6.   Which one of the following explains why voluntary contributions typically do not work as a way of funding public goods and goods with external benefits?

a)   the free rider problem.
b)   the chump problem.
c)   the anonymity problem.
d)   the no-free lunch problem.
e)   a and b.

7. Which one of the following is NOT true of voluntary contributions as a way of funding public goods and goods with external benefits?

a) some citizens will not contribute at all.

b) some citizens will contribute an amount that is small relative to the benefits they receive from the good.

c) voluntary contributions work better than taxes at ensuring that a project is funded.

d) voluntary contributions may increase through programs like "matching contributions" and giving coffee mugs, etc. to contributors.

e) public radio and television have been very successful at overcoming the free rider problem.

8. The free-rider problem is best illustrated with which good?

a) radio talk shows.

b) state universities.

c) a nationally-televised football game.

d) movies.

e) rides at a theme-park.

9. The median voter rule:

a) is that people vote with their feet, i.e. move to communities where their median preferences are reflected.

b) may not be true if people cannot vote on individual issues but must instead vote on packages.

c) suggests that the decisions made by elected officials may not always be the most efficient.

d) implies that candidates for office will take extreme positions.

e) (a) and (c).

10. Public choice economics suggests that government decisions may be based on:

a) the government's desire to make the economy operate more efficiently.

b) the median voter.

c) the self-interest of politicians.

d) people voting with their feet.

e) all of the above.

VI. PRACTICE EXAM: ESSAY QUESTION

1. Suppose that you are the head of a government agency that oversees re-training programs for the unemployed. Discuss whether the service that your agency delivers is a public or private good. Will the private market of demand and supply lead to an efficient outcome? Why or why not? Discuss how your agency is funded. How well do you think a voluntary contribution scheme work in funding your program?

VII. ANSWER KEY: MULTIPLE CHOICE

1. Correct answer: d.

Discussion: A public good is both non-rival and non-excludable in consumption. Non-rival means that one person's consumption of the good does not rival another person's ability to consume/use the good. That is, more than one person can consume/use the good at the same time. Non-excludable means that people who do not pay for the good cannot be excluded from using and receiving the benefits of the good. Thus, even if one person were to pay for the good, others could use it without having to pay for it.

Statement a describes a private good. A private good can only be consumed and thus enjoyed by the consumer. That is, it is rival in consumption. A private good can also only be consumed/used by the person paying for it. That is, a private good is excludable. Reading a book, attending a movie, going to a private school, buying a house, and eating an ice cream cone are some examples.

As an aside, you should remember that a private good can have external benefits as can a public good.

2. Correct answer: b.

Discussion: Public housing is both rival and excludable in consumption even though it is a government-provided good. A free concert in a city park is non-rival and non-excludable. More than one person can enjoy it and people can enjoy it regardless of whether or not they pay for it. Of course, citizens who live around the park who may not prefer the noise of the concert will experience a external (external) cost.

Statement a is an example of two public goods. Statement c is an example of a public good/private good (instead of vice-versa). Statement d is an example of two private goods. Statement e is an example of two public goods.

3. Correct answer: a.

Discussion: Statement a is not true because a government spends money on public goods like highways, law enforcement, and space exploration as well as on education (a private good with external benefits), and housing and food (a private good).

Statement b is true because a public good like the space exploration program can generate external benefits -- high-tech companies may learn new and improved ways to do things from the space exploration program. Private goods like education, health care, and even deodorant create external benefits. Statement c is true because when a private good carries external benefits, not all of the benefits of the good are revealed in the market. That is, not all of the consumers are represented in the demand curve so the market outcome cannot be efficient. Statement d is true -- education generates not only workplace but civic externalities. Statement e is true because the government, by subsidizing particular goods, is attempting to achieve a more desirable (truthful) market outcome.

4. Correct answer: e.

Discussion: All of the above are true of a subsidy. While statement a is true, it does not mean that the government provides subsidies to any and every private good that carry an external benefit. Statement b means that a subsidy forces an external benefit to be reflected in the market demand curve. Statement d suggests that there are many ways in which the government can give money back to citizens for the purchase of a private good. Statement c is also true, as discussed in PET #1.

5. Correct answer: c.

Discussion: Statement c is an example of a public good, not a private good, which has external benefits. All of the other examples are examples of private goods with external benefits.

6. Correct answer: e.

Discussion: E is correct, both statements a and b are correct. The problem of using voluntary contributions to support public goods is known as the free-rider problem. Each person has a financial incentive to try to get the benefits of a public good without paying for it. The flip side of the free-rider problem is the chump problem: no one wants to be the chump the person that gives free rides to other people. C and d are made up options.

7. Correct answer: c.

Discussion: Statement c is not true; taxes work better at ensuring that a project is funded than voluntary contributions. In effect, a tax ensures that everybody pays for the project, not just those willing to contribute.

Statements a and b reflect a common problem with voluntary contributions. Statement d suggests that there are ways (that are costly to somebody, however) to increase voluntary contributions to a specific project. Statement e is true; in fact, public radio and television have used some of the tactics listed in statement d as a way of increasing voluntary contributions.

8. Correct answer: a.

Discussion: The free-rider problem occurs for goods that are non-rival and non-excludable in consumption. Goods with these characteristics are called 'public goods.' A good that is non-rival in consumption means that it is available to anyone to consume whether they pay or not. A good that is non-excludable in consumption means that it is not practical to exclude people who do not pay for the good. The correct answer is a because radio talk shows are available for anyone to listen to by turning on their radio. It is also not practical to exclude people from listening to the talk show who do not to pay for the talk show.

Statements b and c are examples of private goods with external benefits. Students attending state universities pay to attend though the external benefit is to society in the form of a more educated workplace and community. A nationally-televised football game is a private good in the sense that there are ticket holders in the stadium who paid to watch the football game live. But, since it is nationally-televised, the rest of society (those enjoying football!) can enjoy watching the game without paying for it. Thus, society, too, benefits. Statements d (movies) and e (rides at a theme park) are examples of private goods. These are goods for which the person who pays for it receives the benefits and those benefits do not extend to others who do not pay.

9.   Correct answer: b.

Discussion: The median voter rule is that government decisions made by elected officials represent the preferences of the median voter which is the voter whose preferences are exactly midway between the preferences of all of the voters. However, the median voter rule is best applied to government decisions that are made on an individual basis rather than as part of a package. That is, the median voter rule may not be correct if voters vote "yes" or "no" on a package of programs rather than "yes" or "no" on each item in the package. Also, the median voter rule means that the most efficient outcomes are not necessarily guaranteed. Since the median voter's preferences do not necessarily reflect the most efficient outcomes for society, there is no guarantee that the median voter rule will lead to the most efficient government decisions.

Statement b is true as it is harder for the preferences of the median voter to be reflected in a package as compromises will have to be made. Statement a is not the definition of the median voter rule. Statement d is not true of the median voter rule; in fact, the median voter rule implies that candidates will come closer and closer in their positions on issues as election day approaches. Statement c really reflects problems with self interested bureaucrats and not necessarily the median voter model. E is not true because a and c are not true.

10. Correct answer: e.

Discussion: There are many views in public choice economics on how the government actually arrives at the decisions that it makes. All of the above are possible and not necessarily mutually exclusive.

VIII. ANSWER KEY: ESSAY QUESTION

1.   The worker re-training program is a private good with external benefits. It is a private good because only those enrolled in the re-training program are able to use it. Furthermore, only companies that pay for the program, also supported by subsidies from the government, are able to use it. However, there are external benefits to the re-training program. Not only do the unemployed and the companies

using the program benefit, but society benefits as well. People who are employed pay taxes and are less likely to get involved in illegal activities. Since the re-training program has external benefits, the government may subsidize the worker re-training programs. This gets the private market to take advantage of the external benefits.   While my agency is funded through subsidies provided by the government and also through companies paying into the program for its use, the government subsidies ultimately come from tax-paying citizens. A voluntary contribution scheme would probably not lead to the level of support currently provided because of the free-rider problem. What typically happens under a voluntary contribution scheme is that some people who use the program will not contribute anything at all while others will contribute but not in accordance with the actual benefits they receive. Thus, a voluntary contribution scheme would likely lead to an under-funded program which thus may not be able to continue to run. Of course, I might suggest that our agency's fundraising efforts include matching contributions and free gifts. However, somebody will have to pay for these.

We invite you to visit the book's Companion Website at:
http://www.prenhall.com/osullivan/
for further exercises and practice quizzes.

PART 4: MARKET STRUCTURES AND PRICING

CHAPTER 11
PRODUCTION TECHNOLOGY AND COST

I. OVERVIEW

In this chapter, you will learn about the costs a firm incurs when it produces output. You will learn that there are fixed costs and variable costs, and explicit and implicit costs of production. You will learn that a firm's marginal cost changes as it produces more and more (or less and less) output. You will learn that the productivity of a firm's workers affects its marginal cost of production. You will also learn about a firm's short and long run average costs. You will learn that the short and the long run are different time horizons that a firm considers when making decisions about how much to produce, whether to build another plant, hire more workers, or cut back production. You will re-encounter the concept of diminishing returns which is a short run concept. You will learn about economies and diseconomies of scale which are long run concepts.

II. CHECK LIST

By the end of this chapter, you should be able to:

✓ Explain the difference between explicit and implicit costs.

✓ Give some examples of explicit costs and implicit costs.

✓ Explain the difference between the short run and the long run.

✓ Explain the difference between variable and fixed costs and why in the long run, all costs are variable.

✓ Give some examples of variable costs and fixed costs.

✓ Explain why diminishing returns causes marginal cost in the short run to increase.

✓ Draw a short run average fixed cost curve and a short run average variable cost curve and explain their shape.

✓ Draw a long run average cost curve and explain its shape.

✓ Draw a short run marginal cost curve and explain its shape.

✓ Explain the relationship between marginal cost and the average cost curves.

✓ Explain what causes economies and diseconomies of scale.

✓ Define a firm's minimum efficient scale and represent it with a graph.

III. KEY TERMS

explicit cost: The firm's actual cash payments for its inputs.

implicit cost: The opportunity cost of non-purchased inputs.

average fixed cost (AFC): Fixed cost divided by the quantity produced.

short-run average variable cost (AVC): Total variable cost divided by the quantity produced.

short-run average total cost (ATC): Short-run total cost divided by the quantity of output; equal to AFC plus AVC

long-run average cost of production (LAC): Long-run total cost divided by the quantity of output produced.

indivisible input: An input that cannot be scaled down to produce a smaller quantity of output.

minimum efficient scale: The output at which the long-run average cost curve becomes horizontal.

Diseconomies of scale: A situation in which an increase in the quantity produced increases the long-run average cost of production.

variable cost (VC): Cost that varies as the firm changes its output.

short-run total cost (TC): The total cost of production in the short run, when one or more inputs (for example, the production facility) is fixed; equal to fixed cost plus variable cost.

short-run marginal cost (MC): The change in short-run total cost resulting from producing one more unit of the good.

fixed cost (FC): Cost that does not depend on the quantity produced.

long-run total cost (LTC): The total cost of production in the long run when a firm is perfectly flexible in its choice of all inputs and can choose a production facility of any size.

economic cost: Explicit cost plus implicit cost.

total product curve: A curve showing the relationship between the quantity of labor and the quantity of output produced.

economies of scale: A situation in which an increase in the quantity produced decreases the long-run average cost of production.

economies of scale: A situation in which an increase in the quantity produced decreases the long-run average cost of production.

IV. PERFORMANCE ENHANCING TIPS (PETS)

PET #1

For any formula, if you are given two of three missing components, you can always figure out the third component. Likewise for three of four, four of five, and so on.

You encountered this PET in Chapter 5 where it was applied to the elasticity of demand. In this chapter, you can apply it to total, variable, and fixed costs, average total, average variable, and average fixed costs, and output. Let's see how.

Suppose you are told that the total cost of producing 100 units of output is $2,000. What is the average total cost? The average total cost (ATC) is computed using:

ATC = Total Cost/Output

Since you have two of the three missing components to the formula, you can figure out the third component. Thus, the average total cost would be $2,000/100 units = $20/unit.

Now, suppose you are told that the average total cost is $20/unit and that the output level is 100 units. What is the total cost (TC)? The formula above can be re-arranged as below to figure out the total cost:

TC = ATC X Output

Thus, the total cost would be $20/unit X 100 units = $2,000.

Next, suppose you are told that the average total cost is $20/unit and that the total cost is $2,000. How many units of output (Q) must the firm be producing? The formulas above can be re-arranged as below to figure out the output of the firm:

Q = Total Cost/Average Total Cost

Thus, the firm must be producing $2,000/($20/unit) = 100 units.

The same is true for computing variable costs (total or average) and fixed costs (total or average).

You can also apply this PET to the relationship between short run total cost, variable cost and fixed cost and to the relationship between short run average total cost, average variable cost and average fixed cost.

For example, suppose you are told that the variable cost of producing 100 units of output is $1,500 and the fixed cost of producing 100 units of output is $500. What is the short run total cost?

The short run total cost is the sum of the two:

Total Cost = variable cost + fixed cost

Thus, the total cost is $2,000.

Based on the information above, the average variable cost would be $1,500/100 units = $15/unit and the average fixed cost would be $500/100 units $5/unit. Thus, the average total cost would be:

Average Total Cost = average variable cost + average fixed cost

Thus, the average total cost would be $15/unit + $5/unit = $20/ unit.

PET #2

Short run marginal cost is computed by calculating the change in (or addition to) the short run total cost as output increases by one unit. Since the short run total cost is the sum of variable cost plus fixed cost, and since fixed costs do not change as the level of output changes, then marginal cost can also be computed by calculating the change in the short run variable cost as output increases by one unit.

Suppose you are told that the variable cost of producing 10 units of output is $250 and that the fixed cost of producing 10 units of output is $100. Further, you are told that the variable cost of producing 11 units of output is $275. Since fixed costs are fixed, the fixed cost of producing 11 units of output remains at $100. What is the total cost of producing 10 units of output? Of 11 units of output? What is the marginal cost of the 11th unit of output?

Total cost of producing 10 units of output is $250 + $100 = $350.
Total cost of producing 11 units of output is $275 + $100 = $375.

The marginal cost (addition to cost) of producing one more unit of output, the 11th unit is equal to the change in total cost which is also equal to the change in the variable cost. Let's see why:

Marginal Cost of 11th unit = Change in total cost = change in variable cost + change in fixed cost.

The change in total cost is $375 - $350 = $25.
The change in variable cost is $275 - $250 = $25.
The change in fixed cost is $100 - $100 = $0.

Notice that the sum of the change in the variable cost plus the change in the fixed cost equals $25. This is because fixed costs do not change as output changes. That is, the marginal cost associated with fixed inputs is zero. Thus, in the short run, the marginal cost can also be computed as the change in the variable cost.

Remember that in the long run, all costs are variable costs. There are no "fixed" costs.

PET #3

When marginal cost is less than average total (or average variable) cost, average total (or average variable) cost will decrease. When marginal cost is greater than average total (or average variable) cost, average total (or average variable) cost will increase.

Suppose that you are told that the average total cost of producing 300 units of output is $60 and that the marginal cost of producing the 301st unit of output is $65. Will the average total cost of producing 301 units of output be greater or less than $60?

Since the marginal cost of increasing output by one unit to 301 units is greater than the average cost of producing the previous 300 units, then the average cost of producing 301 units will increase.

V. PRACTICE EXAM: MULTIPLE CHOICE QUESTIONS

1. Which one of the following would be considered an implicit cost by a firm?

a) monthly electricity bill.
b) monthly rent for use of a warehouse.
c) weekly wages paid to workers.
d) foregone interest income because an entrepreneur must use her own money to start up a business.
e) payment for installation of a fax line.

2. In the long run, a firm can:

a) alter the number of workers it hires.
b) alter the amount of raw materials it uses.
c) alter the size of the factory.
d) open up new factories or close down factories.
e) all of the above.

3. Use the table below to determine when diminishing marginal returns occurs.

Workers	Output (in units)
1	10
2	25
3	50
4	60
5	68
6	75

a) after the first worker.

b) after the second worker.

c) after the third worker.

d) after the fourth worker.

e) after the fifth worker.

4. Use the table below to determine when diminishing marginal returns occurs.

Workers	Output (in units)
4	1
7	2
9	3
10	4
14	5
20	6

a) after the first unit of output.

b) between the first and second unit of output.

c) after the third unit of output.

d) after the fourth unit of output.

e) after the fifth unit of output.

5. The short run production function (total product curve) is a graph showing the relationship between:

a) output produced and the number of workers, holding everything else constant.
b) the marginal product of a worker and output.
c) output and average cost of production.
d) number of workers and number of other inputs.
e) the marginal cost of production and output.

6. Which one of the following statements is true?

a) short run total cost = variable cost - fixed cost.
b) short run total cost = variable cost + fixed cost.
c) average total cost = average variable cost/average fixed cost.
d) fixed cost = average fixed cost/output.
e) average variable cost = variable cost X output.

7. Which one of the following statements is correct?

a) a firm's average fixed costs increases as output increases. ×
b) in the short run, a firm's marginal cost curve is negatively sloped because of diminishing marginal returns.
c) in the long run, a firm's average total cost curve is U-shaped. ×
d) if the marginal cost of production is less than the average total cost of production, then average total costs will be decreasing.
e) average total costs = average fixed cost - average variable cost. ×

8. Which one of the following explains why a firm's short run marginal cost increases as it produces more and more output?

a) diminishing returns.
b) diseconomies of scale.
c) increasing returns to scale.
d) diminishing marginal utility.
e) diseconomies of scope.

9.   Which one of the following statements is true?

a)   a firm's short run average variable cost first increases and then decreases as output increases. ×

b)   a firm's short run average total cost curve is shaped like a "W." ✓

c)   a firm's average fixed cost always decreases as output increases. ✓

d)   average variable cost increases as output increases because each additional worker becomes less and less productive in the short run.

e)   (c) and (d).

10. Use the following information to answer the question below.

output = 250 units.
fixed cost = $1,000.
average variable cost = $6 per unit.
average total cost = $10 per unit.
marginal cost = $12.

Which one of the following statements is true based on the information above?

a)   average fixed cost = $4 per unit and total cost = $25,000.

b)   variable cost = $1,500 and average fixed cost = $4 per unit.

c)   variable cost = $2,500 and total cost = $1,500.

d)   average fixed cost = $4 per unit and total cost = $22.

e)   total cost = $1,006 and variable cost = $18.

11. Use the following information to answer the question below.

output = 100 units
average fixed cost = $3 per unit.
short run total cost = $800.
marginal cost = $60.

The firm's total variable cost must be:

a) $500.

b) $770.

c) $77.

d) $7,700.

e)   cannot be calculated without more information.

12. Suppose you are told that the average total cost of producing 200,000 dartboards is $4 and that the total fixed costs of operation are $100,000. Based on this, you know that:

a) total variable costs are $700,000.

b) average fixed costs are $2.

c) the marginal cost of production is $1.

d) total costs are $900,000.

e) total profits will be very low.

13. Use the graph below to answer the following question.

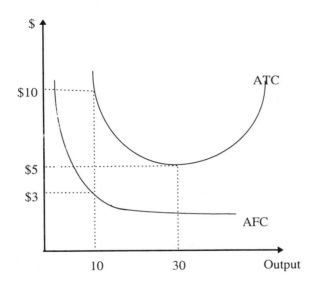

Which one of the following statements is true?

a) the average variable cost of producing 10 units of output is $13 per unit. ✕

b) the total cost of producing 30 units of output is $5. ✗

c) the variable cost of producing 10 units of output is $70.

d) the marginal cost of producing 30 units of output must be less than $5.

e) none of the above are true.

14. Which one of the following defines the long run average cost of production?

a) total cost divided by the quantity of output when the firm cannot alter the number of workers it hires.

b) total cost divided by the quantity of output when the firm can choose a production facility of any size.

c) total cost multiplied by the quantity of output when the firm can choose a production facility of any size.

d) total cost divided by the quantity of output when the firm cannot alter the size of its facilities.

e) total cost divided by the quantity of output when the firm cannot change the number of factories it operates.

15. Which one of the following is a reason for economies of scale?

a) specialization.
b) diminishing returns.
c) divisible inputs.

d) rising marginal costs.
e) comparative advantage.

16. Which one of the following is NOT an example of an indivisible input?

a) an industrial mold for a giant bowl of jello. ✓
b) a large cargo ship. ✓
c) "clean rooms" used by a computer-chip maker.
d) an expensive piece of medical equipment. ✓
e) all of the above are examples of indivisible inputs.

17. Which one of the following statements is NOT true?

a) the minimum efficient scale for production is that output level where average costs are neither increasing nor decreasing, i.e. the long run average cost curve is horizontal. ✓
b) diseconomies of scale may arise from the use of indivisible inputs.
c) diseconomies of scale may occur because of coordination problems that arise as more and more output is produced.
d) diseconomies of scale may occur because input costs increase as a firm produces more and more output.
e) in the long run, a firm does not encounter diminishing returns.

VI. PRACTICE EXAM: ESSAY QUESTIONS

1. Explain why specialization can lead to economies of scale.

2. Distinguish diminishing returns from diseconomies of scale.

VII.ANSWER KEY: MULTIPLE CHOICE QUESTIONS

1. Correct answer: d.

Discussion: An implicit cost is a cost for which there is not an explicit payment by check or money. The textbook lists two types of implicit costs -- the cost of a business owner's time and the cost of a business owner's use of his or her own funds (financial capital). Implicit costs should be included when figuring up economic profit. However, they are not included when figuring up accounting profit.

Statements a, b, c, and e are all examples of explicit costs.

2.   Correct answer: e.

Discussion: The long run is defined as a period of time over which a firm is able to choose the combination of workers, raw materials, size of the factory, and number of factories to operate in order to produce output at the least per unit cost (average cost).

Statements a, b, c, and d are all factors of production that can be altered in the long run. In the short run, however, generally speaking, only the number of workers and the amount of raw material a firm uses can be altered. The size of the factory along with the number of factories currently in operation cannot simply be changed on short notice (say, one week).

3.   Correct answer: c.

Discussion: Diminishing marginal returns is defined as when the change in output begins to decrease. Between the first and second worker, output increases by 15 units. Between the second and third worker, output increases even more by 25 units. So, for this range, the change in output is increasing. However, between the third and fourth worker, the change in output is 10 units. The change in output has decreased from 25 to 10. Between the fourth and fifth worker, the change in output is 8 units and between the fifth and sixth worker, the change in output is 7 units. Thus, after the third worker, the change in output begins to decline. This is one definition of diminishing marginal returns.

4.   Correct answer: d.

Discussion: This table requires that you understand an alternative definition of diminishing marginal returns. Diminishing marginal returns can also be defined as when the addition to an input (labor) must be increased to get the same change in output, in this case one unit. As the table shows, from the first to the second unit of output, three additional workers must be hired. From the second to the third unit of output, two additional workers must be hired, from the third to fourth unit of output, one additional worker must be hired. So, for this range of output, less and less additional labor is needed to get the same increase in output. However, from the fourth to the fifth unit of output, four more workers must be hired to get a one unit increase in output. And, from the fifth to sixth unit of output, six more workers must be hired to produce one more unit of output. In this case, more and more additional labor is needed to get the same increase in output.

5. Correct answer: a.

Discussion: The short-run production function (total product curve) is a graph that shows the relationship between the amount of workers (labor) and the amount of output the workers can produce, assuming a given amount of capital, state of technology, plant size, etc.

6. Correct answer: b.

Discussion: Short run total cost is the sum of variable cost plus fixed cost. That's why it's referred to as "total."

Statement a is not correct because total cost is the sum of, not the difference between, variable cost and fixed cost. Statement c is not correct. It would have been correct if it had read "average total cost = average variable cost + average fixed cost." Statement d is not correct. It would have been correct if it had read "fixed cost = average fixed cost X output." Statement e is not correct. It would have been correct if it had read "average variable cost = variable cost/output." (See PET #2 for review).

7. Correct answer: d.

Discussion: When marginal cost, the addition to total cost, is less than average total cost, it will pull average total cost down. That is, average total cost will decline. See PET #4 for review.

Statement a is not correct because as output increases, a firm's average fixed costs decrease, not increase. Statement b is not correct because a firm's marginal cost curve will be positively, not negatively, sloped when there are diminishing returns. Statement c is not correct because in the long run, the firms average total cost curve is declining and then has a flat portion to it. It is more L-shaped than U-shaped. Statement e is not correct since average total cost is equal to average fixed cost plus average variable cost.

8. Correct answer: a.

Discussion: Diminishing returns means that each additional worker that is hired to produce more output is less productive than the workers hired before him. Thus, it becomes more costly to the firm to get that worker to produce the same level of output as the previous workers. A way to think about it is that that worker would have to work more hours than the other workers (and therefore be paid overtime) in order to produce the same amount of output as the other workers are producing.

Diseconomies of scale is a long run concept. Increasing returns to scale is not a term you have encountered, nor is diseconomies of scope. Diminishing marginal utility is a concept related to consumer "satisfaction" not a firm's cost of production. Thus, statements b, c, d, and e are not correct.

9. Correct answer: e.

Discussion: Statement c is correct because fixed costs do not change with the level of output. Since average fixed cost is calculated as fixed cost/output, as output increases, average fixed cost must decline.

(The number in the denominator gets bigger but the number in the numerator does not change). Statement d is also correct. It is another way of stating that diminishing returns gives rise to increasing average variable cost (as well as increasing marginal cost).

Statement a is not correct because average total cost first decreases and then increases as output increases. Statement b is not correct; a firm's average total cost curve is shaped like a "U." Statements c and d are both correct which is why statement e is the answer.

10. Correct answer: b.

Discussion: Variable cost is computed by multiplying average variable cost by the output level = $6 per unit X 250 units = $1,500. Average fixed cost is computed by dividing fixed cost by the output level = $1,000/250 units = $4/unit.

Statement a is not correct because total cost is $2,500, not $25,000. Total cost can be computed from figuring out variable cost (as above) which is $1,500 and adding to it the fixed cost of $1,000. Statement c is not correct based on the discussion. Statement d is not correct because total cost is not $22. (Total cost is not the sum of marginal cost plus average total cost). Statement e is not correct because total cost is not $1,006 and variable cost is not $18.

11. Correct answer: a.

Discussion: To arrive at the correct answer, you must compute fixed cost using average fixed cost and output. Fixed cost = $3 per unit X 100 units = $300. Then, you can compute variable cost from the difference between total cost and fixed cost = $800 - $300 = $500.

Statements b, c, and d are not correct based on the above discussion. Statement e is not correct because there is enough information (i.e. you don't need to know average variable cost) to compute total variable cost.

12. Correct answer: a.

Discussion: Based on the question, you can calculate the average total cost of production using PET #2. Total cost is equal to $4 X 200,000 units = $800,000. Since you also know that total fixed costs are $100,000, you can compute total variable cost as the difference between total cost and fixed cost. Thus, total variable cost is $800,000 - $100,000 = $700,000.

Statement b is not correct because average fixed costs are $0.50 ($100,000/200,000 units). Statement d is not correct since total costs are $800,000 ($4 X 200,000 units). Statement c cannot be an answer since you do not have enough information to compute marginal cost. You would need to have some information about change in cost and output. Statement e is not correct. You do not know anything about price or even what "very low" would be defined to mean.

13. Correct answer: c.

Discussion: The graph shows the average total cost and average fixed cost associated with different levels of production. Since the average total cost of 10 units of output is $10 per unit and the average fixed cost is $3 per unit, the average variable cost must be $7 per unit. Since the average variable cost is $7 per unit, the variable cost must be $7 per unit X 10 units = $70.

Statement a is not correct because the average variable cost is $7 per unit. Statement b is not correct. It would have been correct if it stated that the average total cost of production was $5. Statement d is not correct because average total cost is increasing beyond 30 units of output. If the average cost is increasing, the marginal cost must be greater than the average cost of $5, not less than $5. Statement e is not correct because statement c is correct.

14. Correct answer: b.

Discussion: Statement b is correct; it indicates a long run concept since the production facility's size can be changed and because an average cost is computed by dividing a total cost by an output level.

Statement a, d, and e are not correct because they imply short run concepts where the firm has some fixed factors of production that cannot be changed. Statement c is not correct because average cost is not computed by multiplying total cost by the output level.

15. Correct answer: a.

Discussion: When workers are able to specialize in the tasks that they do, they become more productive. They know how to do a task well and they don't have to spend time switching from task to task. Statement b is not correct; diminishing returns gives rise to increasing marginal (and variable and total) costs of production. Statement c is not correct; indivisible inputs give rise to economies of scale, not divisible inputs. Statement d is not correct because with economies of scale, marginal costs will be decreasing or not changing. Statement e is not a concept that is applied to economies of scale.

16. Correct answer: e.

Discussion: Indivisible inputs are those inputs that cannot be divided up to accommodate low levels of production. For example, a piece of medical equipment must be purchased by hospital regardless of whether they will use it for one patient, two patients, twenty patients, or one thousand patients. The same is true of an industrial mold, a large cargo ship, and clean rooms used by a computer chip maker. Can you think of other examples?

17. Correct answer: b.

Discussion: Statement b is the only statement that is not true. Indivisible inputs give rise to economies of scale, not diseconomies of scale. All of the other statements are true.

VIII. ANSWER KEY: ESSAY QUESTIONS

1. Specialization is a long run concept. In the long run, a firm is able to alter the amount of equipment each worker has to work with and the amount of space within which each worker works. Thus, in the long run, with more equipment and more space to work, workers can specialize at a task. This means that they can now spend more time on one task (rather than having to move between tasks). This makes workers more productive because time is not lost as workers move between tasks. Thus, each worker is able to produce more output per hour than before. Also, since workers spend more time on the same task, they learn to do the task more efficiently and thus can produce more output per hour than before. Since more output per hour is being produced by the workers and their wages have not changed, the average cost per unit of output will decline in the long run. Economies of scale is defined as a declining average cost as output increases.

2. Diminishing returns is a short run concept and arises because one (or more) of the factors of production with which a firm produces output is fixed, i.e. the amount is not able to be changed in the short run. Typically, plant and equipment are considered the fixed factors of production. Since the amount of plant and equipment is fixed, if a firm wants to produce more output, it must hire more workers but cannot alter the amount of plant and equipment. Consequently, more and more workers are jammed into factory floor space and may have to waste time waiting for a piece of equipment to use to finish their task. What this means is that each additional worker that is hired by the firm will produce less output per hour than the previous worker. This is the definition of diminishing returns.

Diseconomies of scale is a long run concept and arises because of coordination problems and increasing input costs when a firm gets bigger and bigger (produces more and more output). Diseconomies of scale is defined as an increase in long run average cost as output increases. This is the reverse of economies of scale. Coordination problems can contribute to the average cost of production increasing as output increases. Coordination problems may arise because of layers of bureaucracy or management that a business decision must pass through before actually being executed and/or because of personnel problems. Also, as a firm produces more and more output, it increases its demand for inputs which can put upward pressure on the price of inputs. This can thereby contribute to an increase in the average cost of production.

We invite you to visit the book's Companion Website at:
http://www.prenhall.com/osullivan/
for further exercises and practice quizzes.

CHAPTER 12
PERFECT COMPETITION

I. OVERVIEW

In this chapter, you will learn about a perfectly competitive market structure and the characteristics that describe it. You will learn how a firm decides how much output to produce in a perfectly competitive market. You will use the cost concepts and cost curves that you learned about in the previous chapter together with a revenue and marginal revenue curve. You will re-encounter the marginal principle and apply it to determining the level of output that will maximize a firm's profit. You will learn about the factors that influence a firm's decision to either shut down its operation or to continue it even in the face of losses. You will learn what factors might contribute to entry to or exit from a perfectly competitive market. You will see how entry and exit affect the profit levels of the firms that are already operating in the market and how entry, exit, and the ability to alter facility size, in the long run, affect the market supply curve. You will learn about how changes in demand affect the price of a product differently in the short run than in the long run. You will also learn about increasing and constant cost industries which are determined by how productive inputs are as more firms enter (or exit) an industry and how the price of inputs changes as more firms enter (or exit) an industry. You will compare the slope of a short run supply curve to the slope of a long run supply curve.

II. CHECK LIST

By the end of this chapter, you should be able to:

✓ List the characteristics of a perfectly competitive market structure.
✓ Give some real world examples of a perfectly competitive market structure.
✓ Explain the difference between accounting profit and economic profit.
✓ Define total and marginal revenue and represent them with a graph.
✓ Explain why marginal revenue equals price in a perfectly competitive market.
✓ Explain why the rule of picking an output level where price (marginal revenue) equals marginal cost maximizes a firm's profit.
✓ Use a graph to pick the profit-maximizing output level and represent profit on the graph.
✓ Explain when a firm would, in the short run, decide to shut down its operation and when in the long run, it would decide to shut down its operation.
✓ Explain what would happen, in the short run, in a perfectly competitive market to the typical firm earning zero economic profit when there is an increase in market demand (and vice-versa).
✓ Use graphs to show what would happen, in the short run, in a perfectly competitive market to the typical firm earning zero economic profit when there is an increase in market demand (and vice-versa).
✓ Explain the difference between the short and the long run.

✓ Explain what causes firms to enter and exit an industry in a perfectly competitive market structure.

✓ Compare what happens to the quantity supplied by a market as demand (and thus price) of the product increases (or decreases), in the short and the long run, and compare the difference.

✓ Explain what causes a supply curve to be positively sloped and explain what would cause it to be more steeply sloped.

✓ Explain the difference between increasing and constant cost industries and illustrate the difference using a graph of the long run supply curve.

III. KEY TERMS

perfectly competitive market: A market with hundreds of sellers and buyers of a standardized good. Each buyer and seller takes the market price as given. Firms can easily enter or exit the market.

total revenue: The money the firm gets by selling its product; equal to the price times the quantity sold.

economic profit: Total revenue minus total economic cost.

break-even price: The price at which the economic profit is zero; price equals average total cost.

shut-down price: The price at which the firm is indifferent between operating and shutting down; price equals average variable cost.

sunk cost: A cost a firm has already paid or has agreed to pay some time in the future.

short-run supply curve: A curve showing the relationship between the price of a product and the quantity of output supplied by a firm in the short run.

short-run market supply curve: A curve showing the relationship between price and the quantity of output supplied by all firms in the short run.

long-run market supply curve: A curve showing the relationship between the market price and quantity supplied by all firms in the long run.

marginal revenue: The change in total revenue that results from selling one more unit of output.

increasing-cost industry: An industry in which the average cost of production increases as the total output of the industry increases; the long-run supply curve is positively sloped.

constant-cost industry: An industry in which the average cost of production is constant; the long-run supply curve is horizontal.

IV. PERFORMANCE ENHANCING TIPS (PETS)

PET #1

Price and marginal revenue are the same number for a firm in a perfectly competitive market structure.

Let's explore why price and marginal revenue are the same number for a firm in a perfectly competitive market structure. In perfect competition, a firm is a price taker which means that it does not have to lower the price of its product to sell more of it. It can sell all that it wants at the going price. This means that as a firm sells more and more units of its output, it continues to get the same price for its output.

For example, suppose the price of output was $2 per unit. If a firm sells one unit, the total revenue it receives is $2. If a firm sells two units, the total revenue it receives is $4. If a firm sells three units, the total revenue it receives is $6, and so on. Now, what is the marginal revenue (or addition to revenue) from selling one more unit? When the firm sells two units instead of one, it adds $2 to its total revenue ($4 - $2). When the firm sells three units instead of two, it adds $2 to its total revenue ($6 - $4), and so on. Thus, marginal revenue and price are the same for a firm in a perfectly competitive market structure.

PET #2

The rule of picking an output level where price is equal to marginal cost in order to maximize profit can also be expressed as picking an output level where marginal revenue is equal to marginal cost. This happens because in a perfectly competitive market structure, marginal revenue and price are the same number.

In the next few chapters, the rule for maximizing profits you will encounter is to pick an output level where marginal revenue is equal to marginal cost (instead of where price is equal to marginal cost). But, it is really the same rule you have learned in this chapter and the same rationale for why the rule maximizes a firm's profit applies. It may be better to remember the rule as marginal revenue = marginal cost instead of price = marginal cost as long as you understand that price and marginal revenue are the same for a firm operating in a perfectly competitive market.

PET #3

Firms that earn zero economic profit can continue to operate. This is because a firm earning zero economic profit can be earning a positive accounting profit. The positive accounting profit is what a firm may use to fund projects that will allow it to continue to operate in the future. Accounting profit is total revenue minus explicit costs whereas economic profit is total revenue minus explicit and implicit costs.

PET #4

The long run supply curve is flatter than the short run supply curve. This means that quantity supplied is more responsive to a given price change in the long run than is quantity supplied in the short run.

Compare the slope of supply curve (a) to supply curve (b) in the diagram below.

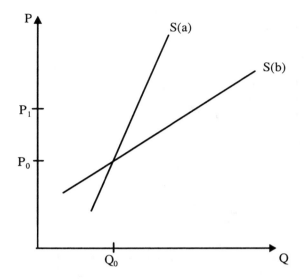

Supply curve (b) is flatter than supply curve (a). What does this mean in practical terms? Let's examine the response of quantity supplied to the same change in price along the two different supply curves. Draw a line from price P_0 across to the supply curves. Where the price line intersects the supply curves, draw a vertical line down to the quantity axis and mark this as the quantity supplied at price P_0 along graph (a) and (b). You will notice that at this price, the quantity supplied in the short and long run is the same amount.

Now, draw a line from price P_1 across to the supply curves. Where the price line intersects the supply curves, draw vertical lines down to the quantity axis and mark these as the quantity supplied at price P_1 along graph (a) and (b). Compare the changes in the quantity supplied along supply curve (a) and (b). You will see that as the price increases, the quantity supplied increases more along supply curve (b) than along supply curve (a). That means that quantity supplied is more responsive to price in the long run than in the short run. Why does this occur? It occurs because in the long run, as the price of a good increases, more firms enter the industry (attracted by profits due to the higher price) and existing firms may have expanded the size of their facility thus enabling them to produce more. Thus, for any given price increase, more is willingly supplied by firms.

PET #5

An increase in demand raises the price of a good by less in the long run than in the short run. A decrease in demand lowers the price of a good by less in the long run than in the short run.

To see this, draw an increase in demand (rightward shift in the demand curve) in the following graph.

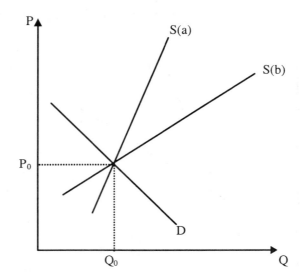

Now, mark the new equilibrium prices along the short run supply curve (a) and along the long run supply curve (b). Compare the change in the price from the initial price of P_0 along the two supply curves. What do you see? You should see that the price has increased by less along supply curve (b) — the flat, long run supply curve — than it has increased along supply curve (a).

Why does this occur? In the long run, remember that in response to a price increase, more firms enter the industry and existing firms will expand the size of their facility; the higher price creates economic profits which motivate entry and expansion in the industry. Thus, in the long run, the industry is better able to satisfy the increased demand for their product. Buyers do not have to bid as fiercely against each other for the ability to purchase the product and thus the price of the product does not rise by as much.

You should work through a decrease in demand on your own.

V. PRACTICE EXAM: MULTIPLE CHOICE QUESTIONS

1. Which one of the following is NOT a characteristic of a perfectly competitive market structure?

a) very large number of firms.
b) standardized (or homogeneous) product.
c) barriers to entry.
d) no control over price.
e) all of the above are characteristics of a perfectly competitive market structure.

2. Which one of the following would be an example of a perfectly competitive industry?

a) restaurants.
b) hog farmers.
c) aircraft industry.
d) auto dealerships.
e) patented sheet-working tools.

3. Use the information below to answer the following question.

quantity sold = 500,000 units
price = $1.00 per unit
explicit costs = $400,000
implicit costs = $150,000

Based on this information, the firm is:

a) earning positive economic profit of $100,000.
b) earning zero economic profit.
c) earning positive accounting profit of $100,000.
d) making an economic loss (negative economic profit) of $50,000.
e) (c) and (d).

4. A firm can maximize its profits by picking an output level where:

a) price > average variable costs.
b) price > average total costs.
c) marginal revenue = marginal cost.
d) price = average variable cost.
e) (b) and (c).

5. Which one of the following statements is always true of a firm in a perfectly competitive market?

a) price = marginal revenue.
b) price = marginal cost.
c) price = total revenue.
d) average total cost = average variable cost.
e) economic profit is positive.

6.   Use the graph below to answer the following question.

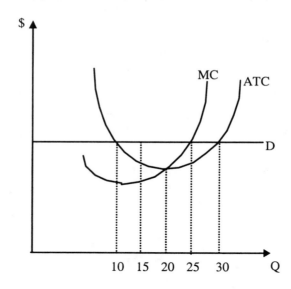

The output level that will maximize the firm's profit is:

a)   10 units.

b)   15 units.

c)   20 units.

d)   25 units.

e)   30 units.

7.   Use the diagram below to compute the profit that the firm is earning.

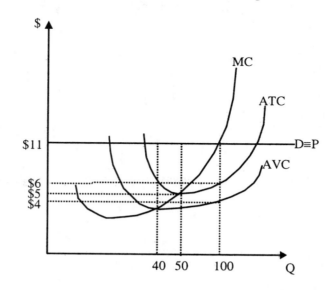

The firm's profit is:

a) $0.
b) $500.
c) $300.
d) $200.
e) $700.

8. Which one of the following statements is correct based on the following information?

price = $5.00 per unit
quantity = 200 units
total variable cost = $400
total fixed cost = $800
marginal cost = $5.00

a) the firm is making a loss but should, in the short run, continue to operate.
b) the firm is making a loss and should shut down its operation.
c) the firm is making a profit of $600.
d) the firm is making zero profit.
e) price is greater than average total cost.

9. Which one of the following statements is correct based on the graph below?

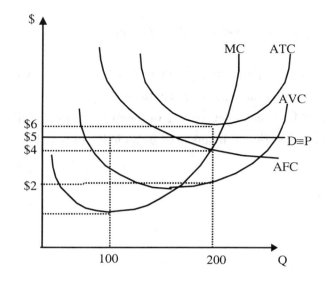

a) the firm is making a loss but should, in the short run, continue to operate.

b) the firm is making a loss and should shut down its operation in the short run.

c) the firm is making a profit of $600.

d) the firm is making zero profit.

e) price is greater than average total cost.

10. Which one of the following statements is true?

a) in the short run, if a firm shuts down it will have zero revenue and zero costs.

b) a firm should shut down if price is greater than average variable cost but less than average total cost.

c) a firm can maximize its profits by producing an output level where price equals marginal revenue.

d) in the short run, if a firm shuts down, it will have a loss equal to the amount of its sunk (or fixed) costs.

e) none of the above.

11. Suppose all firms in a perfectly competitive industry are currently earning zero economic profit. Assume the price of output is $10 per unit. Now, suppose that consumer demand for the industry's product declines. Which one of the following would be least likely to occur?

a) firms may begin to earn a negative economic profit in the short run.

b) price will decline.

c) marginal costs will rise.

d) some firms will exit the industry.

e) producer surplus will decrease in the short run.

12. Which one of the following is the definition of the long run?

a) a period of time over which the demand for a product can increase or decrease.

b) a period of time over which firms can enter and exit an industry.

c) a period of time over which firms can alter the size of their production facility.

d) a period of time over which the price of inputs used by an industry remains constant.

e) (b) and (c).

13. Suppose the average cost of producing a set of golf clubs is $225. Suppose the price at which producers can sell a set of golf clubs is $230. Based on the information you are given, which one of the following best describes the industry response?

a) firms will exit the industry because the economic profit per set of golf clubs is so small.

b) firms will enter the industry because there are positive economic profits to be earned.

c) the quantity of golf clubs supplied by the industry will remain unchanged.

d) demand for golf clubs will increase.

e) the cost of graphite used in making golf clubs will increase.

14. Which one of the following explains why, in the long run, the average cost of production may increase as an industry expands (produces more output)?

a) rising input prices.

b) rising productivity of inputs.

c) falling input prices.

d) increasing fixed costs.

e) (a) and (b).

15. Suppose that a typical farmer sells 10,000 bushels of peaches each season and that the total revenue he earns is $100,000. Further, suppose that the average cost of producing 10,000 bushels is $12 per bushel. Based on this information, which one of the following statements is correct?

a) there are positive economic profits and farmers will enter the industry.

b) there are negative economic profits and some farmers will leave the industry.

c) the average cost of production is rising.

d) the elasticity of supply is 1.2.

e) cannot be answered without information on price per bushel.

16. Which one of the following statements is NOT true?

a) an increasing cost industry has a positively sloped long run supply curve.

b) the long run average cost of production depends, in part, on how productive inputs are.

c) a constant cost industry has a horizontal long run supply curve.

d) diminishing returns explains why the average cost of production decreases in the long run.

e) all of the above statements are true.

17. Consider the taxi industry, which is assumed to be a constant cost industry. If the demand for taxi services decreases, in the short run, the price for taxi services will _____ and in the long run, the price for taxi services will _____.

a) increase; decrease.

b) decrease; decrease.

c) decrease; remain unchanged.

d) remain unchanged; decrease.

e) none of the above.

18. The graph below depicts the situation for a typical firm in a perfectly competitive market structure. Based on the graph, which would be the most likely industry response? Assume the industry is an increasing cost industry.

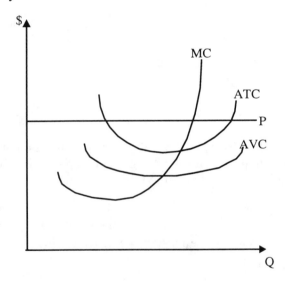

a) there will be entry into the industry.

b) existing firms will expand their production facilities.

c) the prices of inputs will rise.

d) the skill level of the workforce will decline.

e) all of the above.

VI. PRACTICE EXAM: ESSAY QUESTIONS

1. Briefly explain why it is profit-maximizing for a firm to produce output up until the point at which marginal revenue equals marginal cost.

2. Suppose, after graduation, you take a job in a factory in Chile that produces faux leather shoes. One day, your boss comes in and says, "this factory isn't operating at a profit and so we can minimize our

losses by closing up shop." Yikes! You didn't think you'd lose your job that quickly. Your boss continues talking and states that the company is having to pay 300,000 pesos a month for rent, interest on debt, and other non-avoidable costs. He also says that it costs 150,000 pesos a month just to pay you and all the other workers, including paying for the raw materials, to produce the shoes. He states that at current production of 5000 boxes of shoes a month, the company can only expect to get 40 pesos per box of shoes. Do you agree with your boss that the company should close up shop? Why or why not?

3. Explain why the long run supply curve is flatter than the short run supply curve.

4. Consider the market for beef. Suppose that the demand for beef declines because of health concerns. Explain what will happen to the price and quantity of beef supplied in the short and long run assuming the industry is an increasing cost industry.

VII. ANSWER KEY: MULTIPLE CHOICE

1. Correct answer: c.

Discussion: Barriers to entry characterize an oligopolistic and monopolist market structure which you will learn about in later chapters.

A perfectly competitive market structure is one in which there are a very large number of firms each producing a very small portion of overall industry output. The product produced is said to be "standardized" or "homogeneous" which means that consumers don't perceive very much of a difference in buying from one producer than any other. Since there are so many firms providing such a small portion of industry output, the firms have no control over price; it is dictated by the market forces of supply and demand. Firms are said to be "price takers."

2. Correct answer: b.

Discussion: Hog farmers are many and produce a fairly standardized product, the hog.

Pizzerias are an example of a monopolistically competitive market structure since they produce a slightly differentiated product. The same may be true of auto dealerships (although auto manufacturers are considered to be an oligopoly). The aircraft industry is an example of an oligopolistic market structure since there are few firms in the industry that typically operate with economies of scale. A firm that has a patent typically has a monopoly. Thus, patented sheet-working tools are an example of a monopoly.

3. Correct answer: e.

Discussion: The total revenue that the firm is earning is $500,000 ($5 X 100,000 units). The economic cost is $550,000 (= $400,000 + $150,000). Thus, economic profit is -$50,000. That is, the firm is earning a loss.

The accounting profit that the firm is earning is equal to $100,000 ($500,000 - $400,000).   Thus statements c and d are both correct. Statement a and b are not correct because the firm is making negative economic profit.

4.   Correct answer: c.

Discussion: The rule for maximizing profits is to pick an output level where marginal revenue equals marginal cost. There is only one output level where this is true. When a firm follows this principle, it may make positive profit, zero profit, or even a negative profit (in which case we'd say that the firm would be minimizing its losses) but this is the best the firm can do. To assure yourself that this condition will maximize a firm's profit, consider the two other possibilities: (1) marginal revenue > marginal cost and (2) marginal revenue < marginal cost. If condition (1) is true, then a firm could add more to its revenue than to its costs by producing one more unit of output. This means that the firm's profits would increase if it produced more output. Thus, the firm could not be maximizing profits yet. If condition (2) is true, then a firm is adding more to its costs than to its revenue by producing the additional output. By producing this output level, the firm would be cutting into its profits and would be better off reducing production.

Statement a is not correct because there are a number of output levels where this would be true and thus the rule would offer no guidance about which output level to pick. The same is true of statement b. Statement d is not correct but it is the condition that would say that a firm is indifferent between shutting down and remaining open in the short run. Statement e is not correct because statement b is not correct.

5.   Correct answer: a.

Discussion: For a perfectly competitive firm which is a price taker, the firm's revenue from selling each additional unit of output, its marginal revenue, will always equal price.

Statement b is not correct since firms can, in the short run, earn positive or negative economic profit. Statement c is not correct; total revenue is equal to price X quantity. Statement d is not correct since a firm also has fixed costs. Statement e is not correct because a firm does not always earn positive economic profit.

6.   Correct answer: d.

Discussion: The output level that a profit maximizing firm will choose is the output level where marginal revenue (price) equals marginal cost. This occurs at an output level of 25 units (where the price and marginal cost curves intersect).

Statements a, b, c, and e are all incorrect based on the above method for finding a firm's profit maximizing level of output.

7. Correct answer: b.

Discussion: The profit is determined by first selecting the output level that a profit maximizing firm will choose. The profit-maximizing output level is where marginal revenue (price) equals marginal cost. This occurs at an output level of 100 units. Given that output level, the average total cost of 100 units of output is \$6 and the price is \$11. Thus, profit is equal to (\$11 X 100) - (\$6 X 100) = \$500.

Statements a, c, d, and e are all incorrect based on the above method for finding and calculating a firm's profit.

8. Correct answer: a.

The firm's total revenue from operating would be \$1,000 (\$5 X 200 units). The firm's total cost would be \$400 + \$800 = \$1,200. If the firm operates, it will make a loss of \$200. This is less than the firm would lose if it shut down its operation.

If the firm shut down its operation it would not earn any revenue but would still have to pay for its fixed costs. Thus, the firm would lose \$800. Thus, statement b is not correct. Statement c and d are not correct because the firm is not earning a profit. Statement e is not correct because average total cost is \$1,200/200 units = \$6. Thus, price is less than average total cost which is why the firm is making a loss. Notice that since price is equal to marginal cost, the firm is doing the best it can, i.e. minimizing its losses.

9. Correct answer: a.

Discussion: This question is a graphical representation of question (8). To answer this question, you must first establish what the profit-maximizing output level of the firm is. It is found where price and marginal cost are equal (intersect) which is at an output level of 200 units. The average total cost of producing 200 units is \$6. The average variable cost of producing 200 units is \$2. The average fixed cost is \$4. Since price exceeds average variable cost, the firm should continue to operate even though it will earn a loss of \$200.

In order to answer the question, you could also calculate the total cost of producing 200 units of output as \$1,200 and the revenue as \$1,000. Thus, the firm will lose \$200. Then, you could calculate how much the firm will lose if it shuts down. If it shuts down, it will have to pay its fixed costs which can be read off the graph by taking the average fixed cost of \$4 and multiplying it by the output level of 200 units. Thus, the firm's loss would be \$800.

Statements b, c, d, and e are all incorrect for the same reasons mentioned in the answer to question (8).

10. Correct answer: d.

Discussion: If a firm shuts down in the short run, it will have no revenue to offset the sunk or fixed costs that it must continue to pay. Thus, the firm will lose an amount equal to its sunk or fixed costs.

Statement a is not correct because if a firm shuts down in the short run, it will still have some costs to pay. Statement b is not correct. It would have been correct if it had said that a firm should remain open if price is greater than average variable cost but less than average total cost. Statement c is not correct because a perfectly competitive firm maximizes its profits by producing an output level where price (or marginal revenue) equals marginal cost. Statement e is not correct because statement d is correct.

11. Correct answer: c.

Discussion: If demand declines, you learned in Chapter 4 that this would cause price to decline. Thus, statement b is likely to occur. As the price of the product declines, firms that were initially earning zero economic profit will see price drop below their average total cost. This will cause them to make a loss (negative economic profit) in the short run. Thus, statement a is likely to occur. As firms earn negative economic profit, there will be exit from the industry. Thus statement d is likely to occur. As price declines, the profit-maximizing output level for firms will change -- it will decrease. That is, firms will produce less output. Since both price and output have declined, producer surplus must necessarily decline. (The effect on consumer surplus would be ambiguous since the price decline would raise consumer surplus but the quantity decline would reduce it). Thus, statement e is likely to occur. Statement c is least likely to occur because as a firm produces less output, its marginal cost of production will decline.

12. Correct answer: e.

Discussion: The long run is a period of time over which new firms can enter the industry (to capture positive economic profits) or exit the industry (to cut their losses). Over a longer period of time, firms already in the industry can also alter the size of their production facilities; they may wish to expand their operation if economic profits increase or they may wish to shut down some of their operation if they begin to incur losses.

Statements a and d are not correct because the long run is not defined with respect to changes in demand or changes in input prices. Statements b and c are both correct which is why statement e is the correct answer. Thus, statements b and c are both correct

13. Correct answer: b.

Discussion: Since the price that producers can get for a set of golf clubs exceeds the average cost of production by $5, firms will earn $5 of economic profit per set of golf clubs. That is, they will be earning positive economic profit. The positive economic profit will attract other firms into the industry. Entry will stop when economic profit is driven to zero.

Statement a is not correct; any positive economic profit is considered to motivate entry into an industry. Statement c is not correct because the positive economic profit will prompt entry into the industry and thus lead to an increase in the quantity supplied. Statement d is not correct because there is nothing in the information given that gives a reason for why the demand for golf clubs will increase. Statement e is not necessarily correct; it depends on whether the golf club industry is an increasing, decreasing or constant cost industry. If the industry is an increasing cost industry, then the price of graphite will likely increase. However, if the industry is a decreasing or constant cost industry, the price of graphite may actually decrease or not change at all as more golf club producers demand more graphite.

14. Correct answer: a.

Discussion: As an industry expands (produces more output), the demand for inputs increases. This increase in demand for inputs can put upward pressure on the price of inputs and thereby lead to a rise in the cost of the price of inputs. This, in turn, would raise a firm's average cost of production. Thus, statement a is correct.

Statement b is not correct. Rising productivity would actually decrease the average cost of production, not increase it. Statement c is not correct since falling input prices would actually decrease the average cost of production. Statement d is not correct because in the long run, there are no costs that are considered as fixed costs. Statement e is not correct because statement b is not correct.

15. Correct answer: b.

Discussion: In this question, you must determine whether the typical farmer is making a positive, zero, or negative economic profit. You can determine the profit situation of the farmer by either calculating the price per bushel that the typical farmer receives for his peaches or the total cost of producing 10,000 bushels. Once you have made either one of these calculations, you can determine whether there is entry or exit into the industry. The price per bushel can be calculated by dividing total revenue by the number of bushels sold. Since the total revenue is $100,000 and the number of bushels sold is 10,000, the price per bushel is $10. With the average cost of production being $12, the typical farmer will lose $2 on every bushel sold. Alternatively, you could have calculated the total cost of producing 10,000 bushels as $120,000 ($12 X 10,000). In this case, the farmer will lose $20,000 for the lot of 10,000 bushels sold (i.e. $2 for every bushel sold). With either calculation, you should see that the farmer will not be making a positive economic profit. The long run industry response to negative economic profits is for firms (farmers, in this case) to leave the industry.

Statement a is not correct based on the reasoning above. Statement c is not necessarily correct; it depends on whether the industry is an increasing, decreasing or constant cost industry. If the industry is an increasing cost industry, as firms exit, there will be less demand for inputs and the price of inputs would drop. This would mean that the average cost of production would decrease. If the industry is a constant cost industry, the exit of firms will have no effect on the input prices and the average cost of production would remain constant. If the industry is a decreasing cost industry, as firms exit, the cost of inputs will rise which will raise the average cost of production. Statement d is not correct because you are not given enough information to calculate an elasticity of supply. In order to calculate an elasticity, you would need changes in prices and quantity supplied from which you could compute percentage changes. Statement e is not correct because you are given enough information to answer the question.

16. Correct answer: d.

Discussion: Statement d is correct because it is the only statement that is NOT true. Remember that diminishing returns is a short run phenomenon. It arises because a firm, in the short run, cannot alter the size of the capital stock (plant and equipment) that it uses to produce output. On the other hand, average costs of production that decrease in the long run is a long run phenomenon and is a result of entry/exit and alteration of plant size.

Statement a, b, and c are all true. Since statement d is not true, statement e cannot be the correct answer.

17. Correct answer: c.

Discussion: The key to answering this question correctly is to know what the shape of the long run supply curve is when the industry is a constant cost industry. A constant cost industry has a horizontal supply curve. Thus, when demand decreases (shifts left) and moves along a horizontal supply curve, the price of the good will not change from its initial price. However, in the short run, the supply curve is positively sloped. Thus, a decrease in demand will lead to a lower price for the good in the short run.

Statement a and d should be ruled out. From chapter 4 and 5, you should know that a decrease in demand will lower the price of a good, not increase it or leave it unchanged. Statement b is not correct because in the long run, the price of the good will remain unchanged, not decrease. Statement e is not correct because statement c is correct.

18. Correct answer: e.

Discussion: The graph for this question shows that the typical firm is earning positive economic profit. In order to determine this, you must first choose the profit-maximizing output level of the firm. Remember that the profit maximizing rule is to produce at an output level where marginal revenue equals marginal cost. For a perfectly competitive firm, price and marginal revenue are identical numerically. Thus, the profit-maximizing output level is found where the price (marginal revenue) and marginal cost curves intersect. Find this point on the graph and then draw a vertical line down to the quantity axis. This quantity is the profit-maximizing output level. You may wish to label it q*.

Now, you must determine whether the firm is earning a positive, zero, or negative economic profit. To do this, find the average cost of production for producing q* and compare it to the price. The average cost of production is found by drawing a vertical line up from q* to the average cost curve and then over to the $ axis. As you can see, the average cost is less than the price, which means the typical firm is making positive economic profit.

Now that you have determined that the typical firm is making a positive economic profit, you should know that this will attract entry into the industry, lead to expansion of existing firms, put upward pressure on the price of inputs as more are demanded as the industry grows (in an increasing cost industry) and also lead to a decline in the skill level of workers. As the industry grows and produces more output, it will have to hire more workers. However, the firms will not be able to hire the cream of the crop as these workers are already employed in the industry. Thus, firms will end up hiring less skilled (and therefore less productive) workers.

Since statements a - d are all true of an increasing cost industry earning positive economic profit, statement e is the correct answer.

VIII. ANSWER KEY: ESSAY QUESTIONS

1. Note: P = price, MR = marginal revenue, MC = marginal cost.

    When a firm produces output up to that level at which MR = MC, it is always adding more to revenue than it is to costs, and thus adding something (however small) to its profits. If a firm produced at an output level at which MR < MC, the firm is actually taking away from its profits because some of the output costs more to produce than it can be sold for. If a firm produces output where MR > MC, it could continue to expand production and though adding more to cost, could add even more to revenue, thereby adding to its profits. Thus, a firm maximizes profits where MR = MC.

2. Based on short run analysis, you should disagree with your boss:

    The costs of closing up shop in the short run are 300,000 pesos (due to fixed costs). That is, 300,000 pesos must be paid regardless of whether the factory produces no shoes or some shoes. This is the loss the firm would sustain in the short run if it were to close up shop. If the factory were to continue current operation, it could produce 5,000 boxes of shoes and earn revenue of 200,000 pesos which could offset some of the fixed costs. However, by producing, the company would incur another cost - - variable costs in the amount of 150,000 pesos. On net, there is a positive difference of 50,000 pesos between revenue and variable costs. This positive difference can help pay for fixed costs so that if the firm continues to operate, its losses will be 250,000 pesos (Revenue - Fixed Costs - Variable Costs) instead of 300,000 (fixed costs).

    You might also point out that if the company is planning on closing the factory temporarily, it might make customers mad which can have deleterious effects on future sales. Moreover, if the company temporarily lays off workers, they may go find work elsewhere, and thus the company might face some retraining and re-hiring (or search) costs when they re-open the factory.

    On the other hand, if the company is planning on closing the factory permanently, i.e. in the long run, perhaps because of a perceived permanent downturn in demand for faux leather shoes, then your advice may be different. You may advise the company to close the factory and sell its assets (to cover some of its fixed costs, like interest on debt). Also, by closing the factory, the company may be able to avoid fixed costs like rent, as well.

3. The long run supply curve and the short run supply curve both show the relationship between the price of a good and the quantity supplied. However, the time period considered for the relationship is different. In the short run, the number of firms producing for the industry is fixed as is the current size of each firm's facility. In the long run, the number of firms producing for the industry can change as firms enter or exit the industry and the size of the facilities of existing firms can be altered. This means that in the long run, the total industry output can be much more responsive to a price change than in the short run. For example, when the price of a good increases (because of an increase in demand), the short run output response of the industry is constrained by how many firms are already producing for the industry and the current size of their operation. A given amount of firms with a given plant size can only produce so much more in response to a higher price for the output they produce. However, in the long run, a higher price may lure more firms into the industry as well as motivate some firms to alter the size of their operation. Thus, a higher price may elicit a bigger increase in output in the long run than in the short run. Graphically, this would be represented by a

supply curve that is flatter for the long run (and thus steeper for the short run). You may want to take a look at PET #4 of this chapter to inspect the difference between the long and short run supply curves.

4. An increasing cost industry has a long run supply curve that is positively sloped. Of course, the short run supply curve is also positively sloped. However, the long run supply curve is flatter (more elastic) than the short run supply curve as the graph below illustrates. A decline in the demand for beef would be represented by a leftward shift in the supply curve. The reduced demand for beef will in the short and long run lead to a lower price of beef as the graph shows. However, in the short run, the price drop will be bigger than in the long run. The graph also shows that the equilibrium quantity of beef will decline. It will decline by more in the long run than in the short run.

The drop in demand for beef will in the short run cause some firms to shut down their operation altogether. Other firms will continue to operate but they cannot change the size of the capital stock (and thus their fixed costs) that they operate with. In the long run, some firms will make a decision to exit the industry as they sustain losses whereas other firms that remain will likely reduce the size of their operation (lay off workers, shut down some factories, etc). In the long run, the number of firms in the industry will decline and the size of their facility will likely decrease.

We invite you to visit the book's Companion Website at:
http://www.prenhall.com/osullivan/
for further exercises and practice quizzes.

CHAPTER 13
MONOPOLY AND PRICE DISCRIMINATION

I. OVERVIEW

In this chapter, you will learn about the market structure of monopoly in which there is a single supplier of output to a market. You will learn about barriers to market entry that might give rise to a monopoly. You will learn how a monopolist chooses the profit-maximizing level of output and determines the price at which it will sell the output. You will learn that in contrast to a perfectly competitive market structure, price and marginal revenue are different for a monopolist and that a monopolist typically earns positive economic profit. You will learn about the costs and benefits to society of a monopoly. You will also learn about the practice of price discrimination that firms with monopoly power. You will learn that price discrimination is the practice of charging different prices to different groups of customers for the same product and that the elasticity of demand can be used to decide which group of customers should be charged a higher price. You will learn that price discrimination is a way for a firm to increase its profit above that of a single-price policy.

II. CHECKLIST

By the end of this chapter, you should be able to:

✓ Describe the characteristics of a monopoly.
✓ List factors that would give rise to a monopoly.
✓ List some real world examples of a monopoly.
✓ Explain why marginal revenue is less than price for a monopolist but equal to price for a perfectly competitive firm.
✓ Use a graph to depict the profit-maximizing output level a monopolist would produce, the price that would be charged for the product, and the profit the monopolist would earn.
✓ Discuss and compare the relationship of price, marginal revenue, marginal cost, and average cost for a profit-maximizing monopolist.
✓ Compare the price and output decisions of a monopolist to a perfectly competitive firm.
✓ Explain rent seeking.
✓ Discuss the tradeoffs that occur when a patent is granted to a firm which gives the firm monopoly power.
✓ Describe the conditions that make it possible for firms to price discriminate.
✓ Describe how a price discrimination scheme works and which group of customers would be charged a higher price.
✓ Give some real world examples of price discrimination schemes.
✓ Explain how the elasticity of demand is used by a price discriminating firm in setting price.

III. KEY TERMS

deadweight loss from monopoly: A measure of the inefficiency from monopoly; equal to the difference between the consumer-surplus loss from monopoly pricing and the monopoly's profit.

rent seeking: The process under which a firm spends money to persuade the government to erect barriers to entry and pick the firm as the monopolist.

monopoly: A market in which a single firm serves the entire market.

patent: The exclusive right to sell a particular good for some period of time.

price discrimination: The process under which a firm divides consumers into two or more groups and picks a different price for each group

IV. PERFORMANCE ENHANCING TIPS (PETS)

PET #1

The profit-maximizing rule for a monopolist (as for any firm) is to produce an output level where marginal revenue equals marginal cost.

Remember that marginal revenue is the addition to revenue from selling one more unit of output and marginal cost is the addition to cost from producing one more unit of output. As long as the addition to revenue (marginal revenue) exceeds the addition to cost (marginal cost), the monopolist will add to its profits. Thus, the monopolist will maximize its profits by continuing to produce and sell output until marginal revenue is just equal to marginal cost. Beyond that output level, profits will actually be smaller (not maximized).

PET #2

For a profit-maximizing monopolist, the price of its output will be greater than the marginal cost.

This performance enhancing tip is based on two principles: (1) the addition to revenue (marginal revenue) that a monopolist earns from selling one more unit of output is less than the price it receives for selling that one more unit of output, (see your textbook for a good explanation); and (2) a profit-maximizing firm produces an output level where marginal revenue equals marginal cost. Statement (1) says that price > marginal revenue. Statement (2) says that marginal revenue equals marginal cost. Thus, it must be the case that for a monopolist, price > marginal cost.

PET #3

A monopolist produces an output level that is less than a perfectly competitive industry would produce and charges a price that is higher than would prevail under perfect competition.

Under perfect competition, a profit-maximizing firm produces an output level where marginal revenue equals marginal cost, just as does a monopolist. However, for a perfectly competitive firm, marginal revenue and price are identical. This means that a profit-maximizing firm in a perfectly competitive market also ends up producing an output level where price is equal to marginal cost. This is not true of a monopolist as PET #2 discusses. This is the reason that a monopolist will produce a lower output level and charge a higher price for its output than it would if it were a perfectly competitive firm.

To see this, look at the graph below

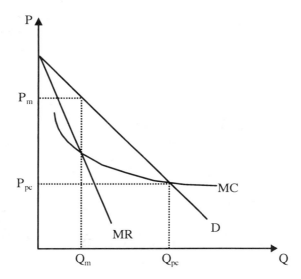

The monopolist will produce output level Q_m which is where marginal revenue and marginal cost are equal. The monopolist will decide on a price for output level Q_m by using the demand curve. At output level Q_m, the demand curve dictates that the price be P_m. Now, suppose the monopolist were to behave as a perfectly competitive firm. It would produce an output level where price equals marginal cost and charge a price dictated by the demand curve for that output level. Price equals marginal cost where the demand and marginal cost curves intersect. The output level in this case would be Q_{pc}. The price charged would be read off the demand curve corresponding to output level Q_{pc} which is P_{pc}. As the graph shows, the monopolist's price exceeds what would be charged by a perfectly competitive firm and produces an output level that is less than would be produced under perfect competition.

PET #4

To increase revenue, a price discriminating firm should increase price to the group of customers with the inelastic demand and reduce price to the group of customers with the elastic demand.

PET #5

A unitary price elasticity of demand (Ed = 1) will occur when the percentage change in quantity demanded is equal to the percentage change in price. An "elastic" demand (Ed > 1) will occur when the percentage change in quantity demanded is greater than the percentage change in price. An "inelastic" demand (Ed < 1) will occur when the percentage change in quantity demanded is less than the percentage change in price.

This is a repeat of PET #4 from Chapter 5 but it is worth reviewing again. You can best understand this PET by an example. Suppose the percentage change in quantity demanded = 4% and the percentage change in price = 4%. Obviously, the elasticity of demand would be 4%/4% = 1. Thus, you can infer that for a unitary elasticity, the percentage change in quantity demanded and price will be equal.

Now, suppose the percentage change in quantity demanded is 4% and the percentage change in price is 2%. Here, the elasticity of demand would be 2 (= 4%/2%) which is characterized as "elastic" since it is a number greater than 1. Notice that in this case, the percentage change in quantity demanded exceeds the percentage change in price. Thus, based on that information alone, without calculating a number for the elasticity, you could infer that the elasticity of demand would be greater than 1 and thus "elastic."

Now, suppose the percentage change in quantity demanded is 4% and the percentage change in price is 8%. Here, the elasticity of demand would be 0.5 (= 4%/8%) which is characterized as "inelastic" since it is a number less than 1. Notice that in this case, the percentage change in quantity demanded is less than the percentage change in price. Thus, based on that information alone, without calculating a number for the elasticity, you could infer that the elasticity of demand would be less than 1 and thus "inelastic."

V. PRACTICE EXAM: MULTIPLE CHOICE QUESTIONS

1. Which one of the following characteristics is true of a monopoly?

a) a large number of firms in the industry.
b) barriers to entry into the industry.
c) firm acts as a price taker.
d) price equals marginal revenue.
e) all of the above.

2. Which one of the following would NOT be an example of a monopoly?

a) a patent granted to a computer company.
b) a franchise awarded to a food service on campus.
c) American Medical Association.
d) Major League Baseball.
e) All of the above are monopolies.

3. A monopolist maximizes profit by picking the output level where:

a) marginal revenue = marginal cost.
b) price = marginal revenue.
c) price = marginal cost.
d) price > average cost.
e) price = average cost.

4. Which one of the following is true for a monopolist?

a) freedom of entry.
b) price > marginal revenue.
c) produces a socially efficient output level.
d) is unable to price discriminate.
e) earns zero economic profit in the long run.

5. Use the diagram below to select the profit-maximizing output level that a monopolist would choose.

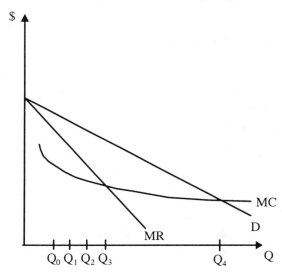

a) Q_0
b) Q_1
c) Q_2
d) Q_3
e) Q_4

6. If the average cost curve is horizontal, say at $2 per unit of output, then at that level of output where the curve is horizontal:

a) marginal cost = $2.

b) marginal cost = $0.

c) marginal cost > $2.

d) marginal cost = $1.

e) cannot be determined with information given.

7. Suppose the price at which a monopolist is selling its output is $12 and the marginal revenue associated with selling the last unit of output is $9. Further, suppose the marginal cost of the last unit of output sold is $10. Which one of the following best describes what the monopolist should do?

a) increase output and raise price.

b) increase output and lower price.

c) decrease output and lower price.

d) decrease output and raise price.

e) shut down.

8. Which one of the following is a cost of a monopoly?

a) price consumers pay is higher than they would under perfect competition.

b) output is less than under perfect competition.

c) rent seeking leads to loss in output in other industries.

d) consumer surplus is less than under perfect competition.

e) all of the above.

9. Which one of the following is a benefit to consumers of a patent-generated monopoly?

a) rent seeking.

b) innovation.

c) deadweight loss.

d) monopoly profits.

e) price discrimination.

10. Which one of the following would NOT be a good example of price discrimination?

a) rebates on washer/dryer combos.

b) no-fee checking to bank customers that keep $500 or more in their checking accounts.

c) restaurant discounts to early bird (before 5:00pm) diners.

d) coupons for dry-cleaning.

e) senior citizen discount for popcorn at the movies.

11. The practice of price discrimination:

a) occurs when a firm sells a product below the marginal cost of production.

b) increases a firm's revenue.

c) will always increase a firm's profit.

d) does not require that a firm have control over the price at which it sells its output.

e) is to charge a higher price to the high elasticity demand group of customers and a lower price to the low elasticity demand group of customers.

12. Which one of the following statements is NOT true of price discrimination?

a) it requires a firm to have some control over its price.

b) firms must have two or more consumer groups who differ in their willingness to pay for the firm's product.

c) resale must not be possible.

d) any type of price discrimination is illegal.

e) all of the above are true of price discrimination.

13. Use the diagrams below to calculate the profit the price discriminating firm will earn from each consumer group when it charges a price of $5 to consumer group I and $10 to consumer group II.

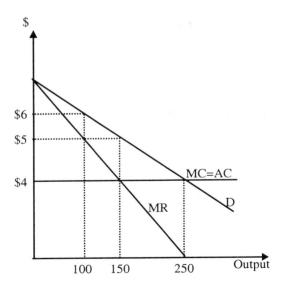
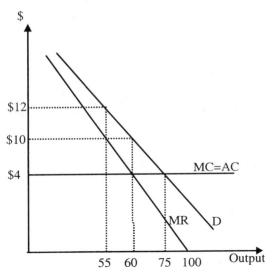

a) $150; $360.

b) $750; $600.

c) $1,000; $300.

d) $100; $110.

e) $600; $240.

14. For which elasticity of demand will an increase from the single price of $200 to $220 lead to biggest increase in revenue?

a) 1.0.

b) 1.25.

c) 0.75.

d) 0.90.

e) 0.50.

15. Which of the following is NOT a characteristic of rent seeking?

a) Hiring lobbyists to persuade legislators to grant monopoly power

b) A firm gets the local government to grant it a sole franchise for its business.

c) The federal government grants a drug company a patent on an antidepressant.

d) Rent seeking creates inefficiencies as firms spend resources to acquire monopoly power..

e) All of the above are characteristics of rent seeking.

VI. PRACTICE EXAM: ESSAY QUESTIONS

1. Discuss the cost and benefits to society of a monopoly that is created because a patent is granted for the product the firm produces.

2. Explain whether a monopoly could increase its revenue and its profits by charging different prices to different groups of customers. You may wish to give a numerical example to illustrate your point.

VII. ANSWER KEY: MULTIPLE CHOICE QUESTIONS

1. Correct answer: b.

Discussion: A monopolistic market structure is characterized by barriers to entry — some barriers are artificial (or government created) and others arise naturally.

Statements a, c, and d are all characteristics of a perfectly competitive market structure.

2.   Correct answer: e.

Discussion: Monopolies can be created by patents (which in the U.S. are awarded for 20 years without an annual renewal fee), franchise and licensing schemes, industrial, sports, and other associations that restrict the number of firms in the market.

3.   Correct answer: a.

Discussion: A monopolist (or any type of firm) will maximize profits by producing an output level where marginal revenue = marginal cost (see PET #1 of this chapter for review).

Statement b describes the relationship between price and marginal revenue for a perfectly competitive firm. Statement c is another version of the profit-maximizing condition for a perfectly competitive firm. Statement d would ensure profit greater than zero but not necessarily the biggest (maximized) profit. Statement e would ensure zero economic profit.

4.   Correct answer: b.

Discussion: A monopolist (unlike for a perfectly competitive firm), must lower the price of its output to all of its customers in order to sell more to a few more customers. This means that the price the monopolist receives from selling the last unit of output is not the addition to revenue (marginal revenue) from selling the last unit of output. The marginal revenue from selling the last unit will be less than the price the firm receives on that last unit because while the firm gets paid $X for the last unit of output, it loses revenue from lowering the price to the previous customers who were paying the higher price. The sum of these two effects makes the marginal revenue earned on the last unit of output sold less than the price received on the last unit of output sold.

Statement a is not correct because a monopolist does not face freedom of entry but rather barriers to entry. Statement c is not correct because a monopolist produces a socially inefficient output level (it produces too little output). Statement d is not correct because a monopolist may be able to price discriminate. Statement e is not correct because a monopolist earns positive economic profit in the long run.

5.   Correct answer: d.

Discussion: A profit-maximizing monopolist picks an output level where marginal revenue equals marginal cost (which occurs where these two curves intersect). The output level at the intersection of these two curves is Q_3. Thus, statement d is correct.

Statements a, b, c, and e are all output levels corresponding to other intersection points. The output level where the demand and marginal cost curves intersect, Q_4, is the output level that would be set if price = marginal cost was the rule the monopolist followed. This would be a socially efficient output level.

6. Correct answer: a.

Discussion: When the average cost curve is horizontal, it means that the average cost per unit of output is not changing as more and more output is produced. If the average cost is not changing. it must be the case that the marginal cost is equal to the average cost. (Your book gives an example using your GPA which is an average of the grades you made in the courses you've already taken. If your GPA is 3.0 and you get a B (= 3.0) on a course you take in the summer (the marginal course), your GPA (average) will remain at 3.0).

Statements b and d are for a marginal cost that is less than the average cost. If this were the case, then the average cost would be "pulled down" or decline and thus not remain constant. Statement c is for a marginal cost that exceeds the average cost; in this case, the average cost would be "pulled up" or increase and thus not remain constant. Statement e is not correct because you are given enough information to get an answer.

7. Correct answer: d.

Discussion: Since marginal cost > marginal revenue, the monopolist is not maximizing its profits and in fact, is producing too much output. If the monopolist is producing too much output, then based on the demand curve, he is charging a price below the profit-maximizing price. Thus, the monopolist should reduce his output level until marginal revenue = marginal cost. By reducing the output level, the monopolist moves back along the demand curve to a higher price for his output.

Statements a and b are not correct because if the monopolist increased his output level, he would continue adding more to his costs than to his revenue and thus profits would decline. Statement c is not correct because the monopolist should not lower price but raise it instead. Statement e is not correct because there is no information that tells you whether the monopolist should shut down.

8. Correct answer: e.

Discussion: A monopolist charges a higher price and produces less output than would arise under perfect competition. This is costly to consumers (see your textbook, PET #3, and essay #1 for further discussion). This also means that consumer surplus (a measure of the benefits to consumers from their purchases) is smaller under a monopolistic market structure than a perfectly competitive one. Monopolies, which often arise as a result of rent seeking undertaken by lobbyists, also entails an opportunity cost to society in that the lobbyists could be employed elsewhere thereby adding to output in other industries which consumers could in turn purchase.

9. Correct answer: b.

Discussion: The awarding of a patent to a firm grants the firm monopoly status (at least for 20 years). The monopoly status means the firm is assured of making positive economic profit. The profit incentive then motivates the firm to actually produce and market the product thereby making it available to consumers. Without the assurance of profit, the firm may not undertake production of the product and thus consumers would lose out on innovative new products.

Statements a and c are costs of a monopoly. Statement d is a benefit to the monopolist but not to consumers. Statement e is not necessarily a benefit to consumers; price discrimination by a monopolist might lead the monopolist to charge some groups of customers a higher price than other groups.

10. Correct answer: e.

Discussion: One of the conditions necessary for price discrimination to work is that it not be possible for customers to resell (or buy for others) the product that is being discounted. In the case of senior citizen discounts for popcorn at movie theaters, the senior citizen can easily purchase the popcorn and then, once inside the movie theater, share it or give it to his or her companion(s) who may not be senior citizens.

Statements a - d are all examples of price discrimination that are practiced. The text also lists similar examples.

11. Correct answer: b.

Discussion: Price discrimination is the practice of charging different groups of customers different prices for the same product with the intent of increasing a firm's revenue.

Statement a is not correct because it is not the definition of price discrimination. Statement c is not correct because a monopolist's profits will not necessarily increase with price discrimination if the cost of serving two or more different customer groups increases. Thus, while price discrimination would raise revenue, it may also raise a monopolist's costs and thus lead to lower, not higher, profit. Statement d is not correct because price discrimination requires that a firm have some control over the price at which it sells its output. Statement e is not correct; it is actually the reverse. A higher price should be charged to the low elasticity of demand customers and a lower price to the high elasticity of demand customers.

12. Correct answer: d.

Discussion: Price discrimination (in the form of discounts, coupons, rebates, etc.) is legal in the United States. However, when price discrimination is used to drive rival firms out of business, its practice is illegal.

Statements a-c are all necessary conditions for price discrimination to work.

13. Correct answer: a.

Discussion: For consumer group I, $5 is the price where marginal revenue equals marginal cost (the MR and MC curves intersect). Based on this, the profit-maximizing quantity for consumer group I is 150 units. Since average cost is constant at $4 per unit, profit, calculated as the difference between revenue (price X quantity) and total cost (average cost X quantity), from consumer group I is $150 (= $5 X 150 - $4 X 150). For consumer group II, marginal revenue equals marginal cost at an output level of 60 units. At a price of $10 per unit and an average cost of $4 per unit, the profit from consumer group II will be $360 (= $10 X 60 - $4 X 60).

Based on the discussion above, none of the other statements can be correct.

14. Correct answer: e.

Discussion: If a firm wants to increase its revenue, it should raise price to the consumer group with the inelastic demand ($Ed < 1$) and lower price to the consumer group with the elastic demand ($Ed > 1$). Since an inelastic demand is characterized as being less than 1, statements c-e represent elasticities of demand for which revenue would increase when price is raised. However, the question asks which elasticity of demand will generate the BIGGEST increase in revenue. In this case, the least elastic demand will generate the biggest increase in revenue. With an elasticity of demand at 0.5, a 10% increase in price will cause a loss in customer base of 5%. The loss in customer base with a 10% increase in price when elasticity of demand is 0.9 is 9% and is 7.5% when elasticity of demand is 0.75. Thus, statements c and d are not correct even though they are elasticities for which revenue will increase with a rise in price.

When elasticity of demand is 1 as in statement a, the price increase will not generate any change in revenue. When elasticity of demand is 1.25 (or any number greater than 1), the price increase will lead to a decline in revenue.

15. Correct answer: e.

Discussion: Rent seeking is the process under which a firm spends money to persuade the government to erect barriers to entry and pick the firm as a monopolist. This is a source of inefficiency as firms will use resources to lobby the government to erect these barriers to entry. These resources could be used in other ways.

Statements a - d are all examples of characteristics of rent seeking. The text also lists similar examples.

VIII. ANSWER KEY: ESSAY QUESTIONS

1. The costs to society of a monopoly are numerous. One cost is that consumers are charged a higher price for the product than they would if entry into the industry could occur as in perfect competition. Also, the industry output under a monopolist is less than would occur if the industry operated as a perfectly competitive one. Thus, society loses on two accounts — they pay a higher price for the output and there are some customers who don't get to purchase the output because not enough is produced. This means that consumer surplus is lower under a monopolistic market structure than under a perfectly competitive market structure. Also, rent seeking behavior is likely to occur and this entails an opportunity cost to society. Rent seeking occurs because, in general, firms prefer to be protected from competition so that they can thereby earn positive economic profits indefinitely. Thus, a firm might hire lobbyists to go to Washington, DC in the hopes that the lobbyists will be able to get the firm some form of protection from competition, i.e. status as a monopoly. The time and effort of the lobbyists, however, entails an opportunity cost in that the lobbyists could be employed in other industries thereby increasing output elsewhere that consumers could purchase.

Of course, there are benefits to the monopolist (a member of society, too). The monopolist earns positive economic profit (at least for the life of the patent). Also, with patent-generated monopolies, a society at least gets the benefit that new products will be produced instead of none at all. That is, innovation benefits society. For example, a new drug that benefits cancer may not be produced unless a patent which ensures the innovating firm positive economic profits is granted. That is, a firm with the technology to produce a new drug may choose not to if they know that as soon as they produce it, other firms will enter the market and drive economic profits to zero.

The problem with patent-granting is that the government does not always know which products will be produced even without a patent. Thus, the government may inadvertently grant monopoly status and thus monopoly profits to a firm that does not otherwise truly need the assurance of monopoly profits to produce the product. In this way, society loses for the reasons mentioned above.

2.   A firm that charges different prices to different customers is practicing price discrimination. First, consider the revenue from a monopolist that is not practicing price discrimination. Suppose the monopolist charges a price of $10 per unit of output and sells 2,000 units. The total revenue earned by the monopolist is $20,000. Price discrimination by the monopolist will be possible if three conditions are met (1) the firm has some control over the price at which it sells its output; (2) different groups of customers must be willing to pay a different price for the same product; (3) resale is not possible. Assuming these conditions are met, a monopolist may wish to split its customer base into two groups (although more than two is also an option). The two groups are established based on the differences in the responsiveness to price changes. Assume one group is very price conscious. That is, a lower price will induce them to buy substantially more and a higher price will induce them to buy substantially less. This is just a way of saying that for this group, the elasticity of demand is high (exceeds 1). The second group is not as price conscious. While a lower price will induce them to buy more, they will not be inclined to buy much more and while a higher price will induce them to buy less, they will not be inclined to cut back their purchases very much. This is just a way of saying that for this group, the elasticity of demand is not very high (is less than 1).

Suppose the elasticity of demand for the price conscious group is 2 and for the "price inconscious" group is 0.4. Based on the differences in the elasticities of demand, the firm's total revenue could actually be greater than $20,000 using the following pricing scheme: charge a price higher than $10 (say 10% higher) to the low elasticity demand group and charge a price lower than $10 (say 10% lower) to the high elasticity demand group. What will happen is the following:

For the group charged the 10% higher price, the quantity sold will, using the elasticity of demand of 0.4, decline by 4%. However, total revenue will still increase because the increase in price in percentage terms exceeds the decrease in quantity demanded in percentage terms. (See Chapter 5 for review).

For the group charged the 10% lower price, the quantity sold will, using the elasticity of demand of 2, increase by 20%. However, total revenue will increase because the increase in the quantity sold in percentage terms exceeds the decrease in the price in percentage terms. (See Chapter 5 for review).

Since both price changes lead to an increase in total revenue, the firm will see its total revenue increase above $20,000.

While the example I used assumed that the monopolist raised price to the low elasticity demand group by the same percentage as it lowered price to the high elasticity demand group, a monopolist could raise and lower the price to the different groups of customers by different percentages and still see its profits increase.

One thing to mention is that while the price discrimination scheme increased the total revenue of the firm, we cannot be sure what happens to the profits of the firm without knowing how or if the total cost of serving two different groups of customers has changed. If the cost does not change, then the price discrimination scheme will increase total revenue and profits. However, it may be possible that the costs increase by more than the revenue increases and thus the firm could end up making less in profit, though more in revenue.

We invite you to visit the book's Companion Website at:
http://www.prenhall.com/osullivan/
for further exercises and practice quizzes.

CHAPTER 14
MARKET ENTRY AND MONOPOLISTIC COMPETITION

I. OVERVIEW

In this chapter, you will learn what entrepreneurs must consider before deciding to enter a particular industry. You will learn that in the case of industries with small economies of scale, there is often a great deal of entry and thus competition amongst firms. This is the case of monopolistic competition. You will learn about some of the characteristics that define a monopolistically competitive market structure and see how it differs from a perfectly competitive market structure and a monopoly. You will learn that in contrast to a monopoly, prices and profits tend to be lower and average costs of production higher in a monopolistically competitive industry. You will also learn that a monopolistically competitive market structure brings with it product variety. You will learn how firms already in an industry are affected by the entry of new firms into the industry.

II. CHECKLIST

By the end of this chapter, you should be able to:

✓ Describe what happens to the price, average costs, output, and profits of firms after a second firm enters a market previously served by only one firm.

✓ Explain why profit for a monopolist declines after a second firm enters the market.

✓ List the characteristics of a monopolistically competitive market structure.

✓ List some real world examples of firms that operate under monopolistic competition.

✓ Discuss the elasticity of demand for products in a monopolistically competitive market.

✓ Describe how monopolistically competitive firms might differentiate their products from other firms in the industry.

✓ Explain the profit-maximizing rule for a monopolistically competitive firm and depict it with a graph for both the short and the long run.

✓ Explain what motivates firms to enter a monopolistically competitive market structure.

✓ Describe what happens to the price, average costs, output, and profits of firms in a monopolistically competitive market structure in the long run.

✓ Discuss the costs and benefits to a monopolistically competitive market structure.

III. KEY TERMS

monopolistic competition: A market served by many (dozens) firms selling slightly different products.

product differentiation: A strategy monopolistic firms use to distinguish their products from competitors'.

IV. PERFORMANCE ENHANCING TIPS (PETS)

PET #1

A monopolistically competitive firm maximizes its profit by producing at an output level where marginal revenue equals marginal cost.

The same reasoning discussed in PET #1 of Chapter 10 applies to a monopolistically competitive firm as well. You may want to review it if you are not comfortable with the principle.

PET #2

The entry of firms into a monopolistically competitive market structure causes the demand curves of all firms to shift to the left since each firm now gets a smaller piece of the consumer market. Since the demand curves shift to the left, the marginal revenue curves also shift to the left.

Since the demand and marginal revenue curves of monopolistically competitive firms shift as entry occurs in the industry, the profit-maximizing output level and corresponding price the firms will charge will also change.

V. PRACTICE EXAM: MULTIPLE CHOICE QUESTIONS

1.   Entry of firms into a market typically occurs if:

a)   there are not large economies of scale in production.
b)   there are currently economic profits being earned by other firms in the market.
c)   price is greater than marginal revenue.
d)   (a) and (b).
e)   (a), (b), and (c).

2.   As entry into a market previously served by a single firm (monopolist) occurs:

a)   the demand curve facing the original firm shifts to the right.

b)   the market price remains at the level set by the original firm.

c)   the output produced by the original firm decreases.

d)   the average cost of production of the original firm declines.

e)   all of the above.

3.   Use the graph below to calculate the firm's profit assuming entry has occurred.

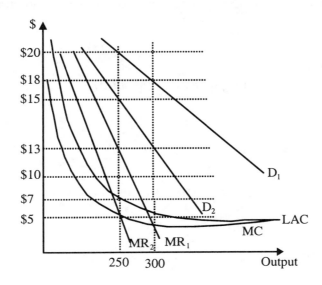

a) $5,000.

b) $2,000.

c) $2,500.

d) $5,400.

e) $3,300.

4.   Which one of the following statements is NOT true?

a)   empirical studies show that market entry reduces price.

b)   The Motor Carrier Act of 1980 caused a decrease in the market value of a firm's trucking license.

c)   deregulation of markets creates competition.

d)   a firm may attempt to differentiate its product from others in the industry by creating a certain image for it.

e)   in a monopolistically competitive market, the demand for products is price inelastic.

5. Which one of the following would NOT be a characteristic of a monopolistically competitive market structure?

a) a homogeneous (or standardized) product.

b) many firms in the industry.

c) elastic demand.

d) no artificial barriers to entry.

e) all of the above are characteristics of a monopolistically competitive market structure.

6. Which one of the following would NOT differentiate one product from another under monopolistic competition?

a) location.

b) special services that go along with the purchase of a product.

c) economies of scale.

d) physical characteristics.

e) product image.

7. Entry into a monopolistically competitive market structure occurs until:

a) demand is zero.

b) economic profits are zero.

c) marginal revenue is zero.

d) marginal revenue equals marginal cost.

e) average cost is minimized.

8. In the long run, firms in a monopolistically competitive market structure:

a) earn zero economic profit.

b) produce an output level where price = marginal cost.

c) do not produce output at minimum average cost.

d) produce an output level where marginal revenue = marginal cost.

e) a, c, and d are true.

9. Under monopolistic competition, entry typically causes price to _____ and profits to _____.

a) decrease; decrease.
b) decrease; increase.
c) increase; increase.
d) increase; decrease.
e) decrease; remain unchanged.

10. Which one of the following would be the best example of a monopolistically competitive firm?

a) sugar farmer.
b) railway transportation.
c) Italian restaurants.
d) drug company.
e) food service at a national park.

11. Which one of the following is NOT a benefit associated with monopolistic competition?

a) lower price.
b) more variety.
c) more locations.
d) lower average cost of production.
e) all of the above are benefits.

VI. PRACTICE EXAM: ESSAY QUESTIONS

1. Consider a small city's dry-cleaning market which is monopolistically competitive. Currently, the typical dry-cleaner is charging $5 an item. The average cost of dry-cleaning is $2. The typical dry-cleaner cleans 1,000 items per week. (Each customer drops off approximately 4 items). Suppose, a new dry-cleaner was to enter the market. Explain what would happen to the price, average cost, output, and profit of a typical dry-cleaner.

2. Discuss the costs and benefits to consumers of having a dry-cleaning market that is monopolistically competitive.

VII. ANSWER KEY: MULTIPLE CHOICE QUESTIONS

1. Correct answer: d.

Discussion: Statements a and b are correct, so statement d is correct. Entry into a market is motivated by profit potential which lures entrepreneurs into opening up new firms. Absent the possibility of economic profit, there would be little motivation for an entrepreneur to start up a new business. Entry into a market is also, and in general, only possible when there are smaller economies of scale in production. In other words, entry into a market can occur when the fixed costs of starting up a business are small. Chapter 10 discusses the reasons for why industries with large fixed costs (and thus, large economies of scale) are typically characterized by only one firm serving the market.

Statement c is not correct. Price is greater than marginal revenue for any type of firm that faces a downward sloping demand curve (instead of a horizontal one). This is not a condition for entry to occur but rather a characteristic related to demand. Since statement c is not correct, statement e is not either.

2. Correct answer: c.

Discussion: As entry by another firm into a market previously served by a single firm, the output produced by the original firm, which was in part based on demand condition, will now be "shared" with the other firm (or firms). That is, there will be a loss of consumers for the original firm because there is more competition.

Statement a is not correct because the demand curve facing the original firm will shift left because the firm will lose customers. This is represented by a leftward shift in demand or a decrease in demand. Statement b is not correct because the market price will decline. Entry promotes competition which in turn reduces the price at which output is sold. Statement d is not correct because average costs of production rise with entry. This is because each firm produces a smaller amount of output than would a single firm serving the market. The lower output levels correspond to higher average costs of production since at lower output levels, economies of scale are less able to be exploited.

3. Correct answer: b.

Discussion: Profit for the firm is based on the demand curve labeled D_2 which represents demand after entry has occurred (it has shifted left). Since demand shifts left, the marginal revenue curve shifts left and so the marginal revenue curve labeled MR_2 must be used to figure out the profit-maximizing output level and price charged by the firm. MR_2 and the marginal cost curve intersect at the output level of 250 units. At that output level, the price charged by the firm, which is read off of the demand curve at the output level of 250 units is $15. At that output level, average cost of production is $7. Thus, the profit of the firm, which is the difference between revenue and total costs is $2000 ($15 X 250 units - $7 X 250 units).

4. Correct answer: e.

Discussion: Statement e is not true because in a monopolistically competitive market structure, products are close substitutes with each other (e.g. toothbrushes). Goods that are close substitutes have elasticities that are characterized as "price elastic." From Chapter 5, "elastic" means an elasticity of demand greater than 1.

5. Correct answer: a.

Discussion: A monopolistically competitive market structure is characterized by product differentiation, real or perceived. A homogeneous product is virtually identical (apples, sugar, wheat, etc) and is characteristic of a perfectly competitive market structure.

Other characteristics of a monopolistically competitive market structure are many firms in the industry (in contrast to monopoly), elastic demand, and no artificial barriers to entry.

6. Correct answer: c.

Discussion: Economies of scale typically characterize monopolies, particularly natural monopolies. Statements a, b, d, and e are all factors that can cause similar products to be differentiated from one another.

7. Correct answer: b.

Discussion: One of the characteristics of perfectly competitive and monopolistically competitive market structure is that there is ease of entry. With ease of entry comes more competition which in turn will thrive until the industry is no longer able to provide a profit for another potential new entrant. Thus, entry stops when economic profits of the industry become zero.

Statement a is not correct. Entry into a monopolistically competitive market structure occurs because there is demand. Statement c is not correct because statement a is not correct. Moreover, if entry stopped when marginal revenue was equal to zero, entering firms would be producing at output levels where marginal revenue would clearly be less than (positive, non-zero) marginal costs. Statement d is not correct; firms maximize profits by producing output where marginal revenue equals marginal cost. Entry is not based on this condition. Statement e is not correct because remember that in a monopolistically competitive industry, firms do not produce at minimum average cost. They all produce at output levels where average cost is higher than minimum. Furthermore, market entry is not dictated by a firm producing at minimum average cost.

8. Correct answer: e.

Discussion: In the long run, competition in the monopolistically competitive market structure leads to entry up until the point at which it is no longer desirable. This occurs where zero economic profits are being earned by the firms in the industry. Monopolistically competitive firms do not produce at minimum average cost because they serve a small portion of the market and because their profit-maximizing strategy is to set marginal revenue = marginal cost. As just mentioned, the profit-maximizing strategy of any firm is to set marginal revenue = marginal cost. Thus, statements a, c, and d are true of a monopolistically competitive market structure.

Statement b describes a version of the profit-maximizing rule that a perfectly competitive firm could use.

9. Correct answer: a.

Discussion: Competition in a monopolistically competitive market structure is what leads to a lower price for the firms' output. This acts to reduce firms' profits. Also, the average cost of production typically rises for monopolistically competitive firms. This too acts to reduce firms' profits. Thus, statement a is the only correct option.

10. Correct answer: c.

Discussion: Statement c is the best example because there are many Italian restaurants each with their own characteristics that differentiate them from each other. Furthermore, entry into the restaurant business is very open.

A sugar farmer is an example of a perfectly competitive firm. Railway transportation is an example of a natural monopoly. A drug company is an example of a patent-generated monopoly. Food service at a national park is an example of a license-generated monopoly.

11. Correct answer: d.

Discussion: Firms in a monopolistically competitive market structure produce at an average cost that is higher than in a perfectly competitive market structure and higher than in a monopoly.

Statements a, b, and c are all examples of benefits from a monopolistically competitive market structure.

VIII. ANSWER KEY: ESSAY QUESTIONS

1. In a monopolistically competitive market, there is ease of entry. The ease of entry, however, means that there will be a lot of competition for customers amongst the firms. Thus, firms that are currently making positive economic profit face the threat of entry by entrepreneurs who believe that they, too, could make a profit in the industry. In fact, entry in a monopolistically competitive market structure typically occurs up until the point at which firms are making zero economic profit. At this point, there is no incentive for more entry into the market.

    In the case of the dry-cleaning business of the small city, the typical dry-cleaner is making $2,000 in profit per week based on the approximately 250 customers served (1,000 items per week/4 items dropped off per customer). If a new dry-cleaner enters the market, there will be some competition from him. This means several things. First, the existing dry-cleaners may have to lower the price of their service in order to hold on to their customer base. Since the new dry-cleaner will likely take away customers from the existing dry-cleaners, their demand curves (and marginal revenue curves) will shift to the left. However, the lower price charged by the dry-cleaners will mean that they may not lose as many customers as anticipated. Second, because the existing dry-cleaners will be serving fewer customers (less output), the average cost of serving each customer will rise. (Remember that average costs decline as output increases and vice-versa, i.e. average costs increase as output declines). Third, since the dry-cleaners will be charging a lower price for their service and incurring a higher average cost of production, the dry-cleaners' profits will be reduced. In the end, entry into the small city's dry-cleaning business will stop when economic profits are driven to zero.

2.   There are costs and benefits to the dry-cleaning business operating under a monopolistically competitive market structure. With ease of entry, there will be a lot of dry-cleaners serving the market each with their own level of customer service, location, etc. Thus, in a monopolistically competitive market structure, customers get the benefits of being able to select from a variety of slightly differentiated products and services. Also, customers will likely see that the travel time to the dry-cleaner they patronize will decrease since more dry-cleaners in the city means more locations being serviced. The customers also benefit in that competition typically leads to a lower price for the product or service being purchased. The cost to society of a monopolistically competitive market is that the average cost of production is higher. From an efficiency standpoint, this is a cost to society since it would be better off if the dry-cleaners could produce where average cost is minimized and correspondingly, the price consumers pay would be the lowest possible. Of course, competition leads to price being reduced to some degree.

We invite you to visit the book's Companion Website at:
http://www.prenhall.com/osullivan/
for further exercises and practice quizzes.

CHAPTER 15
OLIGOPOLY AND STRATEGIC BEHAVIOR

I. OVERVIEW

In this chapter, you will learn about the market structure of oligopoly. You will learn about the characteristics of an oligopoly and what gives rise to an oligopoly. Using game theory, you will also learn how oligopolists make pricing decisions. You will learn that oligopolists act strategically, anticipating the actions of their competitors in response to their own pricing decisions. You will learn that oligopolists may enter into price fixing schemes, price matching schemes, price leadership, or practice entry deterrence in an attempt to avoid the consequences of competition. You will also see that oligopolists attempt to capture the market through advertising. You will use a game tree to analyze the choices and probable strategic outcomes of oligopolists. You will also learn about the kinked demand curve that oligopolists may face. You will learn about contestable markets. You will also learn about an "insecure" monopolist and the steps they may take to deter entry by other firms. You will learn that oligopolists may face an "advertisers' dilemma" which prompts both firms to advertise even though advertising may raise a firm's costs without generating enough offsetting revenue so that profits may actually be less than without advertising.

II. CHECKLIST

By the end of this chapter you should be able to:

✓ Describe the characteristics of an oligopoly.

✓ Explain what gives rise to an oligopoly.

✓ List some real world examples of an oligopolistic market structure.

✓ Discuss the duopolist's (2-firm oligopoly) dilemma.

✓ Discuss and explain the rationale for price-fixing schemes, price matching schemes, price leadership, and predatory pricing. Discuss why such schemes are often likely to breakdown.

✓ Use a game tree to determine what the likely pricing outcome will be between duopolists.

✓ Explain why oligopolists face a kinked demand curve.

✓ Explain the behavior of an insecure monopolist.

✓ Define a concentration ratio and discuss how it might be used to establish whether an oligopoly exists.

✓ Describe the advertisers' dilemma.

III. KEY TERMS

oligopoly: A market served by a few firms.

concentration ratio: A measure of the degree of concentration in a market; the four-firm concentration ratio is the percentage of the market output produced by the 4 largest firms.

price fixing: An arrangement in which two firms coordinate their pricing decisions.

game tree: A graphical representation of the consequences of different strategies.

guaranteed price matching strategy: A strategy where a firm guarantees it will match a lower price by a competitor; also known as a "meet-the-competition" policy.

grim trigger strategy: A strategy where a firm responds to underpricing by choosing a price so low that each firm makes zero economic profit.

tit-for-tat: A strategy where one firm chooses whatever price the other firm chose in the preceding period.

price leadership: An implicit agreement under which firms in a market choose a price leader, observe that firm's price, and match it.

kinked demand curve model: A model under which firms in an oligopoly match price reductions by other firms but do not match price increases by other firms.

dominant strategy: An action that is the best choice under all circumstances.

duopolists' dilemma: A situation in which both firms in a market would be better off if both chose the high price but each chooses the low price.

limit pricing: A scheme under which a monopolist accepts a price below the normal monopoly price to deter other firms from entering the market.

contestable market: A market in which the costs of entering and leaving are low, so the firms that are already in the market are constantly threatened by the entry of new firms.

game theory: A framework to explore the actions and reactions of interdependent decision-makers.

simultaneous decision-making game: A game in which each player makes a choice without the other person knowing what that choice is.

sequential decision-making game: A game in which one person makes a choice before the other.

IV. PERFORMANCE ENHANCING TIPS (PETS)

PET #1

The oligopolist's (or duopolist's) dilemma is that each firm knows that by choosing to sell its output at a high price, the competition will sell at a lower price and thus undercut the high-priced firm's profits. Thus, each firm chooses to sell at the low price but in so doing, each firm ends up with a profit below what they could earn if they collectively agreed to the high price.

The dilemma thus creates an incentive for the oligopolists to collude -- devise pricing schemes that lead to the high price outcome for all firms. However, such schemes are often illegal under anti-trust policy.

PET #2

Cartels and other price-fixing schemes create the incentive for one or more of the participating firms to cheat (undercut the agreed upon price). The cheater is tempted to cheat because his firm's profits will increase at the expense of the other cartel members.

Because of the temptation to cheat, cartels and other price-fixing schemes are often hard to sustain unless there is some enforcement mechanism or punishment that deters the cheater(s) from cheating.

V. PRACTICE EXAM: MULTIPLE CHOICE QUESTIONS

1. Which one of the following is an example of an oligopolistic industry?

a) aircraft and parts.
b) video rental stores.
c) apple growers.
d) sewerage and water treatment.
e) clothing stores.

2. Which one of the following would NOT be true of an oligopolistic market structure?

a) each firm sells a similar product or service.
b) each firm is a price-taker.
c) economies of scale in production.
d) a firm may carry out a big advertising campaign.
e) a few firms serve the market.

3. A cartel is:

a) an industrial association in which research and development is shared.
b) the firm in the industry that sets the going price.
c) a policy designed to prevent mergers that produce a concentration ratio greater than 40%.
d) a group of firms that coordinate their pricing decisions, often by charging the same price.
e) an industry watchdog group that monitors the price of output to ensure that consumers are not being ripped off.

4. Which one of the following statements is true?

a) cartels and price-fixing are legal in the U.S.

b) a four-firm concentration ratio is the percentage of industry profits earned by the four biggest firms.

c) a kinked demand curve is flatter (more elastic) below the kink than above.

d) a grim trigger strategy is when a firm prices its output so low that the competition makes losses and thus is driven out of the market.

e) free trade policy promotes competition.

5. Suppose you are given the following information on a two-firm oligopoly (duopoly).

Firm A will earn $5,000 in profit if it charges a price of $10 and Firm B charges a price of $10; Firm B will earn $5,000 in profit.

Firm A will earn $2,000 in profit if it charges a price of $10 and Firm B charges a price of $7; Firm B will earn $6,000 in profit.

Firm A will earn $6,000 in profit if it charges a price of $7 and Firm B charges a price of $10; Firm B will earn B will earn $2,000 in profit.

Firm A will earn $3,000 in profit if it charges a price of $7 and Firm B charges a price of $7; Firm B will earn $2,000 in profit.

If firm A must pick the price at which it sells its output without knowing what price Firm B will pick and firm B must pick the price at which it sell its output without knowing what price Firm A will pick, what price combination will firms A and B ultimately sell at?

a) $10; $10.

b) $10; $7.

c) $7; $10.

d) $7; $7.

e) cannot be determined without further information.

6. The rational outcome of a guaranteed price matching or "meet-the-competition" policy is that:

a) both firms will sell at the low price.

b) one firm will sell at a high price until the competition sells at a low price; then it will sell at the low price.

c) both firms will sell at the high price.

d) consumers are fooled into thinking the price matching scheme will protect them from high prices.

e) (c) and (d).

7. Which one of the following is NOT a retaliation strategy that firms would apply to one that cheated on a price-fixing scheme by selling at a price below the agreed-upon fixed price?

a) all other firms sell at the same low price as the cheating firm.

b) all other firms sell at a price that ensures zero economic profit for all firms.

c) each period, all other firms sell at the price picked by the cheater in the previous period.

d) all other firms collect a penalty fee from the cheater.

e) all of the above are retaliation schemes used by oligopolists.

8. Which one of the following statements is NOT true?

a) a firm that chooses to cheat on a price-fixing scheme should consider the short-term gain in profits from cheating versus the long-term loss in profits from being punished.

b) the duopoly-pricing strategy leads to negative economic profits.

c) cartels may break down because of the incentive to cheat.

d) price leadership arrangements are an implicit price-fixing scheme.

e) all of the above are true statements.

9. Which one of the following statements is NOT true?

a) a monopolist may act like a firm in a market with many firms, picking a low price and earning a small profit so as to deter entry and thereby guarantee profits for the longer term.

b) a contestable market is one in which firms can enter and leave the market without incurring large costs.

c) government licensing schemes can give rise to oligopolies.

d) price fixing schemes are illegal under antitrust laws.

e) a limit pricing scheme is a decision by a firm to limit the amount by which it lowers its price in response to price cuts by competitors.

10. Which one of the following statements is true?

a) The Sherman Act made it illegal to monopolize a market or to engage in practices that resulted in a "restraint of trade."

b) Airlines used an advanced price listing system to avoid the appearance of explicitly fixing prices.

c) price leadership agreements often lead to garbled signals when the price leader initiates a price cut.

d) in order for price fixing schemes to last, punishment to the price cutter must be enforced.

e) all of the above are true.

11. The advertisers' dilemma is:

a) that two firms advertise even though advertising ultimately reduces each firms' profits.

b) that the elasticity of demand for products increases as a result of advertising.

c) that the most expensive form of advertising increases revenues one-for-one with advertising cost.

d) that there is uncertainty as to whether an advertising campaign will actually increase profits.

e) encountered only for firms that produce products that are close substitutes.

VI. PRACTICE EXAM: ESSAY QUESTIONS

1. Explain why the duopolist's dilemma often leads to price-fixing schemes. Be sure to discuss a number of different price-fixing schemes and what may cause them to break down. Also discuss the enforcement mechanisms that the duopolists might undertake to ensure that a price-fixing scheme does not break down.

2. Suppose you ran the only bakery in town and were currently very profitable. What things might you consider if you wanted to ensure that you continued to enjoy the same success in the future?

VII. ANSWER KEY: MULTIPLE CHOICE QUESTIONS

1. Correct answer: a.

Discussion: Aircraft and parts is an example of an oligopolistic market structure. Video rental stores and clothing stores are examples of a monopolistically competitive market structure. Apple growers is an example of a perfectly competitive market structure and sewerage and water treatment is an example of a natural monopoly.

2. Correct answer: b.

Discussion: In an oligopolistic market structure, firms have some control over price and act strategically in setting price. That means that each firm considers the reaction of the other firms to the price that it may choose to sell its output. Firms are price-takers in a perfectly competitive market structure.

Statements a, c, d, and e are all true of an oligopolistic market structure.

3. Correct answer: d.

Discussion: A cartel is a group of firms that get together to agree to fix the price at which they sell their output. The purpose of the agreement is to ensure higher profits for all firms than if they acted independently.

Statements a, b, c, and e are all incorrect. Statement b is the definition of a price leader.

4. Correct answer: e.

Discussion: Free trade is a policy that does not prohibit foreign firms from selling in the domestic market. As such, free trade policy promotes competition and works to achieve some of the same objectives as anti-trust policy.

Statement a is not correct. Price-fixing agreements are illegal in the U.S. Statement b is not correct. A four-firm concentration ratio is the percentage of industry output that the biggest four firms in the industry produce. Statement c is not correct. The kinked demand curve is flatter (more elastic) above the kink than below. This is because when a firm raises its price (above the kink point), it will lose a lot of customers. This is just a way of saying quantity demanded is very responsive to price above the kink. Statement d is not correct because a grim-trigger strategy is not designed to lead to losses for firms but rather zero economic profits.

5. Correct answer: d.

Discussion: The duopolist's dilemma means that the two firms end up both picking the low price even though it is not the price at which each firm's profits would be maximized. The reasoning is as follows. Firm A knows that if it picks the high price, Firm B will pick the low price since that way, Firm B will get bigger profits. Thus, Firm A does not have the incentive to pick the high price. For the same reasoning, Firm B knows that if it picks the high price, Firm A will pick the low price since that way, Firm A will get bigger profits. Thus, Firm B will not choose the high price. So, if both firms have to pick the price at which they will sell output without knowledge of what price the other has selected, they will both end up picking the low price.

6. Correct answer: e.

Discussion: A guaranteed price matching strategy never actually has to be enacted by the firm that sets the policy. This is because both firms will end up selling at the high price. Thus, consumers may think that they are being protected when, in fact, the protection is just an "empty promise." The reason the policy leads to a high price by both firms is that once the competitor sees the other firm selling at the high price (albeit with the price matching policy), the other firm is now able to select the price that will guarantee it the biggest profit. That price is the higher price and so both firms end up being able to sell at the higher price.

7. Correct answer: d.

Discussion: Statement d is not correct. The book does not discuss any scenario in which firms are able to impose and effectively collect penalties from the cheater.

Statement a is the definition of a duopoly price retaliation strategy. Statement b is the definition of the grim-trigger retaliation strategy. Statement c is the definition of a tit-for-tat pricing strategy. Statement e cannot be correct because statement d is not correct.

8. Correct answer: b.

Discussion: A duopoly-price strategy leads to smaller profits than would arise under a price-fixing agreement. Predatory pricing, on the other hand, leads to negative economic profits.

Statements a, c, and d are all true.

9. Correct answer: e.

Discussion: A limit pricing scheme is a strategy of a firm to pick a price for its output below the monopoly price in an effort to deter entry. Microsoft's decision to sell its version of Windows for $99 is one example of possible limit pricing.

Statements a, b, c, and d are all true. You may wish to look at the answer to essay #2 for a detailed discussion related to statement a. Contestable markets are market structures that may be populated by only one or a few firms yet the behavior of the firms is more like the industry is populated by many firms. The threat of entry is what characterizes a contestable market. Government licensing schemes can limit entry and give rise to oligopolies just as can economies of scale in production and the need for a major advertising campaign. Price fixing schemes are illegal under anti-trust laws.

10. Correct answer: e.

Discussion. Statements a-d are all true.

11. Correct answer: a.

Discussion: The advertisers' dilemma arises because there is an incentive to advertise regardless of whether another firm advertises or not. That is, if a firm advertises (call it Firm A) and its competitor (call it Firm B) does not, Firm A will realize a big increase in sales (and profits, by assumption). But, if Firm A advertises and Firm B also advertises, Firm A's sales (and profits) will at least be bigger than if it (Firm A) had not advertised at all. Thus, the "dominant strategy" or "best response" is for Firm A to advertise. Firm B's thinking is likewise. In the end, both firms advertise but will earn less profit than if neither had advertised to begin with.

VIII. ANSWER KEY: ESSAY QUESTIONS

1. The duopolist's dilemma is that each firm, fearful that its profits will be undercut by its competitor, ends up charging a price lower than they would otherwise want to. Thus, each firm makes a smaller profit than they could if they each charged a higher price. Given this dilemma, there is an incentive for the duopolists to get together and agree to a higher price at which they will both sell their output. That way, they can both be guaranteed profits that are more attractive than when they don't agree to fix the price. While such explicit price-fixing schemes are illegal in the U.S, some firms still engage in price-fixing schemes because the fines and legal fees they might have to pay if they are found guilty are less than the profits they anticipate earning over the time the price-fixing scheme is in operation.

   There are a number of different types of price-fixing schemes. Firms can form a cartel and agree to all sell at a fixed price or agree that some firms can sell at price X while others sell at price Y. A price-matching scheme is another pricing strategy. It is not explicitly illegal. In this strategy, a firm announces (through the media) that it will match the prices of its competitor. It is important that the firm be credible in their policy. Since the competitor believes that any low price they try to sell at will be matched, and thus that their profits will be competed for, they will choose to sell at the same high price, too. Thus, the firm announcing the price-matching policy is able to continue selling at the high price. In this way, both firms enjoy higher profits than if there was no matching policy. Price leadership is another form of price-fixing although it is an implicit agreement. In this set up, the firm that is the price leader sets the price and all other firms simply follow suit. That way, there is no price competition and the price at which firms sell is fixed.

   Price-fixing agreements, whether explicit or implicit, carry a temptation to cheat. The temptation exists because once the price is fixed, the cheaters know that if they sell at below the fixed price, they will get a larger share of the market and thereby reap increased profits. However, cheaters should think about the long term consequences of cheating since the other firms that are selling at the fixed price might punish the cheaters (and unfortunately, themselves as well) by all selling at a lower price, perhaps the one at which the cheaters were selling ("the duopoly price") or even one low enough that all firms earn zero economic profit (the grim trigger strategy). The threat of retaliation which arises in a repeated game sequence may curtail, to some degree, the temptation to cheat.

2. If I ran the only bakery in town and it was very profitable, I would be worried that other entrepreneurs, seeing how profitable I was, would be motivated to open up other bakeries in town. Thus, I would be, in the terms of the textbook, an "insecure monopolist." My insecurity would be that the future success (read profitability) of my bakery may be threatened by the entry of other bakeries into the town. So, what to do? I would consider lowering the price I charge for the array of baked goods I provide to my customers. Of course, I would realize that the lower price might lead to lower economic profits (if my revenue didn't increase and my costs remained the same or even if, at the lower price my revenue increased, but my costs increased by more). The lower price and presumably lower economic profits would make it less attractive for other firms to enter the business and thus I may be able to secure my monopoly status and the long-term prospect of at least positive economic profits.

   On the other hand, if I do nothing to deter entry and it occurs, I will likely see my profits reduced. However, if they do not fall by as much as my "low price deterrence strategy," then it would make sense for me to do nothing.

We invite you to visit the book's Companion Website at:
http://www.prenhall.com/osullivan/
for further exercises and practice quizzes.

CHAPTER 16
MARKET STRUCTURE AND PUBLIC POLICY

I. OVERVIEW

In this chapter, you will learn about public policies toward markets in which there are one or a few firms. In the case of one firm, you will learn about 'natural' monopolies. You will learn that in the case of natural monopolies, government regulation comes in the form of an "average cost pricing policy" which is aimed at achieving a more socially efficient outcome than would arise under an unregulated situation. You will learn that an average cost pricing policy ensures a natural monopoly a guaranteed profit but reduces the incentive for the monopoly to keep its costs of production low. In the case of a few firms, you will learn about antitrust policies which are designed to promote competition in markets dominated by a few large firms. You will also learn about deregulation as a policy aimed at promoting competition. You will briefly review the history of antitrust legislation and learn that antitrust legislation is aimed at breaking up monopolies, preventing corporate mergers, and regulating business practices in instances where competition in the marketplace is threatened. You will learn about some of the strategies used by firms to reduce or eliminate competition. You will learn about real world cases in which antitrust legislation and/or regulation has been used to thwart the efforts of firms that engage in anti-competitive behavior.

II. CHECKLIST

By the end of this chapter, you should be able to:

✓ Explain what gives rise to a natural monopoly.

✓ List some real world examples of natural monopolies.

✓ Explain why natural monopolies are often regulated.

✓ Explain a natural monopoly's reaction to regulation.

✓ Describe the objective and policy used in regulating natural monopolies.

✓ Use a graph to show how an average cost pricing policy works.

✓ Discuss the purpose of antitrust legislation.

✓ Discuss the purpose of government regulation of business practices.

✓ Discuss the circumstances under which the government would permit a merger.

✓ Discuss why the government may prevent a merger between two (or more) rival firms.

✓ Discuss a firm's motives for attempting to reduce competition.

✓ Discuss illegal practices used by firms to increase market concentration.

✓ Discuss some of the major anti-competitive cases that have been ruled on by the Federal Trade Commission.

✓ Explain how an economist might be able to use price information to determine whether a merger will lead to higher prices.

✓ Discuss the major pieces of antitrust legislation.

✓ Discuss de-regulation of the airlines and telecommunications markets.

III. KEY TERMS

tying: A business practice under which a consumer of one product is required to purchase another product.

predatory pricing: A pricing scheme under which a firm decreases its price to drive a rival out of business and increases the price when the other firm disappears.

trust: An arrangement under which the owners of several companies transfer their decision-making powers to a small group of trustees, who then make decisions for all the firms.

merger: A process in which two or more firms combine their operations.

natural monopoly: A market in which the entry of a second firm would make price less than average cost, so a single firm serves the entire market

average-cost pricing policy: A regulatory policy under which the government picks the point on the demand curve at which price equals average cost

IV. PERFORMANCE ENHANCING TIPS (PETS)

PET #1

You may want to review PETS 1-3 from Chapter 13.

PET #2

An average cost pricing policy lowers the price that consumers would pay compared to an unregulated situation and increases the output produced compared to an unregulated situation.

To see this, look at the following graph.

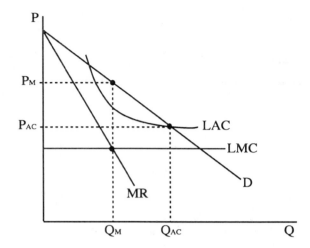

An unregulated natural monopoly would produce an output level where marginal revenue equals marginal cost and charge a price based on what the demand curve would support for that output level. In the graph below, the unregulated natural monopoly would produce an output level Q_m and charge a price P_m.

An average cost pricing policy dictates that the price of output equal the average cost to produce it. This occurs at the intersection of the demand (price) and average cost curves. The graph shows that the output level corresponding to price = average cost is Q_{ac}. Of course, the price associated with this output level (read off of the demand curve) is P_{ac}.

Since $P_{ac} < P_m$ and $Q_{ac} > Q_m$, the average cost pricing policy moves closer to a socially efficient outcome.

PET #3

Antitrust legislation permits mergers as long as they would not threaten competition.

You should be aware that antitrust legislation does not prevent *any and all mergers*. That is, antitrust legislation is designed to block only those mergers that would threaten competition.

V. PRACTICE EXAM: MULTIPLE CHOICE QUESTIONS

1. Which one of the following gives rise to a natural monopoly?

a) patents.
b) increasing average costs of production.
c) economies of scale.
d) inelastic market demand.
e) competition.

2.   Which one of the following would be the best example of a natural monopoly?

a)   video rental stores.

b)   wheat farming.

c)   oil refineries.

d)   sewerage treatment.

e)   auto dealerships.

3.   Based on the graph below, the output level a profit-maximizing natural monopoly would produce is _____ and the output level a regulated natural monopoly would produce is _____.

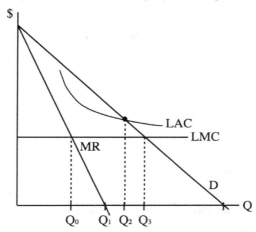

a) Q_0; Q_1.

b) Q_1; Q_2.

c) Q_0; Q_2.

d) Q_1; Q_3.

e) Q_2; Q_3.

4.   Based on the diagram below, the price a profit-maximizing natural monopoly would charge for its output is _____ and the price a regulated natural monopoly would charge is _____.

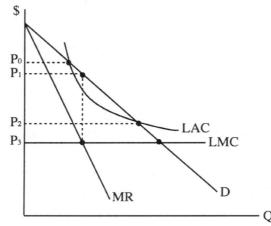

a) P_0; P_1.

b) P_1; P_2.

c) P_0; P_2.

d) P_1; P_3.

e) P_2; P_3.

5. Which one of the following statements is NOT true of an average-cost pricing policy:

a) it will create zero economic profit.

b) it is established where the demand curve intersects the average cost curve.

c) it creates little incentive for the monopolist to control costs.

d) it leads to a higher price than would be charged by an unregulated monopolist.

e) it leads to more output being produced than would arise if the monopoly was not regulated.

6. The purpose of antitrust policies is:

a) to promote competition in markets dominated by a few large firms.

b) to ensure that consumers pay the lowest price possible.

c) to prevent price discrimination by firms.

d) to make sure that firms produce an output level where marginal revenue equals marginal cost.

e) to prevent banks and trust companies from merging.

7. The Sherman Act of 1890:

a) outlawed asset-purchase mergers that substantially reduce competition.

b) extended antitrust legislation to proprietorships and partnerships.

c) made it illegal to monopolize a market or to engage in practices that result in a restraint of trade.

d) outlawed price discrimination.

e) placed a duty (tax) on industries served by fewer than four firms.

8. Which one of the following statements is NOT true of antitrust legislation?

a) the Federal Trade Commission was established to enforce antitrust laws.

b) the Clayton Act outlawed practices that discourage competition.

c) the Robinson-Patman Act permitted the sale of products at "unreasonably low prices" since consumer surplus would increase.

d) the Celler-Kefauver Act outlawed asset-purchase merges that would substantially reduce competition.

e) the Hart-Scott-Rodino Act extended antitrust legislation to proprietorships and partnerships.

9. A "tying contract":

a) protects a firm against buyer injury that may arise from product defect.

b) limits the time period over which a buyer is permitted to return a product.

c) is an agreement between two firms to fix the price at which they sell their output.

d) requires a consumer who buys one product to buy a second product.

e) forces buyers of products to use rope instead of twine to tie up merchandise that will be transported on the top of their vehicle.

10. Predatory pricing occurs when:

a) a firm raises prices temporarily prior to paying dividends to its shareholders.

b) a firm unreasonably lowers the price of its product for the purpose of reducing competition.

c) a group of firms collude to raise prices.

d) a start-up firm lowers its prices as part of a marketing strategy to win new customers.

e) (b) and (d).

11. When firms in an industry transfer the decision-making powers of the owners to a small group of individuals who then make decisions for all the participating firms, the firms have created a:

a) bust.

b) cartel.

c) trust.

d) merger.

e) block.

12. Which one of the following statements is true?

a) antitrust policy is designed to prevent corporate mergers between firms if the merger results in the newly formed firm having more than 50% of the market share.

b) mergers only happen between firms that produce closely substitutable products.

c) the government opposes all mergers.

d) the government may permit mergers that reduce competition if the firms can successfully argue that the merger will reduce costs and lead to lower prices, better products, and better service.

e) all of the above are true.

13. Which one of the following statements is NOT true?

a) a merger between two firms that sell products that are close substitutes creates an incentive for the merged firm to raise prices.

b) predatory pricing may not be a viable strategy since new firms may enter the industry after observing the profits earned by the predatory firm.

c) the motivation behind deregulation is to increase competition and decrease prices.

d) airline deregulation has uniformly led to more competition.

e) all of the above statements are true.

14. Which one of the following statements is true about electricity deregulation?

a) Technological innovations in the 1990s increased the economics of scale in electricity generation.

b) The wholesale price of electricity was allowed to fluctuate in California.

c) The pressure for deregulation of electricity was little variation in prices of electricity prices across states.

d) Deregulation of electricity has caused prices to fall in the states that have adopted deregulation .

e) all of the above are true.

VI. PRACTICE EXAM: ESSAY QUESTIONS

1. Public utilities such as electricity are referred to as natural monopolies and are often subject to regulation by a state authority (the "Public Regulatory Commission"). Explain why a public utility such as electricity is referred to as a "natural monopoly." Explain how and why an average cost pricing policy is applied to public utility. Discuss the effects of the policy on the price and output the utility sells at and produces. Discuss how the policy affects the utility's profits and costs.

2. Explain the circumstances under which a merger would be likely to be granted and under which it would not.

3. Explain why predatory pricing is not a viable long-term strategy.

VII. ANSWER KEY: MULTIPLE CHOICE QUESTIONS

1. Correct answer: c.

Discussion: Economies of scale (average cost declining over large ranges of output) arise because of the fixed costs of starting up a business are very high. This typically occurs if the business requires the use of indivisible inputs.

Statement a is not correct because a patent creates an unnatural or artificial monopoly. Statement b is not correct; decreasing average costs over a large range of output characterize a natural monopoly. Statement d is not correct because the elasticity of demand does not define the market structure. Statement e is not correct; monopolies are characterized by barriers to entry and hence the absence of competition.

2.   Correct answer: d.

Discussion: Natural monopolies typically arise because of the use of indivisible inputs and high fixed costs of start up. A natural monopoly is where there is a single supplier of a good or service. Sewerage treatment is a good example of a natural monopoly.

Since there are typically more than one video rental store per town and because the costs of start up are low, video rental stores are best characterized as monopolistically competitive firms. Wheat farmers produce a homogeneous product and serve a very small portion of the overall market. They also have little control over the price at which they can sell their wheat. Wheat farmers are thus best characterized as perfectly competitive firms. Auto dealerships have a lot in common with video rental stores and are thus characterized as monopolistically competitive firms. While oil refineries may have a high fixed cost of start up and require the use of indivisible inputs, there is typically more than one oil refining company that services a country.

3.   Correct answer: c.

Discussion: An unregulated natural monopoly produces where marginal revenue = marginal cost (the two curves intersect). This occurs at output level Q_0. A regulated natural monopoly produces where price = average cost (demand and average cost curves intersect). This occurs at output level Q_2. Thus, statement c is the only correct answer.

4.   Correct answer: b.

Discussion: To arrive at the correct answer, you must first establish at what output level a profit-maximizing natural monopoly will produce. Once you have determined that output level, you read up to the demand curve and over to the price line to establish the price the natural monopolist would charge. In this case, the profit-maximizing output level occurs where marginal revenue = marginal cost (they intersect) and the price is P_1. For a regulated natural monopoly, price is set equal to average cost. This occurs where the demand and average cost curves intersect. At this point, read over to the vertical axis and that will be the price the regulator sets. In this case, it is P_2. Thus, statement b is the only correct option.

5.   Correct answer: d.

Discussion: One of the aims of an average cost pricing policy is to lower the price that customers must pay for the product or service. Thus, an average cost pricing policy leads to a lower price, not a higher price than would be charged by an unregulated monopolist.

Statements a, b, c, and e are all true of an average cost pricing policy. Since the policy sets price = average cost, the monopoly earns zero economic profit. This price setting policy can be depicted where demand and the average cost curves intersect. Since the regulated monopolist's price will always be set equal to average costs, it has no incentive to hold down its costs. The monopolist knows that whatever costs they incur, they will always be covered by the pricing policy. Another aim of the average cost pricing policy is to force the monopolist to serve as many customers as possible. Thus, the policy will increase the output of the monopolist.

6. Correct answer: a.

Discussion: Antitrust policies have been motivated by a desire to maintain competition in the marketplace and with competition comes lower prices and better quality products.

Statement b is not correct because the purpose of antitrust policies is to ensure competition. Competition, of course, may result in lower prices but that is not the objective of antitrust policies. Statement c is not correct. In fact, as you learned in Chapter 13, price discrimination is not necessarily illegal. It becomes illegal under antitrust legislation if it harms competition. Statement d is not correct. Firms, in their efforts to maximize profits, will obey the dictum of producing an output level where marginal revenue equals marginal cost. Statement e is not correct. Antitrust policies do not have anything to do with banks and trust companies, per se.

7. Correct answer: c.

Discussion: The first piece of antitrust legislation passed was the Sherman Act of 1890. It has subsequently been used to break up the Standard Oil Trust of John Rockefeller in 1911, the American Tobacco Company in 1911, and AT&T in 1982.

Statement a is about the Celler-Kefauver Act. The Celler-Kefauver Act of 1950 outlawed all asset-purchase mergers that would substantially reduce competition. Statement b is about the Hart-Scott-Rodino Act of 1980 which extended antitrust legislation to proprietorships and partnerships. None of the other statements are correct.

8. Correct answer: c.

Discussion: The Robinson-Patman Act prohibited selling products at "unreasonably low prices" with the intent of reducing competition. Unreasonably low prices would naturally increase consumer surplus, albeit temporarily, but the Robinson-Patman Act was legislated with concern about the effects it would have on competition, not on consumer surplus.

All of the other statements are true of antitrust legislation.

9. Correct answer: d.

Discussion: A tying contract requires a consumer who buys one product to buy another. The issue of tying emerged in the Microsoft antitrust case. In one instance, Microsoft was accused of tying the computer's operating system with the browser.

None of the other statements are correct.

10. Correct answer: b.

Discussion: Predatory pricing occurs when a firm unreasonably lowers the price of its product for the purpose of reducing competition. The qualifier "for the purpose of reducing competition" is very important. It is not true that any instance in which a firm unreasonably lowers its prices is predatory pricing. The motivation for the lower prices has to be to drive out competition. Thus, statement d is not an example of predatory pricing. Statements a and c are not correct. Statement e is not correct because statement d is not correct.

11. Correct answer: c.

Discussion: A trust is an arrangement under which owners of several companies transfer their decision-making powers to a small group of trustees, who then make decisions for all the participating firms. In effect, a trust allows for collusion on price and many other facets of decision-making. In effect, a trust acts (illegally) as a monopoly.

Statement b is not correct. In a cartel, participating firms do not relinquish their decision-making powers to a supra-firm organization. Rather, the participating firms effectively remain separate entities and they jointly agree to set prices. None of the other statements are correct.

12. Correct answer: d.

Discussion: Some cases in which a merger will reduce competition are being argued as permissible mergers if the effect of the merger is similar to what would result if there was competition. That is, if two merging companies can argue that their merger will lead to lower prices, better products, and better services (the outcome expected under competition), then the merger may be granted.

Statement a is not correct. There is not a quantifiable figure (like 50% of market share) used in ruling on whether mergers should be permitted or not. Rulings based on antitrust legislation are determined by how the case impacts competition. Statement b is not correct. Mergers can happen not only between closely substitutable products (Office Depot and Staples), but between products that are not substitutes at all. For example, a merger may arise between an auto manufacturer and an auto parts manufacturer. Statement c is not correct. The government does not oppose all mergers. It opposes only those mergers that will reduce competition.

13. Correct answer: d.

Discussion: Airline deregulation has NOT uniformly led to more competition. While the Airline Deregulation Act of 1978 eliminated most of the entry restrictions and price controls, it has not led to increased competition in all airline markets around the nation. Some cities have seen competition decline whereas others have seen it increase. In some cities, airfares have decreased and in other they have increased. So, the effects of airline deregulation are not uniform across cities. However, the consensus among economists is that airline deregulation has generated net benefits on average to the consumer.

Statements a, b, and c are true statements.

14. Correct answer: b.

Discussion: The wholesale price of electricity was allowed to fluctuate in California. Other aspects of the market were not deregulated. The retail price was still under strict controls. The other statements are all false. Option a) is false as technological innovations in the 1990s actually decreased the economics of scale in electricity generation. This created an incentive for deregulation. Option b) is false because one of the pressures for deregulation of electricity stemmed from the fact that there was great variation in prices of electricity prices across states. Option d) is false as deregulation of electricity has caused prices to fall in some states that have adopted deregulation, such as Pennsylvania, but in New York and California prices have risen. E) is false because a, c, and d are false.

VIII. ANSWER KEY: ESSAY QUESTIONS

1. A public utility, such as an electric company, is an example of a natural monopoly. A natural monopoly occurs when there is a single supplier of the output to the market because any more than one firm in the industry would not be profitable. The reason that more than one firm would not be profitable is that a natural monopoly is characterized by very high fixed start up costs and thus very high average costs at low levels of output. This means that with more than one firm in the market, each firm would have only a portion of the overall market and thus will produce for a smaller portion of the market. However, since average costs of production are very high at low levels of output and since each firm is producing for only a portion of the market, each firm will face a very high average cost of production. The firms may not be able to extract a price from their customers that is high enough to cover the costs of providing a service to them and thus each firm will earn negative economic profit. Faced with this prospect, firms typically choose not to enter an industry with high fixed costs of start up where one firm is already present. In other words, the market supports only one firm in the industry. Since this type of monopoly arises naturally, i.e. without the government offering franchises, patents, etc, it is referred to as a natural monopoly.

An average cost pricing policy is often used in the interest of creating a more socially efficient outcome — that is where price is lower and output higher than would arise if the monopolist were unregulated. Under an average cost pricing policy, the regulatory commission effectively sets a price equal to the monopolist's average cost of production and requires that the electric company serve all customers willing to pay the price. In terms of a graph, the regulatory commission forces the utility to produce an output level where the demand and average cost curves intersect. Since price is set equal to average cost, the electric company earns zero economic profit (but positive accounting profit). The average cost pricing policy creates a disincentive for the utility to minimize its costs of production. The reason the disincentive is created is that the utility knows that the regulated price will be set based on the utility's average cost of production; the utility's average cost of production will always be covered and so the utility is always assured of at least zero economic profit, no less. Thus, the utility does not have an incentive to keep costs of production low as would an unregulated firm that desires to maximizes profits.

2. A merger may be granted assuming that it does not reduce or threaten competition and thereby lead to higher prices. Typically, mergers that do not reduce competition are mergers between companies that do not sell the same product or product lines. Additionally, under the newer (1997) guidelines, a merger may be granted if the merging firms can establish that the merger will lead to lower average costs of production and lower prices or better products or better services. Better products or better services effectively act as a price reduction.

    Mergers are typically blocked in cases where competition in the industry will be harmed. Harm to competition also carries with it the expectation that prices will be higher. A merger between Office Depot and Staples was denied because evidence was presented that higher prices would result. Evidence that competition may be harmed has recently come from price data collected from scanners. In the case of Office Depot and Staples, the price data showed that in cities where Office Depot and Staples were both located, prices charged by Staples was lower than in cities where only Staples was located.

3. Predatory pricing is the practice by a firm of lowering the price of its output, unreasonably, i.e. possibly below the average cost of production, for the purpose of driving out rival firms. The firm that is the price predator expects that by dramatically reducing its prices, it will cause the rival firms to lose their customers, or to lose at least enough of them that the rival firms will be forced to shut down their operation. The price predator knows that this pricing strategy will entail a potentially considerable cost when the lower price is announced; the firm may actually operate at a loss temporarily. But the firm weighs this cost against the expected benefit of monopoly power and profits after the rival firms are eliminated. It is a gamble for the predator firm since it does not know for how long the pricing strategy must be held in place in order to obliterate the rival firms. However, even if successful at achieving monopoly status, the predator firm may again have to invoke predatory pricing to maintain its status. This is because once the predator firm secures monopoly status and begins to earn monopoly profits, entrepreneurs will recognize that they too could participate in the profits by opening up a similar business. With entry, the profits of the predator firm will decrease. With enough entry, economic profits may reach zero. Thus, a predatory pricing strategy may ultimately require a perpetual strategy of cutting price unreasonably if the predator firm hopes to continue to earn monopoly profits. (Of course, further predatory pricing will entail further potential temporary losses to the firm).

We invite you to visit the book's Companion Website at:
http://www.prenhall.com/osullivan/
for further exercises and practice quizzes.

PART 5: THE LABOR MARKET AND INCOME DISTRIBUTION

CHAPTER 17
THE LABOR MARKET
AND THE DISTRIBUTION OF INCOME

I. OVERVIEW

In this chapter, you will learn about the labor market using demand and supply analysis where the price of labor is the wage rate. You will learn that demand for labor is a derived demand since the demand for labor is derived from the demand for the output that labor produces. You will learn what will cause the wage rate and employment to change. You will learn why the wage rate differs across occupations and groups of people. You will analyze the effects of a minimum wage law and immigration. You will learn about the distribution of income in the United States and how it has changed. You will learn what explains differences in incomes across households and why the distribution of income has changed.

II. CHECKLIST

By the end of this chapter, you should be able to:

✓ Discuss a firm's short run demand for labor and relate it to diminishing returns.

✓ Explain why the demand for labor is negatively sloped.

✓ Use the marginal principle to determine whether a firm would benefit by hiring one more worker.

✓ Explain why the short run labor demand curve is more steeply sloped than the long run labor demand curve.

✓ Explain the income and substitution effects of an increase in the wage rate. Also explain it in terms of a decrease in the wage rate.

✓ Explain why the market supply of labor is positively sloped.

✓ Explain what will cause the demand for and supply of labor to shift and analyze the effects on the equilibrium wage and employment.

✓ List four explanations for why wages differ across different occupations.

✓ Explain why women and blacks on average earn less for an hour of work than do white males.

✓ Discuss the learning and signaling effect to explain why college graduates typically earn more than high school graduates.

✓ Discuss the tradeoffs associated with a minimum wage law.

✓ Discuss the effects of immigration on wages and prices and who wins and loses.

✓ Explain what quintiles are and how they are used.

✓ Characterize the distribution of income in the United States.

✓ Explain why there are differences in incomes of households in the United States.

✓ Explain how and why the distribution of income has changed in the United States.

III. KEY TERMS

input-substitution effect: The change in the quantity of labor demanded resulting from a change in the cost of labor.

substitution effect for leisure demand: The change in leisure time resulting from a change in the wage (the price of leisure) relative to the price of other goods.

income effect for leisure demand: The change in leisure time resulting from a change in real income caused by a change in the wage.

learning effect: The increase in a person's wage resulting from the learning of skills required for certain occupations.

signaling effect: The increase in a person's wage resulting from the signal of productivity provided by completing college.

long-run demand curve for labor: A curve showing the relationship between the wage and the quantity of labor demanded over the long run, when the number of firms in the market can change and firms already in the market can modify their production facilities.

marginal product of labor: The change in a firm's output from having one additional worker.

marginal revenue product of labor (MRP): The extra revenue generated from one more unit of labor; MRP is equal to the price of output times the marginal product of labor.

market supply curve for labor: A curve showing the relationship between the wage and the quantity of labor supplied.

output effect: The change in the quantity of labor demanded resulting from a change in the quantity of output produced.

short-run demand curve for labor: A curve showing the relationship between the wage and the quantity of labor demanded over the short run, the period when the firm cannot change its production facility

IV. PERFORMANCE ENHANCING TIPS (PETS)

PET #1

The wage rate is the price of labor.

Since the wage rate is the price of the commodity, labor, demand and supply analysis can be used to examine what happens to the price of labor (wage rate) when the demand or supply of labor change.

PET #2

Factors other than a change in the wage rate that are relevant to the labor market may cause the demand and supply curves for labor to shift. Changes in the wage rate cause a movement along the demand and supply curves.

For review, you may wish to review PET #1-5 of Chapter 4 of the Practicum.

PET #3

A higher wage rate will cause some workers to work more (quantity of labor supplied increases) and will cause some workers to work less (quantity of labor supplied decreases).

For workers that work more hours when the wage rate rises, they are behaving according to the law of supply. That is, for these workers, the supply of labor is positively sloped. These workers will reduce the amount of leisure time they take (because the opportunity cost of leisure time has increased since the wage rate has increased) and therefore work more hours. We could say that these workers substitute more work for less leisure time.

For workers that work fewer hours when the wage rate rises, they are not behaving according to the law of supply since they increase the amount of leisure time they take and thus work fewer hours. That is, for these workers, the supply of labor is negatively sloped. A worker may choose to respond this way to a higher wage rate because they recognize that they can now work fewer hours (more leisure time) and still maintain the same income. We could say that these workers substitute more leisure time for less work.

You should be aware this chapter points out some other reasons why the supply curve will be positively sloped.

PET #4

The marginal revenue product of labor is equal to the price at which a firm sells its output multiplied by the marginal product (productivity) of labor.

To see this, note that the price of output (P) is measured as $ per unit of output. The marginal product of labor is measured as the addition to output produced by one more worker (or from one more hour of work). That is, (Δ output/one unit of labor). When price is multiplied by the marginal product of labor, the result is:

$$P \times (\Delta \text{ output/one unit of labor}) = (P \times \Delta \text{ output })/\text{one unit of labor}$$

where ($P \times \Delta$ output) = Marginal Revenue. Thus, the marginal revenue product of labor is the addition to revenue that one more worker generates for the firm.

PET #5

Factors that cause an increase in the demand for output that labor produces will lead to an increase in the demand for labor and thus an increase in the equilibrium wage.

A firm's demand for labor is a derived demand for labor. It is derived from the demand for the output that labor helps to produce. An increase in the demand for output leads to an increase in the price of output. The increase in the price of output means that each worker's work effort (productivity) will add more to the revenue of the firm than before the price increase. That is, the marginal revenue product of labor increases. Using the marginal principle, the marginal benefit to the firm of additional workers has increased. If the wage rate (marginal cost of an additional worker) is unchanged, the firm will find it profit-maximizing to hire more workers.

PET #6

A minimum wage policy is like a minimum price (or price floor, price support).

Remember from Chapter 4 that a minimum price is a price below which the price may not fall. For a minimum price policy to be effective, it must be set above the equilibrium price. In the case of minimum wage policy, a minimum wage that is set above the equilibrium wage will create a surplus of labor (quantity of labor supplied will exceed quantity of labor demanded). If the minimum wage is set below the equilibrium wage, the policy is ineffective since there is no tendency for the equilibrium wage to fall below the minimum wage. You may want to review PET #9 from Chapter 4 of the Practicum.

PET#7

The term 'median' means 'in the middle' – with an equal number above and below.

For example, suppose you had the following information on households and their income:

Household	Income	Rank
Brown	$62,000	5
Jones	$58,000	6
Smith	$87,000	3
White	$55,000	7
Taylor	$46,000	8
York	$101,000	2
Kennedy	$36,000	9
Shealy	$72,000	4
Henderson	$210,000	1

The median income for these nine households would be $62,000, since four families have incomes greater than $62,000 and four families have incomes less than $62,000.

PET #8

The term 'quintile' means '20 percent of a group'. Since each quintile is 20% of the group, there can be five quintiles (adding up to 100%).

For example, imagine that there are 100,000 households in a nation. Quintiles would refer to 20% groupings of the households. In this example, there would be 20,000 households (20% of 100,000) in each quintile. If we were to group the households by quintiles according to their income, the 'top 20%' or 'top quintile' would refer to the 20,000 households who had the highest income of all 100,000 households. The 'bottom 20%' or 'lowest quintile' would refer to the 20,000 households who had the lowest income of all 100,000 households.

PET #9

The term 'share' means 'percentage of' or 'fraction of' or 'proportion of' some amount.

The easiest way to illustrate this PET is with a numerical example. Suppose national income of a country (that is, the earnings of all the households added up) was $100 million (i.e. $100,000,000). Further, suppose the *share* of national income earned by the top quintile is 35%. What does this mean? It means that the top 20% of households or top quintile (see PET #8) collectively earned 35% of $100,000,000. That is, the top quintile collectively earned $35,000,000.

Let's consider another example. Suppose at the end of the semester, your professor reports that out of a class of 50 students, 5 earned A's, 10 earned B's, 10 C's, 20 D's and 5 F's. What is the share of students earning a C or better? The share of students earning a C or better is simply the percentage of the fifty students who earned a C or better. In this case, there were 25 students who earned a C or better. Thus, the share of students earning a C or better would be 50%. Likewise, the share of students earning an A would be 10%.

V. PRACTICE EXAM: MULTIPLE CHOICE QUESTIONS

1. If an increase in the wage rate causes workers to reduce the amount of hours they work and increase the amount of leisure time they take, then:

a) the labor supply curve for these workers is positively sloped.
b) the labor supply curve for these workers is negatively sloped.
c) these workers are obeying the law of supply.
d) the demand for these workers is derived.
e) the marginal product of these workers is negative.

2. Which one of the following would be considered a possible response to a higher wage rate for computer technicians in Palo Alto?

a) a decrease in the amount of hours worked.

b) an increase in the amount of hours worked.

c) an increase in the number of individuals who pick computer technician over other occupations.

d) migration to Palo Alto.

e) all of the above.

3. Which one of the following is an explanation for why the long run demand curve for labor is negatively sloped?

a) an increase in the wage rate raises the price at which output is sold and thus increases the profits of firms.

b) a decrease in the wage rate causes fewer people to be willing to work.

c) a decrease in the wage rate lowers the cost of labor and causes firms to use more labor instead of other more expensive inputs.

d) an increase in the wage rate reduces the productivity of workers.

e) all of the above.

4. The substitution effect of a decrease in the price of labor (wage rate):

a) would lead to a decrease in the amount of hours worked and a decrease in leisure time.

b) would lead to a decrease in the amount of hours worked and an increase in leisure time.

c) would lead to an increase in the amount of hours worked and a decrease in leisure time.

d) would lead to an increase in the amount of hours worked and an increase in leisure time.

e) would have no effect on the amount of hours worked.

5. According to the income effect, a decrease in the price of labor (wage rate):

a) leads to a decrease in the amount of labor supplied.

b) leads to an increase in the demand for goods.

c) leads to a decrease in the demand for leisure time.

d) leads to a decrease in the demand for labor.

e) all of the above.

6. Consider the market for lawyers. Suppose the number of lawyers passing the Bar exam in 1998 is larger than it has ever been in the past. What effect would this have on the market for lawyers?

a) a decrease in the wage rate (salary) paid to lawyers and an increase in the demand for lawyers.

b) a decrease in the wage rate (salary) paid to lawyers and an increase in the supply of lawyers.

c) an increase in the wage rate (salary) paid to lawyers and a decrease in the demand for lawyers.

d) an increase in the wage rate (salary) paid to lawyers and an increase in the supply of lawyers.

e) (a) and (b).

7. Which one of the following would increase the demand for labor?

a) an increase in the price of output that labor produces.

b) an increase in the productivity of labor.

c) an increase in the price of capital.

d) a minimum wage law.

e) (a), (b), and (c).

8. Which one of the following is a reason for why the relative wage of certain occupations is high?

a) few people who have the skills necessary to perform the job.

b) high education and training costs.

c) undesirable job features.

d) licensing boards.

e) all of the above.

9. Which one of the following has NOT been suggested as an explanation for the gender and race gap in earnings?

a) women and blacks have, on average, less education than white males.

b) women and blacks have, on average, less work experience than white males.

c) gender/race discrimination.

d) women and blacks are only a small percentage of the total work force.

e) all of the above.

10. Which one of the following statements is true?

a) In 1999, a typical college graduate earned 80% more than the typical high-school graduate.

b) a college education provides a signal to a potential employer that the job candidate has desirable skills.

c) the "learning effect" of a college education is that students learn new skills that enable them to work in higher-skill jobs.

d) over the last twenty years, technological change has created a big increase in the demand for high-skilled workers

e) all of the above.

11. Suppose the current wage rate in the service industry is $5.00/hour. A minimum wage policy for the service industry that sets the minimum wage at $5.25 will create a _____ of jobs and a minimum wage policy for the service industry that sets the minimum wage at $4.50 will create a _____ of jobs.

a) loss; gain.

b) gain; loss.

c) loss; no effect.

d) no effect; gain.

e) loss; loss.

12. Which one of the following is an explanation for the difference in incomes of U.S. households?

a) differences in the skills of labor.

b) differences in inheritances.

c) luck and misfortune.

d) discrimination.

e) all of the above.

13. Government policies can affect the distribution of income by:

a) taxing high income earners.

b) providing cash transfers to the lowest income earners.

c) reducing racial discrimination.

d) subsidizing education and worker training.

e) all of the above.

14. Which one of the following statements is NOT true?

a) the share of national income earned by the top fifth quintile (top 20% of all income earners) is approximately 25%.

b) the demand for skilled workers has increased relative to the demand of less skilled workers.

c) technological advances have increased the demand for skilled labor.

d) international trade has increased the demand for skilled labor.

e) if the median household income for a country is $30,000, then nearly 50% of the population earns more than $30,000 and nearly 50% earns less than $30,000.

VI. PRACTICE EXAM: ESSAY QUESTIONS

1. Consider the market for graphic designers in Charlotte. Let the current equilibrium wage be $11/hour. Suppose that the demand for graphic designers in Charlotte increases by 10%. Discuss what will happen to the equilibrium wage in the short and long run. Be sure to explain why the results are different. Assume the elasticity of labor supply in the short run is 0.5 and in the long run is 2.

2. Consider the market for construction workers in the United States. If the United States allows more individuals to immigrate to the United States, what will be the effect on the market for construction workers. Use demand and supply diagrams to illustrate.

VII. ANSWER KEY: MULTIPLE CHOICE QUESTIONS

1. Correct answer: b.

Discussion: The labor supply curve is a graph of the wage rate against the amount of labor (or labor time) supplied. An increase in the wage rate that reduces the amount of labor supplied reflects a negative or inverse relationship between the wage rate and the amount of labor supplied.

Statement a is not correct based on the above reasoning. Statement c is not correct because if the workers were obeying the law of supply, then the labor supply curve would be positively sloped. Statement d is not correct because the relationship between the wage rate and labor supplied tells us nothing about the demand for labor.   Statement e is not correct because the marginal product of labor is a component of the demand for labor, not the supply. Furthermore, if the marginal product of workers was negative, no firm would hire them.

2. Correct answer: e.

Discussion: A higher wage rate may induce some workers to work fewer hours (because they can maintain the same income at a higher wage but working fewer hours) and thus take more leisure time.

Some workers may do the opposite -- they may choose to work more hours and thereby increase their earnings substantially. The choice depends on the workers' preferences for leisure time over income (and thus increased consumption and saving). A higher wage rate also has the effect of attracting workers to the profession. Many students choose college majors based on what they expect the wage (salary) to be for that particular job when they graduate. Higher expected wages tend to attract students into those majors. A higher wage rate also causes people to move to those places where they can earn a higher wage.

3.   Correct answer: c.

Discussion: A decrease in the wage rate creates a substitution effect -- the firm finds it less costly to use labor to help produce output than to use other relatively more expensive inputs. Thus, the firm will decide to use more labor and fewer of the other inputs, (e.g. conveyor belt) as a less costly, alternative way to produce output.

Statement a is not correct because it is not an explanation for why the demand curve is negatively sloped. It is also not a correct statement because a higher wage (unless it is an efficiency wage that creates offsetting productivity gains) typically reduces a firm's profits. Statement b is not correct because it is a reference to labor supply not labor demand. Statement d is not correct because it is not an explanation for why the demand curve is negatively sloped. Since statements a, b, and d are not correct, statement e cannot be correct.

4.   Correct answer: b.

Discussion: The substitution effect says that an increase in the price of labor (the wage rate) will increase the amount of hours worked and at the same time, decrease the amount of leisure time an individual takes would lead to a decrease in the amount of hours worked and an increase in leisure time. This works in reverse as well. When the wage rate declines, the amount of hours worked will also decline and correspondingly the amount of leisure time taken will increase. The reason according to the substitution effect is that when the wage rate is lower, the opportunity cost of not working (taking leisure) declines. Thus, since it is, in effect, less costly to take leisure, more of it will be taken.

5.   Correct answer: c

Discussion: The income effect works the opposite of the substitution effect. A decrease in the wage rate, because it reduces the real income, reduces the demand for labor

Statement a is not correct because the income effect says that a decrease in the wage rate will cause individuals to work more (in order to maintain their previous income). When an individual works more, he has less time for leisure. Thus statement b is also incorrect since according to the income effect, a decrease in the wage rate will decrease income and will decrease the demand for all normal goods. Statement d is not correct. The income effect is a concept related to the supply of labor, not the demand for labor. Statement e is not correct since statement c is the correct answer.

6.   Correct answer: b.

Discussion: The big increase in the number of lawyers passing the Bar exam would be represented by a rightward shift in the supply of lawyers. The shift would have the effect of lowering the equilibrium wage (salary) paid to lawyers. As the wage decreased, the quantity of lawyers demanded (movement along the labor demand curve) would increase.

Statement a is not correct because the demand for lawyers does not increase (i.e. labor demand does not shift to the right); the quantity of lawyers demanded increases (movement along the labor demand curve). Statements c and d are not correct because the wage rate decreases, not increases. Statement e is not correct because statement a is not correct.

7.   Correct answer: e.

Discussion: Statement a will cause an increase in the demand for labor. When the price of output that labor produces increases, the marginal revenue each worker generates for the firm increases and thus workers become more valuable to the firm. This would lead to an increase in the demand for labor. Statement b will also cause an increase in the demand for labor. More productive (higher marginal product) workers are more beneficial to a firm (generate more output and thus more revenue). Thus, firms will demand more labor when workers' productivity increases. Statement c will also cause an increase in the demand for labor. When capital becomes more expensive, firms will decide to substitute labor in production for capital (since labor would be relatively less costly). Statement d will cause a decrease in the quantity of labor demanded. That is, a minimum wage policy causes a movement along the demand curve, but not a shift in the demand for labor (decrease in demand).

8.   Correct answer: e.

Discussion: Higher wages are paid to workers who have skills that few people have. This is why chemical engineers are paid more than a clerk at a shoe store. Doctors, professors, lawyers, veterinarians, etc. all are professions which entail more than a college education and thus are more costly professions to enter. Jobs with undesirable features (perhaps risky jobs like oil rig drillers) tend to be paid more because there are fewer people willing to work in dangerous situations. Thus, the supply of labor in these professions is typically not as large as in say, retail sales, and the wages are thus correspondingly higher. Barriers to entry which restrict the supply of workers in the licensed professions can lead to correspondingly higher wages.

9.   Correct answer: d.

Discussion: Statement d has not been used as an explanation for the gender and race gap. The gender and race gap in earnings is that women and blacks typically earn less than a white male counterpart that is doing the same job. The difference in earnings has been explained in several ways (that are not necessarily mutually exclusive). The gender gap may be due to the fact that women and blacks typically have less education and less work experience than white males. That is, these groups of workers, on average, are less valuable to a firm than a worker with more education and work experience. Gender and race discrimination have also been suggested as explanations for the earnings gaps between men and women and white males and black males.

10. Correct answer: e.

Discussion: All of the above are true. Statement a provides evidence that workers who have more education are better paid. Statement b is an example of the "screening" or "signaling" effect that graduation from college provides to potential employers. Statement c suggests that a college education produces workers with higher skills and thereby, admission into better paid professions. Statement d suggests that workers in fields like engineering and computer technology have seen (and may continue to see) increases in wages bigger than those in other professions.

11. Correct answer: c.

Discussion: A minimum wage is a floor below which the wage may not drop. A minimum wage law set at $5.25/hour is a policy that will not permit the wage to drop below that rate. Since the current wage is $5.00/hour, the minimum wage policy raises the wage to $5.25/hour. The increase in the wage rate reduces the quantity of labor demanded (movement along the demand curve) and thus causes a loss of jobs. An increase in the wage rate also raises the quantity of labor supplied (movement along the supply curve). A minimum wage of $4.50/hour is not effective because the equilibrium wage is $5.00/hour. Since $5.00/hour is an equilibrium wage, there is no tendency for it to drop below $5.00/hour. Thus, a restriction that the wage not be permitted to fall below $4.50 is meaningless. This means that the policy will not have an effect on the quantity of labor demanded or supplied or on the equilibrium wage of $5.00/hour. Thus, statement c is the only correct answer.

12. Correct answer: e.

Discussion: There can be many reasons why different people earn different levels of income. The skills and education of people impact their income potential as does who they were born to. Some people receive inheritances from which they can generate an income stream whereas others do not. Also, luck (e.g. winning the lottery) and misfortune (e.g. becoming disabled) can also affect the income potential of individuals. As well, discrimination in the workplace can affect how much people earn. Thus, statements (a) – (d) are all correct.

13. Correct answer: e.

Discussion: The government influences the earnings of households in many different ways. The most notable way is through the tax and transfer system. The income of households is taxed and redistributed (transferred) to those who are at the lower end of the income scale.   The government can also influence the ability to earn income through funding of education and funding of worker re-training programs. The government also has policies and laws to prevent racial discrimination. These policies, too, can influence the earnings of households across the nation. Thus, statements (a) – (d) are all correct.

14. Correct answer: a.

Discussion: Statement (a) is not true. In the United States, the share of national income earned by the top 20% of all income earners amounts to 50% of national income. Let's use a simple example to illustrate. Suppose there are 100,000 households that in total collectively earn $10,000,000. Fifty percent of the total would be $5,000,000. Now, the top 20% of all income earners would correspond to 20,000 households. Thus, we could conclude that the top 20,000 households collectively earn $5,000,000.

VIII. ANSWER KEY: ESSAY QUESTIONS

1. An increase in the demand for graphic designers would be represented by a rightward shift in the demand for graphic designers. The increased demand for graphic designers would raise the wage above $11/hour. The degree to which the wage rises depends on how elastic the labor supply curve is. In the short run, the supply of labor is less elastic than in the long run. This means that the short run supply of graphic designers will be steeper than the long run supply of graphic designers. In the short run, the influence of migration and choice of graphic designer as an occupation cannot be felt on the labor market. That is, the short run is a time period that is not long enough to allow for individuals to migrate to Charlotte to fill the increased demand for graphic designers or for college students and others to alter their career decisions so that they can be hired as a graphic designer. Thus, the increased demand puts a lot more pressure on the wage to rise (because of the limited response on the supply side). If the short run elasticity of supply is 0.5% and the demand for graphic designers increased by 10%, then the increase in the wage rate would be 20%. The formula to be used is analogous to the elasticity of demand formula that was covered in Chapter 5 of your textbook and is reviewed in Chapter 5 of the Practicum. The formula is:

$$\text{Elasticity (E)} = \%\Delta Q / \%\Delta P$$

where in this case, you know that the elasticity of supply is 0.5% and that the $\%\Delta Q$ is 10% since that is how many more graphic designers are demanded. Since we are analyzing the labor market, the $\%\Delta P$ is the $\%\Delta$wage. (The wage rate is the price of labor). Thus, plugging in the numbers and solving for $\%\Delta P$ yields:

$$\%\Delta P \text{ (i.e. wage)} = \%\Delta Q/E = 10\%/0.5 = 20\%.$$

Thus, in the short run, the wage rises by 20% which in dollar terms is equal to (0.20 X $11/hour) = $2.20. The new wage, in the short run, is $13.20/hour.

In the long run, the higher wage and demand for graphic designers causes people to migrate to Charlotte and enter the profession of graphic design. This takes some pressure off of the wage. With a long run elasticity of supply is 2, the equilibrium wage in the long run will change by:

$$\%\Delta P = 10\%/2 = 5\%$$

Thus, in the long run, the wage rises by 5% which in dollar terms is equal to (0.05 X $11/hour) = $0.55. The new wage, in the long run, is $11.55/hour.

In the long run, the wage rises by less than in the short run because the increased demand for graphic designers is matched by a bigger pool of available graphic designers. Existing firms do not have to compete as strongly with each other (by offering better wage rates) in order to attract graphic designers to work for them as they do in the short run when the pool of available graphic designers is limited.

2. Immigration is a policy that permits individuals from other countries to come and live and work in a country that is not their homeland. In many cases, immigrants who come to work in the United States find jobs that do not require a high skill level or education. Immigration policy, therefore, will be likely to increase the pool of workers available to do construction work. Using demand and supply diagrams, immigration policy would be represented by shifting the supply of labor in the market for construction workers to the right, as illustrated below.

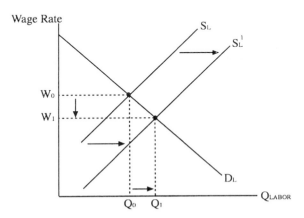

Market for Construction Workers

The increase in the supply of labor (assuming the demand for labor does not change) will cause a reduction in the price of construction workers. That is, the wage paid to construction workers will decline. Since labor is an input into construction, the immigration policy may help keep the costs of construction down.

CHAPTER 18
BEYOND PERFECT COMPETITION: UNIONS, MONOPSONY, AND IMPERFECT INFORMATION

I. OVERVIEW

In this chapter, you will consider how the labor market is affected by labor unions, the presence of a single firm that dominates the demand for labor (a monopsonist), and lack of information by an employer regarding the productivity of its workers. You will consider not only how wages are affected but how productivity and job turnover may be affected, too. You will also cover a brief history of labor unions in the United States.

II. CHECKLIST

By the end of this chapter, you should be able to:

✓ List some examples of craft unions and labor unions.

✓ Discuss three ways in which a labor union attempts to raise the wage of the union members.

✓ Discuss whether unions can create more productive workers.

✓ Explain what monopsony power is and how it can affect wages and employment.

✓ Explain efficiency wages and why they may be paid by a firm.

✓ Discuss the history of labor unions in the United States.

III. KEY TERMS

craft union: A labor organization that includes workers from a particular occupation. Examples include plumbers, bakers, or electricians.

industrial union: A labor organization that includes all types of workers from a single industry, for example, steelworkers or autoworkers.

labor union: An organized group of workers. Unions try to increase job security, improve working conditions, and increase wages and fringe benefits for their members.

marginal labor cost: The increase in total labor cost resulting from hiring one more worker (also known as marginal factor cost)

monopsony: A market in which there is a single buyer of an input.

paying efficiency wages: The practice of a firm paying a higher wage to increase the average productivity of its workforce.

featherbedding: Work rules that increase the amount of labor required to produce a given quantity of output.

collective bargaining: Negotiations between a union and a firm over wages, working conditions, and job security.

IV. PERFORMANCE ENHANCING TIPS (PETS)

PET #1

The wage rate is the price of labor.

Since the wage rate is the price of the commodity, labor, demand and supply analysis can be used to examine what happens to the price of labor (wage rate) when the demand or supply of labor change.

PET #2

For a monopsonist, the wage rate is not equal to the marginal cost of hiring one more worker. To hire one more worker, a monopsonist must not only pay a higher wage rate for that one additional worker, but must pay the higher wage rate to all of its currently employed workers. Thus, to a monposonist, the marginal labor cost of hiring one more worker is greater than (exceeds) the wage rate.

The table below illustrates why the wage rate is less than the marginal cost of labor for the **monopsonist.**

Number of workers	Wage Rate, per hour	Total Labor Cost	Marginal Labor Cost (change in total labor cost)
1	$6	$6	-
2	$7	2 X $7=$14	$8
3	$8	3 X $8 = $24	$10
4	$9	4 X $9 = $36	$12
5	$10	5 X $10 = $50	$14
6	$11	6 X $11 = $66	$16
7	$12	7 X $12 = $84	$18

The table shows that, for example, when the firm moves from hiring one worker to two workers, it adds $8 to its labor cost. Notice that the addition to labor cost is not equal to the wage that must be paid to the second worker. That is, the wage is $7 for the second worker, but the marginal labor cost (addition to labor cost from hiring the second worker) is $8. This difference arises because the firm must pay $7 not only to the second worker, but to the first as well (who was previously being paid $6).

PET #3

An efficiency wage is a wage that is paid by a firm that is above the equilibrium wage (or going market-rate) for a particular job or occupation.

An efficiency wage may be paid by a firm in order to attract high quality, productive workers, to reduce the worker's incentive to shirk (i.e. make them work harder), and to reduce absenteeism and turnover. The higher wages paid by the firm may not necessarily mean that the firm's profits will suffer. The workers may be more productive than their counterparts working for other firms in the same industry who are not being paid an efficiency wage. Thus, even though the firm's wage cost may be higher with efficiency wages, the cost of production may not rise because the productivity increase acts to offset the higher labor costs.

V. PRACTICE EXAM: MULTIPLE CHOICE QUESTIONS

1. Which one of the following statements is NOT true?

a) the Wagner Act guaranteed workers the right to join unions and required each firm to bargain with a union formed by a majority of its workers.

b) the Taft-Hartley Act gave government employees the power to strike when their health or safety was imperiled.

c) The Landrum-Griffin Act guaranteed union members the right to fair elections, made it easier to monitor union finances, and made the theft of union funds a federal offense.

d) Fewer than 20% of all U.S. workers belong to unions.

e) The number of government workers in unions has more than doubled in the last forty years.

2. Which one of the following statements is true?

a) unionization rates are higher in the public sector than in the private sector.

b) unionization rates are lower in the United States than in most other industrialized countries.

c) in the United States, union workers earn about 15% more than nonunion workers doing the same work.

d) one reason why unionization has declined since the 1940s is that there are now laws limiting the amount of hours that can be worked.

e) all of the above.

3.   Unions attempt to increase the wages of their members by:

a)   negotiating with the firm.
b)   advertisements that encourage people to buy products with the union label.
c)   featherbedding.
d)   striking.
e)   all of the above.

4.   Which one of the following is an example of featherbedding?

a)   requiring the government to purchase products produced by unions.
b)   banning imports of a product.
c)   false advertising for products produced by unions.
d)   requiring an auto manufacturer to have a minimum of five factory floor workers assigned to clean up the shop floor.
e)   providing false information to management about the productivity of the workers.

5.   The effect of unions is typically to:

a)   increase wages.
b)   lead to shorter work weeks.
c)   reduce worker turnover.
d)   improve communication between workers and management.
e)   all of the above.

6.   A monopsonist:

a)   is one of many buyers of labor in a particular market.
b)   will find the wage rate for each additional worker is less than the marginal labor cost of hiring that worker.
c)   can hire all the workers it needs at the going wage.
d)   hires workers up to the point at which the wage rate is equal to the marginal revenue product of labor.
e)   will hire more workers than in the perfectly competitive case.

7. Use the graph below to answer the question.

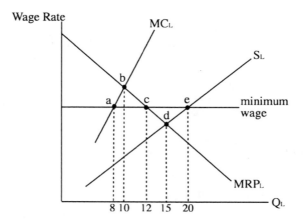

a) a monopsonist will hire 10 workers and a perfectly competitive firm will hire 20 workers.

b) a monopsonist will hire 15 workers and a perfectly competitive firm will hire 20 workers.

c) if there is a minimum wage, the monopsonist will hire 8 workers and the perfectly competitive firm will hire 20 workers.

d) if there is a minimum wage, the monopsonist will hire 12 workers and if there is not a minimum wage, the monopsonist will hire 10 workers.

e) if there is a minimum wage, the monopsonist will hire 8 workers and the perfectly competitive firm will hire 12 workers.

8. Which one of the following statements is true?

a) a firm that pays efficiency wages may see an increased work effort by its employees as well as a reduction in absenteeism and turnover.

b) featherbedding may lead to lower costs of production.

c) a firm knows more about the productivity and skill level of a potential employee than the potential employee knows about his or her own productivity and skill level.

d) a minimum wage decreases employment in the case of monopsony.

e) a monopsonist in the labor market uses its power to increase the wage rate.

9. Which of the following union practices will increase worker productivity?

a) Feather bedding.

b) Reducing worker turnover.

c) Convincing workers to strike.

d) Improving communication between workers and management.

e) b and d.

VI. PRACTICE EXAM: ESSAY QUESTION

1. Discuss the purpose of unions and their intended impact on wages and employment. What are some ways in which union membership leads to more productive workers?

VII. ANSWER KEY: MULTIPLE CHOICE QUESTIONS

1. Correct answer: b.

Discussion: Statement b is not true. The Taft-Hartley Act gave the government the power to break up strikes if they imperiled national health or safety. For example, former president Ronald Reagan fired all striking air traffic controllers and hired non-union air traffic controllers since such a strike imperiled air safety. All of the other statements are true.

2. Correct answer: e.

Discussion: Statements (a) – (d) are all true.

3. Correct answer: e.

Discussion: Statements (a) – (d) are all true. Labor unions (of which the AFL-CIO is the umbrella organization) attempt to increase the wages of their members as well as to improve working conditions and enhance fringe benefits. Unions do this through (1) negotiation with the firm (which may lead to a strike as part of the negotiation tactic), (2) by creating a demand for the product they produce (remember that the demand for labor is a derived demand; the stronger the demand for output, the higher the wage paid to employees that produce the output), and/or (3) through featherbedding (dictating that a firm must hire so many workers for a particular task). That is, featherbedding is designed to increase the demand for labor and thus the wage. Featherbedding, however, can backfire and actually reduce the wage paid to workers. This can happen if featherbedding leads to higher production costs and thus a higher price for the output the workers produce. If the price of the output rises, the amount sold will decline and this will have a tendency to reduce the demand for labor and thus the wage.

4. Correct answer: d.

Discussion: Featherbedding occurs when a union imposes laws that require a firm to hire a minimum numbers of workers to produce a given amount of output. For example, an auto union may impose that at least ten workers be hired for the production of 20 engine blocks.

5. Correct answer: e.

Discussion: Statements (a) – (d) give examples of the effects of unions.

6.   Correct answer: b.

Discussion: For a monopsonist, the additional or marginal cost of hiring one more worker is more than the current wage. PET #2 explains why.

Statement a is not correct. A monopsonist is the only buyer of labor in a given market. Statement c is not correct because a monopsonist cannot hire all the workers it needs at the going wage. It must pay more than the going wage if it wants to attract and hire additional workers. Statement d is not correct. A monopsonist hire workers up to the point at which the marginal cost of labor (which exceeds the wage) is equal to the marginal revenue product from hiring workers. The marginal revenue product of a worker is the addition to revenue the firm earns from selling the output that one more worker produces. This is also called the 'marginal benefit' of that one more worker. Statement e is not correct since a monopsonist will hire fewer workers than in the perfectly competitive case.

7.   Correct answer: d.

Discussion: Statement d is correct because when there is a minimum wage, the marginal cost of labor to the monoposonist is the minimum wage (up until the supply of labor becomes upward sloping). The monoposonist's hiring decision is to employ workers up until the point at which the marginal cost of labor is equal to the marginal benefit of labor. Remember that the marginal benefit of labor is also the 'marginal revenue product' of labor. Since the marginal cost of labor is equal to the minimum wage, hiring by the monopsonist under a minimum wage law occurs at point c on the graph. Thus, the monopsonist will hire 12 workers. If there is not a minimum wage law, the marginal cost of labor is no longer equal to the minimum wage so the upward sloping MC_L curve must be used. It is represented by the marginal cost of labor curve. While the hiring decision is to hire workers up until the marginal cost of labor is equal to the marginal benefit of labor, in this case, the marginal cost of labor is no longer equal to the minimum wage. The marginal cost of labor is greater than the minimum wage. The marginal cost of labor without a minimum wage law is equal to the marginal benefit of labor at point b on the graph. Thus, the monopsonist will hire 10 workers in the absence of a minimum wage law.

Statement a is not correct. While a monopsonist will hire 10 workers (see discussion above), a perfectly competitive firm will hire 15 workers (in the absence of a minimum wage law). For the perfectly competitive firm in the labor market, hiring is also based on equating the marginal cost of labor to the marginal benefit (marginal revenue product) of labor. However, under perfect competition in the labor market, the marginal cost of labor is represented by the supply of labor curve. The supply of labor intersects the marginal revenue product of labor curve at point d indicating that the firm will hire 15 workers. Statement b is not correct. It was established in the discussion above that a monopsonist will hire 10 workers and that a perfectly competitive firm will hire 15. Statement c and e cannot be correct based on the discussion of statements a, b, and d already provided.

8.   Correct answer: a.

Discussion: Efficiency wages may lead workers to work harder (and thus not shirk), but also to reduce the frequency with which they call in sick and their desire to quit the job. When Henry Ford raised the wage he paid his workers from $3/ day to $5/day, he effectively paid them an efficiency wage since the going market rate was $3/day.

Statement b is not true because featherbedding raises costs of production. Statement c is not correct because employees know more about their own productivity and skill level than does a potential employer. Statement d is not correct; in the case of monopsony, a minimum wage law will actually cause employment to be higher than it would be under monopsony. However, employment will still be lower than were there perfect competition and no minimum wage law. Statement e is not correct because a monopsonist uses its power in the market to reduce the wage rate.

9. Correct answer: e.

Discussion: Unions enhance productivity by reducing turnover and increasing communication between labor and management.

Statement a is not true because featherbedding reduces productivity. Statement c is not correct because a strike would reduce output over a period of time and thus reduce productivity.

VIII. ANSWER KEY: ESSAY QUESTION

1. Unions (which came into being in the late 1800s) are organized groups of employees that attempt to negotiate with the firm for higher wages, better working conditions, and better benefits. Unions also attempt to maintain employment for the union members. Since a union is an organization within a firm, the union has more power than an individual in negotiating with the management of the firm.

    While unions attempt to increase the wages of the union members, they confront a problem. A negotiation for higher wages may raise production costs and thus the price of the output the firm sells. If the higher price reduces the amount of output the firm is able to sell, the firm has an incentive to layoff workers. (Remember that the demand for labor is derived from how much output and at what price the output can be sold). Naturally, unions want to avoid any loss of employment for their union members. This is why some unions try to hold membership down. A smaller membership means that a firm would have to think twice about laying off some of its workers because these employees are vital to the firm's operation. Without them, the firm may not be able to operate at all.

    Unions also recognize that there are other ways to increase wages without directly asking for higher wages. Unions may promote products produced under the union label. That is, unions attempt (through advertising) to increase the demand for the product(s) that they produce. Unions may also advocate work rules that establish how many workers must be used to fulfill certain tasks. This is called "featherbedding." For example, unions may dictate that a roadside construction crew consists of 4 workers when perhaps 3 could do the job just as well. Featherbedding thus leads to an artificially increased demand for labor and supposedly would lead to a higher wage -- just what the union is after in the first place. However, featherbedding can backfire. If featherbedding leads to higher production costs and thereby a higher price for the output the workers are producing, the demand for labor could actually decline. This is because a higher price of output will reduce the amount of output sold and thus fewer workers are needed.

    In terms of a graph, featherbedding is designed to shift out (to the right) the demand for labor. Thus, the wage will rise and employment will increase. However, as the price of output rises, the demand for labor shifts back in (to the left). If the price increase is big enough, the demand for labor could shift back in by enough that the new wage and employment level are below what the initial wage and employment level were.

To see this, look at the graph below.

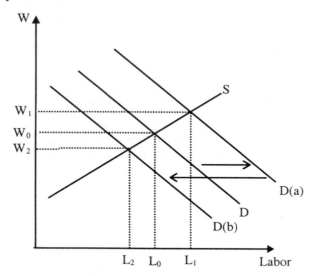

The curves labeled S and D are the initial supply and demand curves prior to featherbedding. The hoped for impact of featherbedding is to increase the demand for labor to D(a). However, as the price of output rises (because of production cost increases associated with the featherbedding), the demand curve may shift back to D or even worse D(b). At D(b), the new equilibrium wage and employment level is below what the starting wage and employment level were.

One of the assumptions so far has been that the higher wage that union members are paid is not offset by an increase in union member productivity. That is, the higher wage (without any corresponding rise in worker productivity) is what leads to higher production costs and a higher price for the output which, unfortunately for the union, reduces the demand for labor. However, this turn of events can be avoided if the higher wage leads to more productive workers. That is, if the higher wage is offset by employees becoming more productive, the firm's production costs may not increase and thus the price at which output is sold need not necessarily increase with the higher wage rate. There are two ways in which union members may have an incentive to be more productive. First, since the union promotes communication between the management of the firm and the workers, workers may be more satisfied on the job because any problems they have may be dealt with more swiftly by management. Furthermore, the more satisfied workers are, the less likely they are to quit. Thus, turnover rates of union members may be lower. This translates to more experienced workers (the longer one stays on the job the more experienced he becomes). More experienced workers are assumed to be more productive. Second, the higher wage may be viewed as an "efficiency" wage in the sense that the higher wage motivates workers to work hard (so as to keep their well-paying jobs).

PART 6: THE INTERNATIONAL ECONOMY

CHAPTER 19
INTERNATIONAL TRADE AND PUBLIC POLICY

I. OVERVIEW

In this chapter, you will learn why trade can be mutually beneficial to countries. You will re-encounter the principle of opportunity cost and use it to determine comparative advantage. You will learn that free trade can lower the price that consumers would pay for goods compared to the prices they would pay if they did not trade (autarky). You will also learn that there are resource movements from one industry to another associated with moving from a position of no trade (autarky) to a position of free trade. These resource movements mean that free trade will, in the short run, create employment losses and factory closings in some industries but expansion in others. You will learn about policies that restrict trade -- tariffs, bans on imports, quotas, and voluntary export restraints. You will learn that protectionist trade policies are typically designed to protect job losses in specific industries. However, protectionist trade policies impose costs on consumers. Thus, you will see that protectionism creates some winners and losers within a country. You will learn that protectionist trade policies initiated by one country may invite retaliation by a trading partner. You will learn about the rationale for protectionist trade policies and criticisms of these arguments. You will learn about some recent trade policy debates over foreign producers "dumping" their products in the U.S., over the impact of trade agreements on the environment, and about whether free trade causes income inequality. You will also learn about some recent trade agreements.

II. CHECKLIST

By the end of this chapter, you should be able to:

✓ Explain the benefits from specialization and trade as compared to autarky.

✓ Use an output table to calculate the opportunity costs of production in two countries for two different types of goods and determine in which good a country has a comparative advantage.

✓ Draw a production possibilities curve using information from an output table. Explain what the different points on the production possibilities curve represent.

✓ Explain what determines the range of terms of trade that would be mutually beneficial to two countries.

✓ Draw a consumption possibilities curve using information about the terms of trade. Explain what the different points on the consumption possibilities curve represent.

✓ Describe the employment effects of free trade.

✓ Explain who the winners and losers are from free trade.

✓ List the different types of protectionist trade policies.

✓ Explain how the different protectionist trade policies work and their effects on import prices.

✓ Compare and contrast the effects of an import ban to an import quota on equilibrium price and quantity using demand and supply curves.

✓ Compare and contrast an import quota to a tariff.

✓ Explain how the threat of retaliation by one country can persuade another country to loosen its protectionist policies.

✓ Explain why import restrictions might lead to smuggling.

✓ Define the Smoot-Hawley Tariff Bill.

✓ Discuss some arguments (or rationales) for protectionist trade policies.

✓ Describe the practice of dumping and predatory dumping (pricing).

✓ Explain why some firms might dump their products in other countries.

✓ Discuss why trade policy and environmental issues have become linked.

✓ Explain how trade might cause income inequality to widen.

✓ Discuss some recent trade agreements.

III. KEY TERMS

Production possibilities curve: A curve showing the combinations of two goods that can be produced by an economy, assuming that all resources are fully employed.

Autarky: A situation in which each country is self-sufficient, so there is no trade.

Comparative advantage: The ability of one person or nation to produce a good at an opportunity cost that is lower than the opportunity cost of another person or nation.

Absolute advantage: The ability of one person or nation to produce a good at a lower absolute cost than another person or nation.

Terms of trade: The rate at which two goods will be exchanged.

Consumption possibilities curve: A curve showing the combinations of two goods that can be consumed when a nation specializes in a particular good and trades with another nation.

Voluntary export restraint (VER): A scheme under which an exporting country voluntarily decreases its exports.

Import quota: A limit on the amount of a good that can be imported.

Import licenses: Rights, issued by a government, to import goods.

Tariff: A tax on an imported good.

Learning by doing: Knowledge gained during production that increases productivity.

Infant industries: Industries that are at an early stage of development.

General Agreement on Tariffs and Trade (GATT): An international agreement that has lowered trade barriers between the United States and other nations.

World Trade Organization (WTO): An organization that oversees GATT and other international trade agreements.

Dumping: A situation in which the price a firm charges in a foreign market is lower than either the price it charges in its home market or the production cost.

Price discrimination: The process under which a firm divides consumers into two or more groups and picks a different price for each group.

Predatory pricing: A pricing scheme under which a firm decreases its price to drive a rival out of business, and increases the price when the other firm disappears.

IV. PERFORMANCE ENHANCING TIPS (PETS)

PET #1

In autarky, a country is constrained to consume what it produces. With trade, a country is able to consume a bundle of goods different from what it produces. Trade permits consumption beyond the production possibilities frontier and thus makes a country potentially better off.

PET #2

Opportunity cost calculations used to determine comparative advantage should be based on a per unit comparison.

(This is a review of PET #1 from Chapter 3.) Suppose you are given the following information:

	Country A	Country B
Wood products per hour	10	8
High-tech products per hour	15	4

The information in the table tells you that Country A can produce 10 units of wood products in one hour (with its resources) and 15 units of high-tech products in one hour. Country B can produce 8 units of wood products in one hour (with its resources) and 4 units of high-tech products in one hour. How can this information be used to determine which country has a comparative advantage in wood production and which country has a comparative advantage in high-tech production?

The easiest way to compute comparative advantage is to determine what the opportunity cost of production is for each good for each country, on a per unit basis. To do this, you must first answer how much Country

A must give up if it were to specialize in the production of wood. For every additional hour of effort devoted to producing wood products, Country A would give up the production of 15 units of high-tech products. (Of course, it is then able to produce 10 more units of wood products.) On a per unit basis, Country A must give up 1.5 units of high-tech products for each 1 unit of wood products = (15 high-tech products/hour)/(10 wood products/hour) = 1.5 high-tech products/1 wood product. You would read this as "for Country A, the opportunity cost of 1 wood product is 1.5 high-tech products." For Country B, for every additional hour of effort devoted to producing wood products, it must give up 4 units of high-tech products. (Of course, it is then able to produce 8 more units of wood products.) On a per unit basis, Country B must give up 0.5 units of high-tech products for each 1 unit of wood products = (4 high-tech products/hour)/(8 wood products/hour). You would read this as "for Country B, the opportunity cost of 1 wood product is 0.5 high-tech products." Thus, Country B has the lower opportunity cost of producing wood products since it has to give up fewer high-tech products.

Since Country B has the lower opportunity cost of wood production, it should specialize in wood production. (Wood production is "less costly" in Country B than in Country A). If this is true, then it must also be true that Country A has the lower opportunity cost of high-tech production and thus should specialize in producing high-tech goods.

Let's see if this is true using the numbers from the table above. For Country A, the opportunity cost of producing more high-tech products is that for every additional hour of producing high-tech products, it must give up producing 10 units of wood products. (Of course, it is then able to produce 15 more units of high-tech products). On a per unit basis, Country A must give up 0.67 wood products for every 1 high-tech product = (10 wood products/hour)/(15 high-tech products per hour). You would read this as "for Country A, the opportunity cost of 1 high-tech product is 0.67 wood products." For Country B, the opportunity cost of producing more high-tech products is that, for every additional hour of producing high-tech products, it must give up producing 8 units of wood products. (Of course, it is then able to produce 4 more units of high-tech products.) On a per unit basis, Country B must give up 2 wood products for every one unit of high-tech products = (8 wood products/hour)/(4 high-tech products/hour). Thus, Country A has the lower opportunity cost of producing high-tech products since it has to give up fewer wood products. (High-tech production is "less costly" in Country A than in Country B.)

PET #3

Opportunity cost calculations used to determine comparative advantage are also used to determine a range for the terms of trade that would create mutually beneficial exchanges between two countries.

In PET #2 above, the opportunity cost in Country A of producing wood products is 1.5 high-tech products (i.e., 1.5 high-tech products/1 wood product). In Country B, the opportunity cost of producing wood products is 0.5 high-tech products (i.e., 0.5 high-tech products/1 wood product). Thus, the terms of trade range that would be beneficial to both countries must be between 0.5 high tech/1 wood product and 1.5 high-tech products/1 wood product.

For example, a mutually beneficial terms of trade might be 1 high-tech product/1 wood product. Country A would only have to give up (trade) 1 high-tech product in return for 1 wood product if it trades. If Country A produces for itself, it will have to cut production by 1.5 high-tech products to get back 1 wood product. The extra 0.5 high-tech product the country "saves" can then be used to buy more from the foreign country. Thus, Country A gains from trade. On the other hand, Country B would give up (trade) 1 wood product to Country A and get in return 1 high-tech product. If Country B produces for itself, it will only get back 0.5 high-tech products by reducing wood production by 1 unit. Thus, Country B gains, as well.

PET #4

Trade protection reduces the total supply of a good in a country. The reduced supply will increase the price a country pays for the protected good.

Your textbook mentions different types of trade protection -- import bans, import quotas, voluntary export restraints, and tariffs -- all of which act to raise the price of the goods and services that a country imports from other countries. Protectionist trade policies effectively reduce the total supply of a good (where the total supply comes from domestic production plus foreign imports) by restricting the amount of foreign imports. Thus, in terms of supply and demand analysis, protectionist trade policies shift the supply curve to the left. A leftward shift in the supply curve raises the price of a good. (See the box in PET #7 in Chapter 4 for review.)

V. PRACTICE EXAM: MULTIPLE CHOICE QUESTIONS

1. Use the table below to answer the question. Assume that each country can use its resources to produce either stuffed animals or pineapples.

	Country A	Country B
Stuffed Toys (per day)	200	300
Pineapples (per day)	400	900

a) Country B has a comparative advantage in the production of both goods.

b) Country A has a comparative advantage in the production of stuffed toys and Country B has a comparative advantage in the production of pineapples.

c) Country B has a comparative advantage in the production of stuffed toys and Country A has a comparative advantage in the production of pineapples.

d) Country A has a comparative advantage in the production of both goods.

e) neither country has a comparative advantage in the production of stuffed toys.

2. Suppose the opportunity cost of producing one unit of lumber in Canada is 3 units of auto parts and that the opportunity cost of producing one unit of lumber in Japan is 6 units of auto parts. If the terms of trade are one unit of lumber for 8 auto parts, then:

a) Canada and Japan will be able to engage in mutually beneficial trade.

b) Japan will benefit from trade but Canada will not.

c) Canada will benefit from trade but Japan will not.

d) Canada will specialize in the production of auto parts.

e) (a) and (d).

3. Use the graph below to complete the following question.

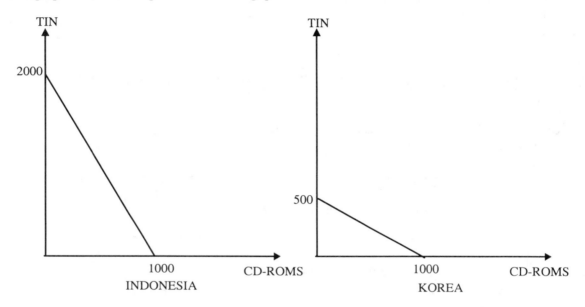

a) Indonesia will specialize in tin production.

b) a terms of trade of 250 units of tin for 100 CD ROMs will lead to greater consumption possibilities for Indonesia than its consumption possibilities in autarky.

c) a mutually beneficial terms of trade would be 1.5 units of tin for 1.0 units of CD ROMs.

d) if trade occurs, workers in the CD ROM industry in Korea will become unemployed.

e) (a) and (c).

4. Which one of the following is NOT an example of a protectionist trade policy?

a) ban on imports.

b) voluntary export restraint.

c) tariff.

d) import quota.

e) all of the above are protectionist trade policies.

5. Which one of the following trade policies would create the biggest increase in the price of the protected good?

a) an import ban.
b) a voluntary export restraint.
c) an import quota.
d) a tariff.
e) a WTO license.

6. Which one of the following would NOT be a result of a tariff imposed by the U.S. on footwear imported from Brazil?

a) U.S. footwear firms will be winners.
b) employment in the U.S. footwear industry will be higher than compared to a situation of free trade.
c) the price that U.S. consumers pay for footwear produced in the U.S. will be lower than compared to a situation of free trade.
d) U.S. citizens should prefer a tariff on footwear to an import quota.
e) all of the above would result from the tariff on Brazilian footwear.

7. Which one of the following statements is true?

a) under an import quota, if the government sells import licenses to importers, then importers may not make money from the quota.
b) Japan's agreement to a voluntary export restraint on its automobile exports to the U.S. resulted in a decrease in the price of U.S.-made automobiles.
c) the threat of retaliation may persuade a country to impose harsher protectionist trade policies on its trading partners.
d) the Smoot-Hawley Tariff bill was designed to gradually lead to the removal of tariffs around the world.
e) the NAFTA agreement turned a U.S. trade surplus with Mexico into a U.S. trade deficit.

8. Which one of the following would NOT be a likely result of protectionist trade policies?

a) retaliation.
b) smuggling.
c) consumers paying a higher price for the protected good.
d) unemployment in the protected industry.
e) inefficient production.

9.   Which one of the following statements is true?

a)   protectionist trade policies often obtain Congressional approval because of the lobbying efforts of a limited group of people most likely to benefit from the protection.

b)   the infant industry argument for trade protection is that it promotes learning by doing and thus can enable a new industry to be able to compete with other producers from around the world.

c)   a problem with granting trade protection to an infant industry is that the protection is not likely to be removed as the industry matures.

d)   by protecting infant industries from foreign competition, trade protection may lead to inefficient production by the protected industries.

e)   all of the above are true.

10. Which one of the following is a problem with a government subsidizing an industry in the hope of establishing a world-wide monopoly?

a)   the taxpayers ultimately pay for the government subsidy.

b)   there is no guarantee that country will be able to profit from securing the monopoly.

c)   another country may also grant a subsidy to the same industry.

d)   the government may end up subsidizing an industry in which there are not economies of scale.

e)   all of the above are problems.

11. Which one of the following statements is NOT true?

a)   dumping occurs when a firm charges a price in a foreign market that is below its cost of production.

b)   dumping is illegal under international trade agreements.

c)   predatory dumping is an attempt to drive competitors out of the industry so that the dumping firm can gain monopoly status.

d)   countries are permitted to restrict imports from other countries if the production methods used by other countries cause harm to the environment.

e)   the wages of skilled labor in the U.S. have risen relative to the wages of unskilled labor as world trade has increased.

VI. PRACTICE EXAM: ESSAY QUESTIONS

1.   Suppose the U.S. initially has no trade restrictions on imports of copper. Explain how a tariff on copper creates winners and losers within the U.S. Where might resources (labor and capital) move after the tariff is imposed? Be sure to address the government's use of the tax revenues earned by the tariff. Use demand and supply analysis to show the effects of the tariff.

2.   Discuss some of the arguments made in favor of trade protection.

VII. ANSWER KEY: MULTIPLE CHOICE QUESTIONS

1. Correct answer: b.

Discussion: Country A's opportunity cost of producing 1 stuffed toy is 2 pineapples (i.e., 400 pineapples per day/200 stuffed toys per day = 2 pineapples/1 stuffed toy). That is, in order to produce 1 more stuffed toy, Country A would have to take resources out of pineapple production and put them into stuffed toy production. Thus, pineapple production would decrease by 2 units. Country B's opportunity cost of producing 1 stuffed toy is 3 pineapples (i.e., 900 pineapples per day/300 stuffed toys per day = 3 pineapples/1 stuffed toy). That is, in order to produce 1 more stuffed toy, Country B would have to take resources out of pineapple production and put them into stuffed toy production. Thus, pineapple production would decrease by 3 units in Country B. Thus, it "costs" less to produce stuffed toys in Country A (in terms of what must be given up) than it does in Country B. Since Country A has the comparative advantage in stuffed toy production, Country B must have a comparative advantage in pineapple production. To assure yourself that this is true, you can invert the ratios above so that Country A must give up producing 1/2 stuffed toy in order to produce 1 more pineapple whereas Country B must give up producing 1/3 stuffed toy in order to produce 1 more pineapple. Thus, pineapple production is less "costly" (in terms of what must be given up) in Country B than in Country A.

Based on the above discussion, none of the other statements are correct.

2. Correct answer: c.

Discussion: A mutually beneficial terms of trade must be between 3 auto parts/1 unit of lumber and 6 auto parts/1 unit of lumber. Since Canada's opportunity cost of producing lumber is less than Japan's opportunity cost of producing lumber, Canada has a comparative advantage in lumber production and thus should trade lumber for auto parts. Japan should do the reverse. At a terms of trade of 8 auto parts/1 unit of lumber, Canada will benefit since in autarky, she could only exchange one unit of lumber for 3 auto parts; with trade she would get 5 **more** auto parts per unit of lumber. However, at a terms of trade of 8 auto parts/1 unit of lumber, Japan will not benefit since in autarky, she would have to give up 6 auto parts in order to produce one unit of lumber whereas with trade, she would have to give up 2 **more** auto parts in order to purchase lumber from Canada. Thus, Japan would be worse off with trade than producing lumber for herself. (See PET #3 above for review.)

Statement a is not correct. For trade to benefit both countries, the terms of trade must range between 3 auto parts/1 unit of lumber and 6 auto parts/1 unit of lumber. Otherwise, one country will gain and the other country will lose. Statement b is not correct based on the discussion above. Statement d is not correct because Canada will specialize in lumber production. Statement e is not correct because neither statement a or d are correct.

3. Correct answer: e.

Discussion: The slope of the production possibilities curve gives the opportunity cost of producing tin (or CD ROMs). The slope of the production possibilities curve for Indonesia shows that the production of 1 CD ROM "costs" 2 units of tin. For Korea, the opportunity cost of producing 1 CD ROM is 0.5 units of tin. Since CD ROMs incur a lower opportunity cost in Korea than Indonesia, Korea will specialize in and export

CD ROMs while Indonesia will specialize in and export tin. Thus, statement a is correct. Since the terms of trade are between 0.5 units of tin/1 CD ROM and 2 units of tin/1 CD ROM, trade can be mutually beneficial. Thus, statement c is correct.

Statement b is not correct. Statement b implies a terms of trade of 2.5 units of tin/1 CD ROM. While this terms of trade would be beneficial to Korea, it would not be beneficial to Indonesia. (See PET #3 above for review.) Statement d is not correct. Since Korea will specialize in CD ROM production, labor and capital will have to move to the CD ROM industry. Thus, workers will become, at least temporarily, unemployed in the tin industry, not in the CD ROM industry.

4.   Correct answer: e.

Discussion: None necessary.

5.   Correct answer: a.

Discussion: An import ban completely eliminates any imports of the good. For example, an import ban on cigarettes imposed by the U.S. would mean that no cigarettes produced in foreign countries would be permitted into the U.S. Thus, the total supply of cigarettes available to the U.S. market would be reduced. In this case, the total supply of cigarettes available to the U.S. market would have to come solely from U.S. production of cigarettes. The import ban would thus be represented by a leftward shift in the supply curve where the new supply curve would now be that attributed to domestic production only. Since this policy is the most restrictive on imports, the increase in the price of cigarettes will be the biggest of any of the policies.

Statement b, c, and d are not correct. An import quota and a voluntary export restraint do not drive imports to zero but instead simply restrict the amount of imports to sum number (greater than zero). A tariff is a tax on the price of the imported good and also acts to reduce the supply of the imported good, but not to zero. Statement e is not correct. There is no such thing as a WTO license.

6.   Correct answer: c.

Discussion: Statement c is not correct. A tariff on footwear from Brazil will raise the price to U.S. consumers of footwear, regardless of whether the footwear is produced in Brazil or the U.S.

Statement a is correct. U.S. footwear firms will be winners in the sense that they will be able to get a higher price for the footwear that they sell to U.S. consumers. Statement b is correct. In free trade, there would be less production of footwear by U.S. producers and more by foreign producers. Thus, under free trade, employment in the U.S. footwear industry would be lower than when footwear is subject to a tariff, which is to say employment in the U.S. footwear industry would be higher with the tariff than in free trade. Statement d is correct. A tariff raises the price of the protected good (footwear in this case) less than does an import quota. Moreover, the government collects tariff revenue that the government could then use to fund government programs that benefit consumers (or to even give them tax refunds!).

7. Correct answer: a.

Discussion: When the government establishes an import quota, it gives licenses to importers which dictate how much of a good they are permitted to import. Naturally, importers are aware that they can profit by having an import license because they can buy the good from the foreign Country At the unrestricted price and sell in the home Country At the quota-induced price which is higher. However, if importers have to pay for the import licenses, then some of the profit that they expect to make from the import quota will be "eaten up" by the cost of the import license. That is, paying for the import license is a cost that an importer would have to consider in determining how profitable it would be to have the license.

Statement b is not true. Japan's agreement to a voluntary export restraint (VER) on its automobile exports to the U.S. resulted in a higher, not lower price of U.S.-made automobiles. U.S. consumers paid approximately $660 more for a U.S.-made automobile after the VER. Statement c is not true. The threat of retaliation may persuade a country to impose less harsh (i.e., less restrictive) protectionist trade policies on its trading partners, not harsher policies. Statement d is not correct. The Smoot-Hawley Tariff bill raised U.S. tariffs by an average of 59% and is pointed to as a policy that may have worsened the U.S. depression of the 1930s. Statement e is not correct. The devaluation of the peso is much more likely to have turned the U.S. trade surplus with Mexico into a U.S. trade deficit. The devaluation of the peso effectively made Mexican products much cheaper than U.S.-made products.

8. Correct answer: d.

Discussion: Protectionist trade policies are "protectionist" because they protect workers in the domestic industry from job losses that might occur were the industry left open to foreign competition. Thus, protectionist trade policies typically (at least in the short run) enhance employment in the protected industry.

All of the others may be a result of protectionist trade policies.

9. Correct answer: e.

Discussion: None necessary.

10. Correct answer: e.

Discussion: When a government subsidizes an industry, it gives money to the industry. The money the government has to give to the industry is ultimately provided by taxpayers. There is no guarantee that a country will be able to profit from securing a monopoly in a particular industry since other governments, may have, at the same time, chosen to subsidize the same industry. In this case, one or both countries may end up earning losses. The government also may choose to subsidize an industry thinking that the industry has large economies of scale (low average cost of production at very large levels of output) and thus is much more likely to exist as a monopoly (single producer). However, if it turns out that the industry is actually able to exist with more than one producer, the government-subsidized industry may find itself having to compete with producers from other firms around the world. In this case, monopoly profits anticipated by the government may not materialize.

11. Correct answer: d.

Discussion: Statement d is not true. Countries are NOT permitted to restrict imports from other countries if the production methods used by other countries cause harm to the environment. For example, suppose that Chile produces aluminum using a method that creates a lot of air pollution (more than what would be permitted under U.S. standards). Under World Trade Organization (WTO) laws, the U.S. would not be permitted to restrict the importation of Chilean aluminum into the U.S. even though the production methods used by Chilean producers would be outlawed in the U.S.

VIII. ANSWER KEY: ESSAY QUESTIONS

1. First of all, one might wonder why the U.S. decided to institute a tariff on a previously freely traded good. There are a few explanations. One explanation might be that the U.S. imposed the tariff as a retaliatory action to its trading partner's decision to impose a tariff on a U.S. good(s). The retaliation may be used as a device to prompt the trading partner to remove their tariff on a U.S. good(s). An alternative explanation might be that workers in the U.S. copper industry felt threatened by the competition from copper producers in foreign countries. Fearing that the competition might mean that U.S. copper producers would lose their market to foreign producers (and thus jobs and profits), workers/management in the U.S. copper industry may have lobbied Congress for trade protection.

When a tariff is introduced on foreign imports of copper, there will be winners and losers in the U.S. The winners will be the copper producers and workers in the copper industry. The price at which producers can sell copper will increase (as the graph below shows) and thus their profits may increase as well.

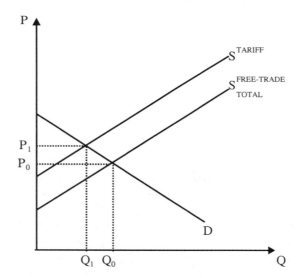

More workers and capital may now be needed in the copper industry, so resources may be taken out of other industries and moved into copper production. Thus, workers with skills in the copper industry will benefit. However, since the tariff raises the price of copper, users (buyers) of copper will lose.

Since the tariff generates tariff revenue for the government, the government may be able to use the revenue to offset some of the higher costs to copper users (i.e., subsidize copper users). Alternatively, the government may be able to use the tariff revenue to reduce income taxes on all workers, i.e., all workers might be given a tax refund. Or, the government could use the tariff revenue to help pay for other government programs that the citizens of the country feel are worth supporting.

2. There are several arguments made in favor of trade protection. One argument is that trade protection should be granted to industries that are just starting out -- so-called "infant industries." The argument is that the infant industries need protection from international competition in the early stages of development so that they become competitive themselves. Without the protection, the industry may not be successful, so the country loses out on establishing an industry that it may want. Another argument made in favor of trade protection is that trade protection "keeps jobs at home." Here, the argument is that without trade protection, the industry will be unable to compete against foreign competitors and so the domestic industry will go out of business. Thus, by granting protection to a domestic industry, a government can prevent the industry from going out of business and thereby prevent any attendant job losses that would result. Another argument made in favor of protection is that monopoly profits may be obtained. In this case, protection would be granted to industries which are likely to survive as monopolies. By granting protection to a monopoly industry, the country becomes the sole producer of the industry output and may thus be able to extract monopoly profits from sales around the world. The government may encourage this if it is able to share in the profits with the producer. Another argument that can be made in favor of protection is that it can be used to get trading partners to loosen their trade restrictions. For example, a country may threaten to or actually impose stiff tariffs against a good or set of goods imported from another country to prompt the country to reduce its tariffs. The U.S. used this type of threat against Japan and was successful in getting Japan to loosen some of its trade restrictions against the U.S. Another argument made in favor of protection is that it will "level the playing field." This is a tit-for-tat application of protectionism. For example, if one country's government subsidizes a particular industry, then its production costs are unfairly low relative to the production costs of the same industry in other country that is not subsidizing the industry. Thus, to compete on a level ground, trade protection is considered to be a fair response.

This discussion provides arguments made in favor of trade protection. To be sure, there are many arguments that can be made against trade protection.

We invite you to visit the book's Companion Website at:
http://www.prenhall.com/osullivan/
for further exercises and practice quizzes.
